W9-CRT-445

Pelican Books

The Best of *I. F. Stone's Weekly*

I. F. Stone was born in the middle west of the
U.S.A. and enjoys an international reputation as a
political journalist and television broadcaster. He
began his career by writing witty and polemical
pieces in the now defunct papers, *PM, New York
Star* and the *Daily Compass*. The first issue of
I. F. Stone's Weekly appeared in Washington on
17 January 1953, and it ran for nineteen years
until 1971, becoming a bi-weekly in its last six years.
The paper began with a circulation of about 5,000
which grew to 75,000 and became the best known
and most influential political paper in the U.S.A.
Written, edited and produced almost single-handed,
it commented on all aspects of America's political
life as well as other wide-ranging topics. It was
I. F. Stone's Weekly that, almost alone, stood out
against McCarthy and survived every attack – and
these were considerable. I. F. Stone is a regular
contributor and editor for the *New York Review
of Books*. His publications include *The Haunted
Fifties, In Time of Torment, Polemics and
Prophecies, The Hidden History of the
Korean War* and *The Kent State Killings*.

The
Best of
I. F. Stone's
Weekly

Pages from a
radical newspaper

Edited and
introduced by
Neil Middleton

Penguin Books

Penguin Books Ltd, Harmondsworth,
Middlesex, England
Penguin Books Inc., 7110 Ambassador Road,
Baltimore, Maryland 21207, U.S.A.
Penguin Books Australia Ltd, Ringwood,
Victoria, Australia

This selection published by Pelican Books 1973

Made and printed in Great Britain by
Cox & Wyman Ltd,
London, Reading and Fakenham
Set in Intertype Times

Contents

For this is not the liberty which we can hope, that no grievance ever should arise in the Commonwealth, that let no man in this world expect; but when complaints are freely heard, deeply considered, and speedily reformed, then is the utmost bound of civil liberty attained that wise men look for.

John Milton, *Areopagitica*

Introduction

I. F. Stone established his reputation as a radical journalist early in his life. His witty and polemical pieces had appeared in the now defunct papers *P.M.*, the *New York Star* and the *Daily Compass*. On 17 January 1953 the first issue of his own paper, *I. F. Stone's Weekly*, appeared in Washington; this was during the height of the 'McCarthy era'. The paper became a bi-weekly in 1968 and finally closed down in December 1971. Closure meant the end of one of the most astonishing feats in the history of journalism. With a few exceptions every issue of the paper was written, from cover to cover, by I. F. Stone himself. The range of affairs covered in the nineteen years of its existence was enormous and the style in which Stone approached them was as varied as it is possible for one man to get. The early years were especially hard: rather than trying to promote the paper and make it grow into a business proposition Stone decided to concentrate instead on writing, and, as he says, '. . . doing as good a job as possible and hope that the quality would sooner or later attract a large audience'. It took ten years for the circulation to reach 20,000, but by then the *Weekly*'s reputation was firmly established and with the last issue the circulation had risen to over 70,000.

What made the paper unique was not only the undoubted energy of its author and the intense hard work that went into his inquiries, but also his consistency. Izzy Stone is widely considered to be among the most stringent critics of the U.S. government – one of the ways in which the largely conformist mass media has sought to remove some of the sting from his writing has been to cast him in the role of eccentric, to label him as a professional 'gadfly' and thus make him acceptable as a 'character' and render him harmless. For those anxious to defuse Stone in this fashion his exposure of folly and corruption must be presented as merely embarrassing. But to see Stone as setting out just to embarrass the government is wilfully to misrepresent his work, for the whole point of his attacks on folly and corruption is that they are part of his passionate defence of civil liberty. From the first issue of the journal to the last, every attack, every analysis, every joke has this defence at its base. He has used his enormous journalistic skills repeatedly to make clear that the world also belongs to the ordinary people who live in it.

The fifties were probably America's most paranoid period; the 'red menace' had never loomed so large and the witch hunts threatened to scare off any political activity to the left of a watery Eisenhower paternalism. Senator Joseph McCarthy ('low blow Joe'), a cartoon monster with real power, dominated the headlines with his crusades against those unfortunates whom he and his fellows had selected for destruction. Stone's voice was one of the few to be raised against McCarthy and the perversion of American society that he represented. It was an effective protest; as liberal journal after liberal journal collapsed under McCarthyist attack, those suffering personally from the witch hunts and those who recognized them as a threat to democratic norms increasingly came to depend on the *Weekly* as one of the few weapons of defence left to them. Once the worst of the McCarthy/McCarren period was over and its sequels began to be felt – the race war, crystallization of the Cold War, the troubles in South-East Asia and so on – Stone was again to be found perpetually writing in defence of people and their liberties. What this demanded, as I hope this selection from his writing will make clear, was not simply an examination of those instances where obvious injustice was at issue, but also a considerable insight into the larger political structures of U.S. domestic and foreign policy.

Stone has often identified his intellectual heroes; high among them are Erasmus and More, with Milton and Kropotkin following close behind. Milton's great blast against the censorship of books, the *Areopagitica*, is very close to his heart. These choices are significant not only because of what those men wrote and stood for in their own time, but because they are the kind of writer people tend to have in mind when they talk of preserving what is best in the western liberal tradition. All

Stone's attacks on the existing social-democratic governments of the west flow from his view that in behaving oppressively what they represent is a deformity of that tradition rather than something which is essentially of their nature. Thus, while he frequently identifies with young radicals because they bear the brunt of oppressive governmental attack, he is often suspicious of the way they think because he feels that they, too, fail to recognize all that is excellent in the history of western liberalism.

Anyone who has read the *Weekly* with attention can see that this has led him to some painful places. One of the most interesting in many ways is his writing about Israel. Stone is not only a dedicated American liberal, he is also proudly Jewish – when he talks of 'my people' it is not simply a rhetorical flourish. He watched the emergence of the survivors from Nazi concentration camps, he travelled with illegal immigrants to Palestine and he covered the Arab–Jewish war in the late forties for *P.M.* His desire for the restoration of Israel was intense. When it came it seems clear that he hoped Israel might be the country that would most nearly conform to his liberal dream, and his emotional stake in its survival and success was, and is, considerable. The articles I have chosen on the subject (pp. 278–97) reflect this concern, but they also reflect the personal conflict produced by his unfailing devotion to liberalism. He discovered that the things he hated most, racialism, intolerance and class division, were all being reproduced in the very country where above all they ought to have been left behind for ever. Perhaps his ability to criticize even the dream country is what makes his writing so remarkable.

When searching for parallels to I. F. Stone's achievement, what comes most obviously to mind is the work of William Cobbett, whose *Weekly Political Register* (1802–35) was for so long the vehicle of his Tory Radicalism and whose political and journalistic life was dedicated to the eradication of 'Old Corruption' and to the championing of the working classes. It has been remarked that Cobbett was just naturally *with* the people, and the same is true of Stone. However, the parallel goes farther than this, for when Cobbett attacked the situation in which

agricultural labourers were reduced to starvation what he remembered was a past in which there had been a broader, freer
England of unenclosed common land on which the poor had at
least been able to feed themselves adequately. He identified the
depopulation of the countryside and the immiseration of the
people with the enclosures – a policy which he identified as,
among others, designed only to serve the interests of a corrupt
ruling class and its government. Similarly I. F. Stone often
seems to have an image of a world in which the great liberal
values are not eroded – his historical sense is, of course, stronger
than Cobbett's and he does not fall into the trap of supposing
that such a world has ever existed. But it could be created, the
seeds of it are present in our own, and it will, if it comes to be,
embody all those values conceived and nurtured through a long
and great liberal past.

If I am right and this does approximate to the way in which
Stone sees the world then he is offering what is in fact a radical
and revolutionary view. No one man can do everything, and it
is not a criticism to say that he has failed to suggest a strategy
for the achievement of the liberal revolution – perhaps in retiring from the pressure of weekly journalism he might want to
turn his thoughts in that direction. Be that as it may, it is clear
that despite his frequent support for Marxists in various parts
of the world who have suffered at the hands of the American
government he is very far from accepting their world-picture.
He sees a good deal of what Marx and Engels had to say as
belonging firmly to that liberal tradition he so much respects,
but beyond that Marxism as such, in all its forms, holds little
attraction for him. It may well be that, rather like the modern
western Communist parties, he is hankering after something in
the nature of a marriage of Marx and Milton.

When I began making this selection my object was to do two
things. First I wanted to select articles which would, within the
limited space at my disposal, give a portrait of the world from
within American politics. It is a measure of the scope of Stone's
writings that one could even think in these terms. Second, by
arranging the articles I chose according to themes, I wanted to
show, as time and the debates went on, how Stone's own think-

ing developed. I did not then know that by the time I had completed my selection the *Weekly* would have been brought to an end. The author/editor had lived for a long time under the pressure of weekly production; while he was still young enough he wanted to write at greater length about the things that are of importance to him. The *New York Review of Books* has had the admirable sense to take him on as a regular contributor so that his supreme ability as a political journalist will not be entirely lost. But what we may now look forward to are the books he has always wanted to write but for which there has never been time.

He is, naturally, aware that his *Weekly* has been of some considerable importance in American political journalism – what I suspect he cannot know is the extent to which, over the years, it has been a thoroughgoing introduction to the social and political life of the U.S.A. The campaigns and causes are all there, but so too is the feeling of what it is like to live with both the frustrations and the victories in the battle against bureaucracy. During eighteenth- and nineteenth-century England it was common enough to find journalists who were effectively writing social histories of their times. This was true not only of Cobbett but also of writers as different, for example, as Addison and Mayhew. It is a tradition that has largely vanished in England but which has survived in the U.S.A., and the *Weekly* is one of the best examples of it. It has not been possible in this volume to do more than suggest this – there were times while I was working on it when it seemed as if the only sensible course for a publisher to pursue would be simply to re-issue the entire *Weekly*.

The kind of detailed analysis offered by I. F. Stone in the fifties and sixties was unique in American journalism. Since then it has been taken up by a hundred small magazines and specialist publications. Perhaps one will emerge which will take over where the *Weekly* left off. If we are very fortunate it may even be as good – but it can never be the same. We are lucky that Stone is still writing, but the folding of his paper feels a bit like the ending of an age. I find that my regret for its passing is already tinged with nostalgia – thus what began as a book specifically designed to introduce English readers to the work of the *Weekly* I now offer as a tribute to its founder, author and editor.

Neil Middleton

Exposing A Crooked Little Game in The Senate and at The UN

Marching With Jefferson?

"According to the President, the thousands of young Americans now in Vietnam are 'marching with Jefferson'."
—*Baltimore Sun from El Toro, Cal., November 1.*
Marching with Jefferson—in defense of an Asian military regime which gags the press, riggs its elections and still holds under arrest without charges the peace candidate who came in second for President last September? Marching with Jefferson—under an American President who broke his election pledge not to get us into a land war in Asia, who embarked on that war without consulting Congress, who is making unquestioning support of that war a test of loyalty and threatening to induct into the Army any young men who dare to oppose it? Is this marching with Jefferson—or steadily away from him?

I. F. Stone's Weekly

VOL. XV, NO. 27   NOVEMBER 20, 1967 191   WASHINGTON, D. C.   15 CENTS

All We Ask of the Viet Cong Is Their Surrender

Ambassador Goldberg's appearance before the Senate Foreign Relations Committee Nov. 2 created the impression that the United States had softened its position toward the National Liberation Front and taken a new step toward a negotiated settlement. The truth, as will be seen when the printed record is available, is that this was another in the many phoney peace performances of the Johnson Administration. It will be seen that we are asking nothing less than the disarming and demobilization of the Viet Cong as the price of peace.

The New Pre-Condition

If anything, the U.S. attitude toward the NLF has hardened. On Jan. 31, 1966, Goldberg submitted a resolution to the UN Security Council calling for a cease-fire in Vietnam and "immediate discussions without preconditions." The new UN resolution he made public for the first time at the November 2 hearing would have the Security Council lay down as a pre-condition, "That there should be no military forces or bases maintained or supported in North and South Vietnam *other than those under control of the respective governments,* and all other troops and personnel should be withdrawn or *demobilized* [emphasis added]." Though Goldberg read the text of both resolutions to the Committee, no Senator called attention to this vital difference between them. It was not until the hearing was almost over that Pell of Rhode Island asked Goldberg—

Would it be conceivable in your view that that portion of South Vietnam which is under Communist discipline or Viet Cong discipline would willingly drop its weapons and demobilize while those portions which are under the Thieu government's regime maintain their weapons?

Goldberg never answered the question. He said, "This is what the Geneva Accords in our view provide."

, No one asked Goldberg whether he thought there was any chance at all of the Security Council underwriting any such preposterous and one-sided a condition for a settlement. Even the earlier resolution, as Goldberg admitted in his opening statement to the Committee, had obtained the necessary nine votes for inscription on the agenda of the Security Council only "on the understanding [as Goldberg put it] that the Council would not proceed forthwith to consider the matter substantively." Three weeks later Matsui of Japan,

A Question Rusk Would Rather Not Discuss

Sen. McCarthy (D. Minn.): The consideration of whether you would withdraw is limited to what might happen in Vietnam. Does this have reference to other parts of southeastern Asia or not?

Amb. Goldberg: We are also very interested in observance of the 1962 accords in Laos, very much so. We would like the Laos accord to be complied with.

Sen. McCarthy: Where would this leave us in the light of what the Secretary of State said in his rather well-publicized press conference of October 12 when he talked about the threat of a billion Chinese with nuclear weapons to all Southeastern Asia and beyond that to the U.S. itself? Are we going to leave this critical area open to a billion Chinese if the question of South Vietnam should be settled within the limits you have defined or not?

Amb. Goldberg: I think that question ought to be-addressed to the Secretary of State.

Sen. McCarthy: All right, I will ask the Secretary.

Sen. Pell: When?

Sen. Morse: Where? (Laughter)

—*Before Senate Foreign Relations Committee Nov 2.*

then President of the Council, shelved the U.S. resolution altogether, reporting "a general feeling that it would be inopportune for the Council to hold further debate at this time." The fact is, as Goldberg well knows, that no one at the UN takes seriously the idea of UN intervention. Neither North Vietnam nor Communist China, as non-members, will accept the jurisdiction of the UN. Only a reconvened Geneva conference can be the forum for a negotiated settlement. The Jan. 31, 1966, resolution was seen at the UN as an attempt to divert attention from U.S. unwillingness to accept U Thant's 3-point plan for peace, which called for unconditional cessation of the bombing in the North as the necessary first step toward negotiations.

Goldberg disclosed at the November 2 hearing that the new UN resolution was prepared last September "largely at the initiative of Senator Mansfield and Senator Morse." One wonders why they would lend themselves to this empty charade. Goldberg admitted in his prepared statement that a "recent canvass once again shows a general unwillingness for

(Continued on Page Two)

(Continued from Page One)

the Security Council either to resume its consideration of the agenda item and draft resolution which we proposed in early 1966, *or to consider the new draft, or to take any other action on the matter.*" [Emphasis added.] At the UN the whole idea is a dead duck. There the new resolution is made the more distasteful by the recollection of the proposal Goldberg put forward in his address of Sept. 22, 1966, to the UN Assembly. Then he said that the U.S. was prepared to accept "a time schedule for the supervised withdrawal of all *external forces* [emphasis added]—those of North Vietnam as well as those from the U.S." Now Goldberg is asking the UN to require not just the withdrawal of the Northern forces but the disarming of the indigenous Southern Viet Cong as a precondition for peace.

G.O.P. Hawks Reassured

That earlier speech by Goldberg proved to be tricky and disingenuous in its use of the term "external forces". It was assumed that this referred to the North Vietnamese. This assumption was strengthened by a speech a few days later (Oct. 12, 1966) in which Secretary Rusk said that if the invaders from the North were withdrawn, the "indigenous element" in the Viet Cong would be "well within the capacity of the South Vietnamese to handle." Laird of Wisconsin, chairman of the House Republican Conference, was so alarmed by the Goldberg speech that he wrote a letter to Secretary McNamara six days later asking whether the views of the Joint Chiefs of Staff had been sought before the speech was made and what was "the current estimate of the Joint Chiefs regarding the ability of the South Vietnamese Army to cope with Viet Cong elements which apparently would be free to continue the war." The reply, almost a month later, from McNamara's office, said the views of the Joint Chiefs of Staff had not been sought on this latter question because "the Department of Defense believes Ambassador Goldberg's speech includes the intent that Viet Cong military units would be deactivated in any proposed withdrawal of external forces from North Vietnam." * It is against this background that one should read the phrase "all other troops . . . should be withdrawn or demobilized" in the new UN resolution and the phrase which follows "and all other military bases abolished as quickly as possible and in accordance with an agreed time schedule." The U.S. would withdraw from its bases in South Vietnam only after the Viet Cong had laid down its arms. This is what the UN was asked to ratify.

* Little attention was paid to this exchange of letters when it was finally made public by Laird. Their text was published in this Weekly for Nov. 7, 1966.

The Propaganda Ploy

Sen. Aiken: I think it is perfectly obvious that there is a substantial percentage of the UN members who think that the U.S. is to blame, and wholly to blame, for the war going on in Southeast Asia, and what I wanted to ask you next is if we take this matter to the Security Council and indicate beyond a doubt that we want a political settlement of this trouble, would that in your opinion change the minds of any of these countries that now think the U.S. alone is to blame, assuming that our efforts are blocked by other countries, other members, particularly Russia or France.

Amb. Goldberg: I think it would be helpful.

—Before Senate Foreign Relations Nov. 2.

Perhaps one reason the committee let Goldberg get away with this comedy is that so many Senators, like the Administration itself, are using appeal to the UN as a way to make it look as if they are for peace. No less than 55 members of the Senate are sponsoring S. Res. 180 by Mansfield. This empty piece of fluff merely expresses "the sense of the Senate that the President consider taking the appropriate initiative through his representative at the UN to assure that the U.S. resolution of January 31, 1966, or any other resolution of equivalent purpose be brought before the Security Council for consideration." *

Even Morse, though not a co-sponsor, has endorsed the Mansfield resolution while introducing a UN resolution of his own, S. Con. Res. 44. His discussion with Goldberg at the hearing leads one to fear that he is shifting from a critic of Johnson on the war to a collaborator. Morse said that he had discussed taking the war to the UN with Goldberg after his appointment as Ambassador and then again at the time of "the steel case" when they were both at the White House "and the President asked us to talk about it further." Morse said he endorsed the Mansfield resolution because "I thought it was important that we build a bridge between the Congress and this Administration in trying to resolve some of these foreign policy differences." Morse declared that many

* The co-sponsors, beside Fulbright, Bobby Kennedy, McCarthy, McGovern, Hartke, Church, Aiken, Clark, Cooper, Morton, Pell, and Young of Ohio, all of whom should know better, includes Anderson, Bartlett, Bayh, Boggs, Brewster, Brooke, Burdick, Byrd of W. Va., Cannon, Carlson, Case, Ervin, Griffin, Harris, Hart, Inouye, Javits, Jordan of Idaho, Teddy Kennedy, Lausche, Long of Missouri, Metcalf, Mondale, Monroney, Montoya, Moss, Muskie, Nelson, Pastore, Pearson, Prouty, Proxmire, Randolph, Ribicoff, Spong, Symington, Talmadge, Tydings, Williams of N.J., Yarborough, Young of North Dakota and a hawk like Tower of Texas whose willingness to co-sponsor this "peace move" shows how meaningless it is.

people did not know that Johnson had favored UN intervention "from the very beginning" and "has always welcomed *appropriate* [our italics] UN participation and intervention in trying to seek a peace in Southeast Asia." In this, as in hailing Goldberg's statement to the Committee as "historic," Morse made himself a partner in deception.

Morse's own resolution is very different from Mansfield's. Morse's would direct the President to ask the UN Security Council to end the war in Vietnam, "pledging the U.S. in advance to accept and carry out any decision on the matter by the Council." But there is—as Morse should know better than anyone else—not the slightest chance that Johnson would accept a UN Security Council decision. On the contrary, as the new U.S. resolution at the UN shows, we are not even willing to let the Security Council act without tying its hands by making it accept our own preconditions, preconditions which require a Viet Cong surrender.

Goldberg's Evasive Language

The supposed concession to the NLF which made the headlines never appeared in Goldberg's statement at all. It came up under questioning by Gore, who is not a co-sponsor of the Mansfield resolution and subjected Goldberg to the only thorough grilling that he got (see bottom of p. 3). Gore wanted to know what the position of the U.S. would be about inviting the NLF to participate in a Security Council discussion. Goldberg said "we would not stand in the way ... We would not prevent it from happening." Gore wanted to know what would happen if there were eight votes for the invitation, would the U.S. supply the necessary ninth vote? Again Goldberg was unwilling to give a direct answer. "Well," was all he would say, "in light of the statements I have filed with you, Senator, the U.S. would not initiate an invitation. But if the Security Council, there was a feeling in the Security Council that they ought to be invited we would join in that invitation." That does not say we would supply the missing vote. *

As for the NLF's position at a Geneva conference, Gold-

---

* The invitation wouldn't be worth much anyway since groups or individuals invited to present their case under Rule 39 have no vote.

---

berg said in answer to a question by Symington that "we would recognize the competence of the conference to decide the invitees, the scope and to enter into resolution of any disputed question of interpretations." At a State Department press conference next day, however, it was made clear that this did not mean we would actually accept the decisions of a Geneva conference on disputed questions. "Just for clarification," State Department spokesman Robert McCloskey was asked, "you said, quoting the Ambassador, that the U.S. government would accept the judgment of the conference. Concerning what? Concerning the invitation or the participation? Or concerning the whole question?" This followed—

A. Participation and—

Q. Only?

A. —and the form that participation would take.

Q. So this statement is restricted only to the participation, that the U.S. would accept judgment.

A. That's right.

Even the willingness to have the NLF participate was considerably attenuated by Goldberg's only other reference to the

(Continued on Page Four)

Gore Shows How Johnson and Goldberg Misread the Geneva Accords

Sen. Gore (D. Tenn): In order that I put the point, I refer to a speech which President Johnson made before the Tennessee General Assembly in March of this year and I quote: "We believe that the Geneva accords of 1954 and 1962 could serve as the central element of a peaceful settlement. These accords provide in essence that both South and North Vietnam should be free from external interference while at the same time they would be free INDEPENDENTLY to determine their position on the question of reunification." [Emphasis added.]

Now that seems to be the position which both you and the President and the State Department have consistently taken. Yet I do not find it, as the President has said, in accord with the Geneva Agreement. Let me read you this, this is the final declaration of the Geneva Conference, July 21, 1954: "The Conference recognizes that the essential purpose of the agreement relating to Vietnam is to settle military questions with a view to ending hostilities and that the military demarcation line is provisional and

should not in any way be interpreted as constituting a political or territorial boundary." ... Yet you and President Johnson refer to the two political entities acting independently. This ... appears to be a contradiction.

Ambassador Goldberg: ... What I am saying is that under the Geneva Accords as we understand them, and we have not heard Hanoi dispute this, there would be an election in the South as to whether they want to be reunited ... (and) there would be an election in the North ... If the two peoples North and South decide they want to be reunited we would not interpose any barriers.

—Before Senate Foreign Relations Committee Nov. 2.

So the Thieu-Ky government, that has just come to power through rigged elections, would run the election in the South to determine whether the people wanted reunification! The new U.S. resolution at the UN does provide for "international supervision of the foregoing through such machinery as may be agreed upon." But how effective that might be is problematical.

The Simple Reply the State Dept. Declined to Give

(Continued from Page Three)

NLF's role and by McCloskey's gloss on it next day. Toward the close of the hearing Senator Pell told Goldberg, "I think we have made a great step forward in my mind here today in the assertion of our willingness, if necessary, to deal with it [the NLF], not deal with, but negotiate with the representatives of the NLF." Goldberg's reply was "Well, I think the President has frequently said that is not an insurmountable problem, *and I was repeating it in that context*." [Italics added.] But in that context the U.S. has never said it was ready to *negotiate* with the NLF. The President's exact words as quoted by McCloskey at the State Department next day were from the speech of July 28, 1965, in which Johnson said, "The Viet Cong would have no difficulty in being represented and having their views presented if Hanoi for a moment decides to cease her aggression." McCloskey said Goldberg's statement was to be read in the light of that Presidential declaration. The colloquy that followed left the matter murky:

Q. Bob, to clarify the business of the relationship with these statements to previous ones in your statement. The

Sen. Pell: I think the record should show very clearly that every witness who has come here on this [Mansfield] resolution [to refer the Vietnam war to the UN Security Council] has specifically stated that the resolution did not have a Chinaman's chance or to use more diplomatic words to that effect unless there was a cessation of the bombing.

—*Senate Foreign Relations Committee Nov. 2.*

emphasis—at least in private—has always been that the Viet Cong participation and the presentation of VC views would be through Hanoi, the North Vietnamese delegation. Is that what Mr. Goldberg means?

Mr. McCloskey: Look, I'm just not going to add to the multiplication of language on this subject. I've made an effort to clarify . . .

Q. Are you clarifying or reiterating what he said?

A. Both.

Q. You did a better job at the latter than the former.

The simple, the clarifying, answer would have been that Goldberg meant the U.S. was now prepared to accept direct NLF participation if the conference so decided. Mr. McCloskey was unwilling to give that answer.

OWNERSHIP, MANAGEMENT AND CIRCULATION

(Act of October 23, 1962; Section 4369, Title 39, United States Code)
1. Date of Filing November 3, 1967.
2. Title of Publication: I. F. Stone's Weekly.
3. Frequency of issue: Every Monday except last In December and first In January; bi-weekly in July; not published in August.
4. Location of known office of publication: 5618 Nebraska Avenue, N.W., Washington, D. C. 20015.
5. Location of the headquarters or general business offices of the publishers: 5618 Nebraska Avenue, N.W., Washington, D. C. 20015.
6. Names and addresses of publisher, editor, and managing editor: I. F. Stone, same address.
7. Owner (if owned by a partnership or other unincorporated firm, its name and address, as well as that of each individual must be given): I. F. Stone, 5618 Nebraska Avenue, N. W., Washington, D. C. 20015; Esther M. Stone, same address.
8. Known bondholders, mortgagees, and other security holders owning or holding 1 percent or more of total amount of bonds, mortgages or other securities (if there are none, so state): none.
9. Paragraphs 7 and 8 include, in cases where the stockholder or security holder appears upon the books of the company as trustee or in any other fiduciary relation, the name of the person or corporation for whom such trustee is acting, also the statements in the two paragraphs show the

affiant's full knowledge and belief as to the circumstances and conditions under which stockholders and security holders who do not appear upon the books of the company as trustees, hold stock and securities in a capacity other than that of a bonafide owner.

	Average No. Copies Each Issue During Preceding 12 months	Single Issue Nearest To Filing Date
A. Total No. Copies Printed	34,500	38,500
B. Paid Circulation		
1. Sales Through Agents, News Dealers or Otherwise	1,570	2,854
2. To Term Subscribers by Mail, Carrier Delivery, or by other means	32,053	35,371
C. Total Paid Circulation	33,623	37,425
D. Free Distribution (including samples) by Mail, Carrier Delivery, or by Other Means	400	500
E. Total No. of Copies Distributed	34,023	37,925
F. Office Use, Etc.	477	575
G. Total	34,500	38,500

I certify that the statements made by me above are correct and complete. I. F. Stone, editor.

We'll Send Free Sample Copies of This Issue to Your Friends If You Send Us Stamped, Addressed Envelopes

I. F. Stone's Weekly   5618 Nebraska Ave., N. W. Washington, D. C. 20015

For the enclosed $6.95 send I. F. Stone's new book:

(To) Name ....

Street ....

City .... Zip .... State ....

Indicate if gift announcement wished ☐

Please renew (or enter) a sub for the enclosed $5:

Name ....

Street ....

City .... Zip .... State ....

11/20/67

I. F. Stone's Weekly

5618 Nebraska Ave., N. W.
Washington, D. C. 20015

NEWSPAPER

Second class postage paid at Washington, D. C.

I. F. Stone's Weekly. Second Class Postage Paid at Washington, D. C. Published every Monday except in August, the last week in December and the first week in January and Bi-Weekly during July at 5618 Nebraska Ave., N.W., Washington, D. C. An independent weekly published and edited by I. F. Stone; Circulation Manager, Esther M. Stone. Subscription: $5 in the U.S.; $6 in Canada; $10 elsewhere. Air Mail rates: $17 to Europe; $20 to Israel, Asia and Africa.

Part One:
Four Themes
and a
Footnote

How Earth Day was Polluted

The week the devoted band of youngsters who ran the Vietnam Moratorium gave up in despair was the week in which other youngsters all over the country, with the full support of the Establishment and its press, celebrated Earth Day. On the grassy slopes of the Sylvan Theatre in the shadow of the Washington Monument, where so many anti-war teach-ins have been held, a predominantly youthful audience jumped with joy as the rock bands played. Looking out at that tumultuous sea of sweet faces, in their long hair and bizarre costumes, I felt that just as the Caesars once used bread and circuses so ours were at last learning to use rock-and-roll, idealism and non-inflammatory social issues to turn the youth off from more urgent concerns which might really threaten the power structure. And I said so in my speech.

The pollution issue is real enough, though a little exaggerated, but it cannot be solved in isolation. From one viewpoint, the Earth Day affair was a gigantic snow job. Here was the country slipping into a wider war in South-East Asia. Even as we spoke the news was leaking that U.S. officers in civilian clothes, either C.I.A. or military, were directing a South Vietnamese offensive into Cambodia and that six days earlier the U.S. had already promised the new Cambodian regime a few thousand rifles but had asked them (*New York Times*, 23 April 1970) to keep the shipment secret. Two days before the Earth Day rally, Secretary of Defence Laird had made a speech to the Associated Press which can only be read as a deliberate effort to sabotage the S.A.L.T. talks, but here we were talking as if we had nothing to worry about but our drains.

The anti-pollution campaign was saved providentially from a Nixon message but half the Cabinet were on the day's soapboxes. The only bright note was provided by the oldest section of the American revolutionary movement, the D.A.R. Their convention denounced anti-pollution as a subversive movement. The clear proof: It was being entertained by Pete Seeger, 'a documented Communist'. 'It's strange, isn't it,' one D.A.R. speaker noted astutely (ah, if only the C.I.A. and the F.B.I. were as sharp as these old dowagers!), 'that today is Lenin Day and Earth Day.' If it was anybody else in the White House but Richard Nixon they'd have been calling him Vladimir Ilyich.

The Nixon budget should clear him of suspicion. He called air and water pollution a 'now or never' task but turned in a budget which allocates 52 cents of every general revenue dollar to the military and space, but only four-tenths of one cent per dollar to air and water pollution. New weaponry alone gets $5.4 billion while air and water pollution get $569 million. Senator Tydings at the University of Maryland Earth Day said we ought to be spending on pollution what we are spending on the Vietnam war. But nobody knows what that is. Laird said months ago it would be $17 billion but this year for the first time in history part of the military budget is blacked out, and no figures are given for certain items, Vietnam among them.

Unless there is a sharp change of course we are already in the first stages of a wider and more costly second Indo-Chinese War. Our secret services brought it on, upsetting the status quo in Cambodia by encouraging the anti-Sihanouk coup, as they upset the Laotian status quo with their Plain of Jars offensive last year. The enemy took up the challenge, and now Nixon's latest Vietnam message has raised the stakes by putting Cambodia and Laos squarely into the area of our concern. We must either get out altogether or plunge in further, for the military consequences otherwise would leave South Vietnam outflanked. You can kiss good-bye to any hope of controlling inflation if Nixon takes the plunge.

What a time to talk about pollution! What a time to fill the campuses, the press, the radio and TV, with Earth Day talk when such momentous secret decisions are being made. Education on the complex tasks of air and water control are all to the good, and should be sharpened to a fundamental discussion of governmental and corporate policy the Establishment doesn't want. But how much more urgent and important to educate the public while there is still time to the more critical issues of the widening war in South-East Asia and the S.A.L.T. talks in Vienna. On both Nixon is waging a con game, and Earth Day distracted from it. In the former he remains a prisoner of the terrible power of inertia. He still wants to avoid humiliation. How to avoid some humiliation for so many disastrous mistakes? He still wants victory of some sort: indeed he speaks as if it were possible and imminent. And what is the meaning of the message leaked through James Reston (*New York Times*, 22 April 1970) that he will use 'any' weapon to prevent a major military defeat as and when more troops are withdrawn? Are we back in desperation to the lunatic nonsense of threatening to use nuclear weapons?

The campuses and the communications media should be full of these questions, as they should be full of discussion about S.A.L.T. There the battle to curb the arms race is being lost even as it begins. The day the S.A.L.T. talks opened, Nixon had leading Senators in for a snow job. What Nixon is really trying to pull off was indicated four days earlier when Nixon won the support of Mendel Rivers and House Armed Services for a $1.4 billion expansion of the A.B.M. in return for $300 million more for the Navy. The A.B.M. expansion was cleared publicly the day the S.A.L.T. talks reopened. Seen from the other side this signals a U.S. drive for an area defence and an area defence is a necessity for a first strike strategy. The night before the S.A.L.T. talks opened, Secretary Rogers chose the significant vehicle of an interview with Radio Free Berlin to declare again our intention to go ahead with M.I.R.V. Add M.I.R.V. to A.B.M. and there is nothing for S.A.L.T. to do but ratify a new spiral in the arms race. That has been Nixon's intention from the beginning.

Senator Jackson, whom Nixon wanted as Secretary of Defence, is working hard on the Hill, and Laird, whom Nixon took as second choice, is working hard out of the Pentagon to make sure that S.A.L.T. does not succeed. The Laird speech to the A.P. 20 April is the most mendacious performance by a U.S. official since the days of John Foster Dulles. The Soviets are several years behind us in nuclear proficiency. They have just begun to deploy a solid fuel equivalent of Minuteman. They have just begun to develop M.R.V. We had it several years ago and are already developing M.I.R.V. The latest report of the London Institute of Strategic Studies released 11 April showed that thanks to M.I.R.V. our present total of 4,200 deliverable warheads (as against the Soviet's just under 1,900) would become 11,000 by 1975 – a stupendous imbalance, clearly raising the threat of a first strike. Yet Laird told the A.P. editors we had been standing still for five years while the Russians have been forging ahead!

Laird achieved this bit of trickery by ignoring the enormous qualitative advances we have made in those five years and focusing on the Soviet's effort to make up in numbers and in megatonnage (which is wasteful) for their lag in accuracy, multiple independently targeted warheads *and* numbers. He continued to impute to the Russians a desire to achieve what our Air Force has long sought – first strike capacity. If the roles were reversed and a Soviet official were to present so false and inflammatory a picture of the power balance we would decide that it was time to pack our bags and head for home. Let pollution buffs notice Dr Panofsky's testimony that we already have enough weapons between us to make the entire Northern Hemisphere unlivable in one swift nuclear exchange. If S.A.L.T. fails and we up the firepower, we may wake up one morning and find there is nothing left on Earth to pollute.

23 April 1970, vol. 18, no. 9

Imperialism is not Internationalism

Internationalism made its appearance in American foreign policy with the administration of Woodrow Wilson. It rested on three premises whose validity was demonstrated by the great power rivalry which culminated in World War I. The first was that balance of power politics could not be relied on to preserve peace but only exacerbated mutual suspicion. The second was that the arms race which accompanied balance of power politics had itself become a primary source of tension and war. The third was the need for a world organization as a framework for peaceful settlement of international disputes and for the reduction of national armies to levels necessary only for internal order. This was the grand design with which Wilson declared America's intervention in Europe a 'war to end war' and sought unsuccessfully to make that a reality by leading the United States into the League of Nations. By those standards Nixon is not an internationalist but an imperialist.

On several occasions Nixon has wrapped himself in the mantle of Wilson and invoked the rhetoric of World War I to support the Vietnamese conflict.* But the policies outlined by Nixon in his interview with C. L. Sulzberger, as in his new state of the world message, clearly outline an attempt single-handedly to police the world. The supposed 'low posture' of the Nixon Doctrine turns out to be little more than an optical illusion to appease a public sick of unilateral intervention. 'Of course,' Nixon told Sulzberger, 'we're not going to get into every little firefight everywhere.' But where other nations 'are ready to fight a fire' we 'should be able to furnish the hose and water'. These homely but deceptive analogies apply only to the sideshows. 'Our responsibilities,' Nixon said grandly, 'are not limited to this great continent, but include Europe, the Middle East, South-East Asia, East Asia, many areas whose fate affects the peace of the world.' This covers just about every place on earth except the South Pole. Of course our motives, Nixon says, are benign. But there has never been an imperialism yet from Kipling's 'white man's burden' to the Kaiser's 'Kultur' which did not claim to be altruistic.

Considering the territorial sweep of the Nixon Doctrine, it is hard to see how he can 'seriously doubt' that 'we will ever have another war' and add as he did, 'This is probably the very last one.' For a man who claims 'I know this world' how can he overlook the scores of national rivalries and conflicts in this vast area, any one of them capable of flaring up into a good-sized 'firefight' at any time? No cop ever volunteered for a wider and

---

* I am describing Wilsonianism at its best. At its worst, in dealing with Latin America, it was as imperialistic as the 'dollar diplomacy' of Roosevelt and Taft which the Democrats had criticized.

more dangerous beat. Yet Nixon could also say in the same interview that the period of 'expansion as typified by Theodore Roosevelt and the idea of Manifest Destiny' is 'fortunately gone.' No one ever dreamt in T.R.'s day that we would some day consider it our destiny to impose a Pax Americana on the whole world, or to wield a Big Stick as big as our present Pentagon. Nixon told Sulzberger we confronted two great powers, Russia and China 'motivated by a philosophy which announces itself as expansionist in character'. What could be more expansionist than the Nixon Doctrine itself? It is dangerous to have a leader so unaware of any mote in his own eye.

In a realm of discourse in which words have lost all normal meaning, it is not surprising to hear that Nixon also told Sulzberger, 'I rate myself as a deeply committed pacifist.' Many men have been 'committed' for less obvious lapses from reality. His is a pacifism which does not require extended surveillance by military intelligence. Nixon's pacifism implies a perpetual arms race. 'We can't,' he said, 'foolishly fall behind in the arms competition.' This from the leader of the world's most heavily armed nation, with an arms budget almost as big as the rest of the world's combined!

Even Laird, whose whoppers fill one with reluctant admiration, has never gone as far in misrepresentation as Nixon did when he told Sulzberger, 'The Soviets now have three times the missile strength of ourselves . . . By 1974 they will pass us in subs carrying nuclear missiles.' Table 2 of Laird's new posture report shows that we can launch 2,600 nuclear 'force loadings' or more than twice as many as the Soviets. By 1974 the Soviets pass us in the number of nuclear submarines but only because we plan to concentrate on M.I.R.V.-ing our fleet, increasing the number and accuracy of its warheads rather than the number of submarines.* The Institute for Strategic Studies estimates that by 1975 our strategic forces will have 11,000 nuclear warheads

---

* As with land-based I.C.B.M.s where we have also concentrated on M.I.R.V. ing Minutemen. The Soviets may be ahead of us in numbers of I.C.B.M.s but many are obsolete and few are solid-fuel. For a full picture see my 'Memo to the A.P.: How Laird Lied' in the *New York Review of Books* last June 4.

while the Soviets in this insane race may reach 5,000, or still less than half as many. Then if war comes our overkill will be four times – and the Soviet's $2\frac{1}{2}$ times – what it is today. That should make us all feel more secure. Yet Nixon closed the Sulzberger interview with an argument for giving arms expenditure higher priority than health, education and environment. 'After all,' Nixon said brightly, 'if we manage to improve the environment and living conditions in this country we must also assure that we will be around to enjoy these improvements'. We haven't heard such clinchers since we left high school.

Nixon's philosophy of representative government matches his foreign and military policy. Here, too, what he says and how he portrays himself do not match what he is doing. Only Jules Feiffer has begun to do justice to his quick-change artistry, now a Pentagon pacifist, in a Ghandi loincloth; now, with the 'power to the people' theme in his State of the Union message, prac- tically a Black Panther in a dashiki. The point Senator Sym- ington tried to make in his 'Kissinger syndrome' speech in the Senate 2 March is that Nixon has been insulating himself more and more from Congressional and popular control by con- centrating power in a greatly enlarged White House staff. The press, always avid for personality clashes, focused on Kissinger and Rogers. It overlooked the fundamentals of what Symington was trying to say. Though Nixon talked in the 1968 campaign of 'streamlining' the White House staff, its numbers have more than doubled and its cost has tripled. By moving more and more of the decision-making process particularly in foreign policy into the White House, where those who take part are protected by 'executive privilege' from interrogation by Congress, Nixon has covertly moved power further away from, not closer to, 'the people'.

The anti-imperialists who fought the annexation of the Philippines in the 1890s warned that imperialism would weaken democracy. Even they could hardly have imagined that a future government could carry on a war in Indo-China so plainly against the popular will. 'Frankly,' Nixon told Sulzberger in talking of opposition to the war among the elite, 'I have far more confidence in our people than in the Establishment.' He shows it in strange ways. At one point he said to Sulzberger, 'In 1966 and 1967 – culminating in 1968 – the American people began to tire of playing a role in the world.' What they tired of was the war in Vietnam and heavy military spending, of interventionism and the Pax Americana, not of 'playing a role in the world' but of Lyndon Johnson's conception of that role and Nixon's which is really the same as L.B.J.'s. That all this is contrary to popular will was admitted by Nixon himself when he said in the Sulzberger interview that he was 'certain a Gallup poll would show' (in fact the polls *have* shown) that 'the great majority' want to get out of Vietnam, to reduce our military forces in Europe and 'cut our defence budget'. Then he added lamely, 'But polls are not the answer.' Two years ago Nixon was appealing to a silent majority. Now that it is no longer silent, he is saying that it must be ignored. This is the Caesarism inseparable from empire.

14 March 1971, vol. 19, no. 6

The Crisis Coming for a Free Press

In the Pentagon Papers, the government had a poor case on the facts. It had an even poorer case on the law. It is a pity that the upshot was not the kind of historic defence of a free press that the weak pleading and the grave circumstances called for. *The press did its duty but the Supreme Court did not.* Its splintered opinions left a bigger loophole than before for prior restraint – something English law abandoned in 1695 and the American press has never experienced. In addition five of the nine Justices encouraged the government to believe that they would give it wide latitude if it sought to punish editors for publishing official secrets *after* they did so instead of trying to enjoin them in advance. Two Justices indeed spent most of their opinions helpfully spelling out possibilities for successful criminal prosecution. It will be a miracle if this Administration, which is almost paranoid in its attitude towards the media, is not encouraged to include editors and reporters among the 'all those who have violated Federal criminal laws' the Attorney General now says he will prosecute.

The coming attempt to prosecute for violation of the government's classification orders involves nothing less than the future of representative government. For if the government can continue to abuse its secrecy stamps to keep the press, the Congress and the people from knowing what it is really doing – then the basic decisions in our country are in the hands of a small army of faceless bureaucrats, mostly military. The struggle comes at a climactic moment when Hanoi's new peace offer and public weariness with the war make it all the more necessary for the bureaucratic machine to prevent new leaks by intimidating its own mavericks and the press. Duplicity is more requisite than ever when the other side makes it necessary plainly to choose between release of the prisoners or continued pursuit of a military-political victory in South Vietnam. From every indication, Nixon's answer, however veiled, will be to pursue the war. This will intensify his conflict with the media.

First, as to the facts: Trial of the government's action against the *New York Times* and the *Washington Post* proceeded on the assumption that two documents in their entirety were in the hands of these newspapers – a 47-volume Pentagon history of our involvement in Vietnam from 1945 to 1968, and a 'Command and Control' report on the Tonkin Gulf incidents of 1964. The government was invited to 'pinpoint' for the trial judges, the two Courts of Appeal and the Supreme Court precisely which portions of these documents were so sensitive that their publication warranted an order forbidding the papers to publish them. To give the government greater leeway, it was allowed to present much of its evidence in secret. This was the first secret proceeding of its kind ever held in the U.S. courts, itself a disturbing precedent for the future. Yet of the 27 Federal judges who passed on the government's pleadings not a single one thought the evidence impressive enough to warrant a preliminary injunction. The government was able to obtain nothing more than temporary restraining orders pending trial and appeal, and those who dissented on the appeals courts and the Supreme Court did no more than argue for a remand for further hearing. This is the best measure of just how dubious the government's system of classification looked even to sympathetic judges in secret hearings.

Some of the dissenting judges thought the case was disposed of too hastily, and that the government should have had more time. But the government had had ample time to review the two documents involved. The Senate Foreign Relations Committee has been negotiating with the Pentagon for the Command and Control document since early in 1968 and the so-called Pentagon Papers since November 1969. At least half a dozen letters have passed between Chairman Fulbright and Secretary Laird about these documents, and the Pentagon classification officer who was assigned to review them as a result of Fulbright's repeated requests testified during the trial. The government had plenty of time to decide what in the documents was really sensitive. Apparently the judges didn't think very much was. But only as this is written the Senate Foreign Relations Committee has finally received copies of both. It took a tidal wave of a leak to pry them loose but they arrived still stamped 'Top Secret'! The truth about the Tonkin Gulf incidents may be buried in the Command and Control report but the *New York Times* completed its series without disclosing what was in this document and the Senate Foreign Relations Committee is still forbidden by the 'Top Secret' stamp from discussing the contents publicly. It will be seven years next month since the Tonkin Gulf incidents occurred and we still don't know the full truth about them, though they were used to get a blank cheque for war from Congress.

The two dissenting judges who were most impressed with the government's case were Judge Wilkey on the Court of Appeals for the District of Columbia and Mr Justice Blackmun on the Supreme Court. They felt that *if* the newspapers, had, and *if* they published, certain documents dealing with diplomatic negotiations this would do great harm. But Dr Ellsberg at his press conference in Cambridge 28 June said he withheld 'several' of the 47-volume Pentagon Papers from the newspapers because they involved secret negotiations with Hanoi, Moscow and other foreign capitals. On N.B.C.'s *Today* show 2 July he said he gave the full set to the Senate Foreign Relations Committee but did not retain any copy of these diplomatic volumes 'since I had no intention of giving them to the newspapers at any time'. In oral argument before the Supreme Court, the Solicitor General said he had 'pinpointed' ten sensitive items in his secret brief and that one of them was made up of four volumes 'all dealing with one specific subject'. Are these the volumes Dr Ellsberg withheld?

The newspapers provided the court with inventories of the documents in their possession. The Solicitor General told the Supreme Court that the government's experts had difficulty in matching this inventory against the 47-volume Pentagon Papers. There may have been difficulty in matching individual items but it is hard to understand why they could not match up an 'item' as large as four related volumes. A week before the oral argument, the *Christian Science Monitor* (19 June) carried a story from Washington saying that Pentagon experts, after they compared the published reports in the *Times* 'with the still guarded and highly classified originals', decided that the disclosures were 'something less than catastrophic'. They informed higher officials 'that some potentially damaging material, *particularly in terms of America's relations with other nations* (our italics) had been omitted'. This sounds as if they spotted the material Ellsberg withheld. It is a pity the secret record cannot be opened up to resolve this mystery. The government's most impressive cause for alarm would have been eliminated by the admission that these volumes had never reached the newspapers at all.

All this may explain the curious vagueness and equanimity displayed by Deputy Under Secretary of State Macomber on the *Today* show 5 July, the day the *New York Times* series ended. He admitted that Dr Ellsberg had withheld some sensitive documents and that the newspapers themselves had withheld others. When asked whether the *New York Times* or the *Washington Post* had published items 'the government has pointed to as particularly sensitive', he replied, 'I don't think the *Washington Post* has. I think the *New York Times* may have. I don't want to say it has. I'm not sure.' So this is the molehill to which the government's mountainous original charges dwindled.

The government made an even poorer showing on the law. Solicitor General Griswold's argument was downright trivial and the few precedents he cited were irrelevant and quoted out of context. Unfortunately the newspaper lawyers were no better. Never was a great case argued so feebly. No one took the First Amendment as his client. The defence lawyers argued the case as narrowly as possible in order to get their newspaper clients off the hook. Professor Alexander Bickel whom the *New York Times* retained specially for the occasion, is no firm defender of the First Amendment; he holds the 'balancing' view Frankfurter among others propounded. This holds, as Griswold flatly said during argument, that where the First Amendment says 'Congress shall make no law ... abridging freedom of the press', it does not mean what the plain words say but only that freedom of the press must be 'balanced' against other public considerations. Bickel agrees with Griswold. This nullifies the intention of the Framers.

The crisis for which the bar and the press must mobilize lies in the fact that never before have the courts had to confront the freedom of the press issue in this form. The publication of secret government papers is hardly new. A patriot newspaper in Boston, thanks to a leak from Benjamin Franklin, published the Royal Governor's correspondence on the eve of the Revolution. The furore over the Sedition Act began in 1798 when John Franklin Bache (Benjamin's grandson) published secret diplomatic documents to attack the covert Federalist war against France. But this was before the days of 'classification' and leaks of this kind were prosecuted as seditious libels intended to bring the government into disrepute. What we face now are the first prosecutions of the press for upsetting the government's system of classification. The freedom of the press issue is thereby entangled with the question of national security.

A government cannot be denied the right to some secrets, especially in wartime. But what makes this case so crucial is that Dr Ellsberg's leak and its publication in the press represented the first open revolt against a system of secrecy which has reached cancerous proportions and threatens unless checked to destroy free government itself. The amount of information now stamped secret and withheld from the press and Congress is staggering. The *Washington Star* estimates (8 July) that Pentagon Xerox machines produce about 100 million documents a year. A recently retired Air Force security officer told a House Government Information subcommittee 24 June, 'I would guess that there are at least 20 million classified documents, including reproduced copies, in existence' and added, 'I sincerely believe that less than one-half of one per cent of the different documents actually contain information qualifying even for the lowest defence classification.'

The Pentagon Papers showed that the government has been carrying on secret warfare in Indo-China since 1954. They disclosed for the first time the full dimensions of the arrogance, duplicity and inhumanity with which successive Administrations got us into this horrible mess which is tearing the country apart and demoralizing the armed forces themselves. It was the height of Nixon-era banality for Chief Justice Burger to say that a newspaper editor, handed such documents, should, like a taxi driver who finds stolen goods in his cab, turn them over to the police! To reduce such historic revelations in the midst of an agonized public debate over the war to the dimensions of a simple case of larceny and receiving stolen goods is utterly to miss the function of a free press in a free society.

Representative government is menaced today by a cloud of secrecy. The Daniel Ellsbergs and Neil Sheehans are too few; a Senator like Gravel willing to challenge the classification system in which Congress has acquiesced for so many years, is unique. We need more such rebels, not fewer, if free government is to survive.

In the fight against government secrecy we need to apply in a fresh form the philosophy of risk which laid the foundations for real freedom of the press in the earlier struggle against the law of seditious libel. It is often forgotten that after prior restraint or censorship ended almost three centuries ago, the press was still shackled by the common law of seditious libel. Editors went to jail for bringing government into disrepute; the rule was that the greater the truth of their publications the greater the offence; royal governors decided the law and made conviction by the jury almost a foregone conclusion. The reformers sought to protect the press by making the jury the judge of the law as well as the facts, and to make truth a defence. The Sedition Act of 1798, so notorious in our history, actually embodied these reforms, though its purpose was repressive. Like Fox's historic Libel Act six years earlier in England, it made the jury the judge of the law as well as the facts; in addition the Sedition Act made truth a defence, something English law did not achieve until 1843.

But these long-sought reforms proved illusory. In the heat of partisan passion, only one jury failed to convict in a Sedition Act case and 'truth' proved difficult to determine. It became clear that freedom of the press could only be secure if the press were allowed to propagate error. Otherwise censorship was only replaced by prosecution after publication. It was in the battle against the Sedition Act that the Jeffersonians for the first time* hammered out the libertarian doctrines which have made ours the freest press in the world. The philosophy to which we are indebted runs in a great line from Madison, the Father of the Constitution, to Brandeis, and from them to Black and Douglas. It says that freedom is impossible without risk of repression. This is what the best young people yearn for under Communist rule and this is what we are in danger of forgetting in the Nixon era.

We must apply the philosophy of risk to the new circumstances. Talk of reforming the classification system will soon evaporate. Successful prosecutions would only nail it down. The path of least resistance is that which Nixon has already charted: to cut down the number of persons with access to secret documents and to tighten up on security. It would in any case take a small army many years to review the classification of all our secret documents. The only hope lies in jury acquittals in the coming prosecutions, and in arguing that the only possible check on the abuses of overclassification and secrecy is to allow

* One may find this ably developed in Leonard W. Levy's book, *Freedom of Speech and Press in Early American History*.

unpunished the leak and publication of documents like the Pentagon Papers. Congress by twice refusing to enact an Official Secrets Act in wartime has shown itself of a similar mind. Men of courage are all too rare; the circumstances which bring establishment papers to print such documents are even rarer. This is the only safety valve we have if the people's right to know is not entirely to disappear.

9 July 1971, vol. 19 no. 14

Heading for a Bigger Arms Race in the 70s

Despite euphoric reports about the S.A.L.T. talks and the $5.9 billion cut in the final defence budget this fiscal year, the military monster is far from being subdued. It takes a long time before cuts in Congressional authorization and appropriation bills actually lead to cuts in expenditure. The best guide to actual expenditures is the daily U.S. Treasury statement. Its 2 January statement covering all but the last two days of the first half of the 1970 fiscal year is not encouraging. The cash deficit for the six months was $12.4 billion as against $7.8 billion in the same period last year. To this deficit the military establishment was a prime contributor, despite the first withdrawals from Vietnam and talk of reduced commitments. In the first half of the fiscal year the military drew more than half a billion ($685 million) *more* from the Treasury than in the corresponding period a year ago. The *rate* of increase seemed to be going up. In December alone military spending was more than $1 billion higher than in December a year ago. The tempo of military spending is still feeding the fires of inflation.

The Tax Foundation estimates that in 1970 the average tax burden per American family for defence will be $1,250 a year. For those families lucky enough to be on the gravy train of the military-industrial complex, this tax is easily outweighed by their earnings. Indeed from an economic point of view the arms race is a device for taxing the poor to profit the well-to-do. The prospect for a change in the seventies is dim. The Arms Control and Disarmament Agency estimates that the world has spent $4,000 billion on arms since 1900 and at the current rate of increase will spend that much again in the coming decade alone. That, too, will not help our chronic inflationary fevers.

There is little reason to believe that the Strategic Arms Limitation Talks (S.A.L.T.) will change the picture much, if at all. The two biggest escalations which lie ahead are those to be sparked by M.I.R.V., the multiple, independently targeted missile warheads, and the A.B.M. the anti-ballistic missile. There is no sign that Washington or Moscow is prepared to halt either. The constant and pleased assurances from the State Department and the Pentagon that the Russians at Helsinki were behaving splendidly and avoiding 'propaganda' are – in our opinion – cause for depression, not optimism. If Moscow were militantly for disarmament or arms control, we may be sure this would be stigmatized as 'propaganda'.

Disarmament buffs had naïvely assumed that a main purpose of the S.A.L.T. talks was to block M.I.R.V., for once the missiles on both sides are outfitted with the multiple warheads, it will be impossible for either side to know by aerial surveillance how many warheads there are atop each missile on the other. The fog and the fear will come down again, and it will be hard to keep the arms race within any bounds at all. But the Pentagon is now leaking the revelation that there has never been much if any intention on our side to curb M.I.R.V. William Beecher, who covers the Pentagon for the *New York Times*, reported in a dispatch to his paper 31 December that while the Johnson Administration in the summer of 1968 was prepared to propose a freeze on strategic weapons, there was to be no limitation on 'improvements of systems within the limited numbers', including M.I.R.V.s. This was the first public disclosure of the Johnson negotiating position. George C. Wilson, who covers the Pentagon for the *Washington Post*, reported (1 January) from a similar briefing with unnamed officials that 'the Nixon Administration view is that multiple-warhead submarines are a fact of life already' so M.I.R.V. discussion would focus on the land-based missiles 'but, according to informed sources, the Soviets showed little interest at the S.A.L.T. talks in calling off the flight tests of M.I.R.V. missiles'. Clearly the Nixon Administration shares this lack of interest.

The second biggest item of future arms spending is the A.B.M. The Pentagon is beginning to leak stories designed to build up support for its escalation. Beecher reported in the *New York Times* (2 January), 'Administration Expected to Back A.B.M. Expansion'. The Associated Press was given a similar backgrounder, 'Soviet Buildup Spurs New Anti-Missile plans' (*Washington Star*, 3 January). This was an effort to revive the first-strike scare of last spring. The A.P. was told that if the Russians continue building SS9s at the current rate, they will have 420 by 1974–5 and that these 420 would then be able to wipe out 95 per cent of our 1,000 Minutemen in a surprise attack. The arithmetic sounds like pure Pentagon Munchhausen. Unanswered is the question of why anyone would risk a first strike at our Minutemen when this would expose the Soviet Union to destruction from our submarine missile fleet. Another question no one raised at the backgrounder was – if land based missiles are now so vulnerable to first attack, are they not obsolete? Indeed the House Appropriations Committee report on the new defence budget (3 December, p. 78) suggests that instead of spending millions to bury the missiles in 'very costly' hard rock siloes and in defending them with more A.B.M.s, it would be better to replace them altogether with submarine or mobile land missiles. 'The final argument for expansion,' the A.P. account said, with unintended irony, 'is that it would cost less now than later in the face of rising prices and inflation.'

The House report noted that the fiscal 1969 military budget was seven times the military budget of 1948, just two decades ago. It may easily double and redouble within the next ten years. The reductions in the 1970 budget were mostly cuts in fat and waste; old ships were mothballed, headquarter staffs – military and civilian – were cut down. Development contracts were stretched out. The budget cuts were a tactical retreat. In that retreat the Pentagon saved the major new weapons systems whose costs will proliferate into billions during the next decade. Senator Hatfield (R. Ore.) spelled out a few of them in his

speech on final passage 15 December. There was $100 million
for A.M.S.A., the new strategic bomber; it will eventually cost
from $8 to $23 billion. The $450 million for the new F-14 plane
launches a programme that will cost from $15 to $30 billion.
The $425 million for a new nuclear attack aircraft carrier will
give us fifteen such task forces eventually; each costs $1 billion.
The $5 million for the new Navy underwater missile system
(U.L.M.S.) is another item which will escalate into billions.
These are but a few samples of the spiralling expenditures
ahead.

Most important of all, despite talk of cutbacks, the new troop-
level strength next June will still be 3.2 million men, down only
260,000 from the previous June, and three quarters of a million
men higher than in the first Kennedy year when the military
buildup began. This huge force is the embodiment of a continued Pax Americana, 'a projection of threats and con-
tingencies,' Hatfield said, 'that are far overdrawn and bear little
relation to the contemporary realities of international affairs'.
This year's appropriation though reduced somewhat still 'allows
us to station troops on foreign soil throughout the globe, where
their mere presence often contributes more to the undermin-
ing of our relations with foreign nations than to our own
security'.

12 January 1970, vol. 18, no. 1

Another Way to Elude the Censor and See the Fate in Store for that 'Peace Dividend'

There is another clue (beside those mentioned in our last issue)
to the military spending figures blacked out in the new Nixon
budget projections. At page 8 of the *Economic Report of the
President* there is a Table 14, which gives projected Federal
expenditures from 1970 to 1975 inclusive in 1969 prices. This is
part of what the Nixon Administration says is its effort 'to formulate the larger choices it faces in the allocation of national
output in the light of competing options'. They include military
spending but the military projections are nowhere given.

One way to get some conception of the military spending is to start with the figures this table gives on Federal purchases of goods and services. From a table on p. 177, one can with a little arithmetic learn that 78 per cent of all Federal purchases of goods and services in fiscal 1969 were for national defence. From p. 587 of the budget message one can also figure out that 97 per cent of all national defence expenditures are for goods and services. Assuming that these two ratios will remain about the same, we can then apply them to the yearly projections for goods and services and deduce how much will be spent on national defence in those six years 1970 to 1975. The total is $415 billion.

In the first six fiscal years of the sixties before the cost of the Vietnam war played havoc with the budget, the total spent on national defence was $300 billion. That was a period of rapid military expansion. Yet it looks as though the first six years of the seventies will be a third, or $100 billion higher.

One can take the five fiscal years 1965–9 inclusive when we spent about $100 billion on the Vietnam war and compare it with this projection for the five fiscal years 1971–5 inclusive when (we have been led by Nixon to believe) we should be out of Vietnam. The total spent in 1965–9 was $338 billion. The total projected for 1971–5 is $342 billion. Even allowing for inflation that looks as if most of the 'peace dividend' will be absorbed by the Pentagon.

Another way to look at it: The table at p. 80 shows projected spending year by year from 1970 to 1975 for 'new initiatives'. These include welfare, pollution and education. These start at $1 billion in fiscal 1970 and rise to $15 billion in fiscal 1975, a total of $58 billion for six years. But national defence in those same years will absorb $100 billion *more* than in the first six years of the sixties or $342 billion, roughly as much as we spent during the Vietnam war years! No wonder the Nixon Administration would rather keep these figures secret. But why is there so little protest in Congress over this secrecy? How can it debate the priorities when the military figures are hidden from it?

23 March 1970, vol. 18, no. 6

Part Two:
McCarthy
and the
Cold War

1: McCarthy and the Witch-Hunt

Time for a Deportation – to Wisconsin

McCarthy will never be beaten on the defensive. He loses one fight and starts two new ones. Charges are always more exciting than their refutation, and he thereby dominates the front pages. He is becoming the biggest thing on the national landscape, and frontal collision with the President and his own party leadership adds to his prestige. He has hardly begun to hit his stride as master of the Big Lie. Like Hitler and Goebbels, he knows the value of ceaseless reiteration. He has their complete lack of scruple, and sets as low an estimate as they on the popular mind's capacity to remember. His defeat in the fight against Bohlen is a minor episode in the perspective of his ambition and his potentialities.

If – the fatal *if* that shadows democratic governments in their contest with fascist pretenders – *if* this Administration had guts, it would move now to act on the findings of the buried McCarthy report submitted by the Senate subcommittee on privileges and elections. The new Attorney General, in a cheap and vulgar St Patrick's Day speech, announced a heightened deportation campaign against so-called 'subversives'. The most subversive force in America today is Joe McCarthy. No one is so effectively importing alien conceptions into American government. No one is doing so much to damage the country's prestige abroad and its power to act effectively at home. If 'subversion' is to be met by deportation, then it is time to deport McCarthy back to Wisconsin. Families are being broken up, long-time residents driven into exile, men face permanent detention, on charges which are far more tenuous than those made against McCarthy by the Senate inquiry under the Benton resolution.

Far stronger than the inference of guilt McCarthy sees in every invocation of the Fifth Amendment is the inference created by his own failure six times to show up when invited by the subcommittee to rebut the charges made against him. His repeated fliers in stock and commodity speculation, the unexplained $105,000 in his bank accounts and those of his administrative assistants, the diversion to speculation of funds contributed to fight Communism, his hectic borrowings and his ability to bank more than $170,000 in four years on a Senator's salary (his assistant banked another $96,000 in the same period) – all this cries out for investigation. The subcommittee raises serious question as to whether Wisconsin banking and Federal election laws have been violated. Here lies the means of stopping McCarthy before he has grown too big to be stopped.

There may never be a more favourable opportunity. Young William Randolph Hearst, who has several times put the damper on Pegler, last week got off the McCarthy bandwagon and declared (*New York Journal*, 26 March), 'We've had enough of this kind of malicious mischief in American life. Joe McCarthy has pulled a strategical boner with his opposition to the Bohlen appointment.' The hitherto favourable Scripps-Howard press (*Washington News*, 26 March) attacked McCarthy for his 'back-alley tactics' and said, 'The amazing thing is that this loud-mouthed rowdy has attracted a Senate following, which has assisted him in dragging that body into the gutter with him.' The magisterial *Washington Star*, the most influential paper in the capital, said of McCarthy and McCarran in the Bohlen fight (29 March), 'Their attack was vicious and thoroughly unprincipled. Their weapons were the familiar ones of sly hint and ugly insinuation ... With this dirtiest of dirty business there should be no compromise.'

Though McCarthy at one point in his career was happy to have Communist support, he now likes to picture himself as a remorseless foe of Communism. But the affair of the Greek shipowners last week shows how differently McCarthy treats suspected Communist collaborators who are men of means from the way he treats poor schoolteachers. These shipowners – the breed of the wily Ulysses – have been supplying Communist customers in ships acquired cut-rate from America. Owners of 242 such ships have got an immunity bath from McCarthy in return for a paper promise he admits is unenforceable. These subtle-minded Greek operators are men who know their way around politically.

One would have expected McCarthy to denounce them for having grown wealthy by taking America's favours and supplying America's enemies. Yet they are not to be exposed, harassed or punished. The Attorney General is not to be denounced for failure to recover these ships. Instead these shipowners by their private deal with McCarthy may find therein some protection against the seizures and mortgage foreclosures the Eisenhower government had begun to institute in these cases. McCarthy's mandate from the Senate to investigate the operations of government may be broad but it is not broad enough to allow him to invade the sphere of foreign policy and to arrange 'agreements' by which possible law violations may be excused. It is no wonder he kept his negotiations secret from the State and Justice Departments! His sudden emergence as a combination Secretary of State and Attorney General in this arrangement with the Greek shipowners calls for investigation.

Ever since that famous $10,000 pamphlet for Lustron (let's hope it doesn't turn out that McCarthy is also writing pamphlets now on the Greek merchant marine), the Senator has been moving more and more into the domain of literature. His inquiry last week into the overseas information programme should give the State Department a lesson in diplomacy. The Department has placed 2,000,000 books abroad by more than 85,000 authors, among them Owen Latimore's *Ordeal by Slander*. But when McCarthy asked whether any of his own books were in the overseas libraries, it appeared there was not a single one on the list. The State Department never committed a greater *faux pas*.

Louis Budenz was on hand as an expert witness, and the often incredible Roy Cohn put this to him:

MR COHN: I will ask you this question, Professor Budenz: Have you at the request of the committee examined a partial list of some authors whose books we have been advised by the Library of Congress are currently being used by the State Department in its information programme?

MR BUDENZ: Yes, sir, I have gone over that list.

MR COHN: On that list did you find any authors who were known to you as Communists?

MR BUDENZ: Yes, sir, I did.

MR COHN: Approximately how many?

MR BUDENZ: At least seventy-five. And four that had very close connections with the Communist Party.

The answer is intriguing since it implies that one can be a Communist without having 'very close connections with the Communist Party'. Naturally Cohn did not press him on the point. After all a lot of people named by Budenz as Communists never had 'very close connections' with the party.

The F.B.I. ought to check one unexplored angle of McCarthy's interrogation of Earl Browder, some of whose works were in libraries abroad. In 1950 International Publishers put on sale a book about the Rajk trial in Hungary called *Tito's Plot Against Europe*. It was written by Derek Kartun, the foreign editor of the London *Daily Worker*. In it on pages 20–21, Kartun says a counter-revolutionary group in 1944 were primed for dirty work in Hungary by the O.S.S. which gave them copies of Browder's books *Teheran* and *Victory and After*.

Kartun explains that Browder's theories 'would have emasculated the revolutionary movement. The U.S. intelligence service understood immediately the value of the Browder theories in confusing and paralysing the European Communist parties, and had distributed large numbers of the Browder books . . .' If this is correct, then McCarthy in discouraging the State Department from circulating these books abroad must be acting as a Communist agent. How the plots do thicken!

4 April 1953, vol. I, no. 12

Time for a Change

Every year about this time the House Appropriations Committee releases the annual testimony of J. Edgar Hoover on the F.B.I. budget. Each year he gives the committee the latest figure on the membership of the Communist Party – an exact count, down to the last subversive digit, as if the comrades had been herded through a special turnstile by the F.B.I. The membership figures as he has given them during the last five years follow:

1949	54,174
1950	52,669
1951	43,217
1952	31,608
1953	24,796

As anyone can see by running his eye down the figures, the Communist Party, according to Hoover, has lost more than fifty per cent of its members in the last five years.

But while the number of Communists has been dwindling, the number of F.B.I. men employed to watch them has been growing. The F.B.I. budget has been rising at just about the same rate that Communist Party membership has been falling. In the fiscal year ended 30 June 1948, the F.B.I. budget was less than $30,000,000. For the fiscal year beginning next 1 July Hoover is asking $77,000,000. The number of Communists is less than half what it was five years ago but the F.B.I. budget is more than double what it was then.

This is not because the F.B.I. is spending more time chasing bank robbers. Its main business is 'internal security', i.e. acting as a political police. Some readers will recall that last year just about this time Attorney General McGranery fired Newbold Morris as special investigator of corruption in government, declaring that if he saw any corruption around he would 'straighten it out' himself with the aid of the F.B.I.

Morris replied that the F.B.I. was too busy to investigate corruption. He said Hoover 'told me it was impossible for his department to do anything except the task before them of counter-espionage'.

It would appear from Hoover's testimony this year that the F.B.I. is not doing too well at that task. Hoover told the House Committee 'the enemy espionage rings are more intensively operated today than they have been at any previous time in the history of the country'.

A statement of this kind, from any other official so long a part of the Roosevelt–Truman Administration, would provoke a storm in Congress, if not an investigation to determine whether Hoover himself might not be ... well, you never can tell.

The number of Communists has been cut in half, the F.B.I. budget has been doubled, the government has been turned turvy by one loyalty purge after another, yet Hoover says enemy spy rings are working here more intensively than ever before. Either the enemy must be devilishly clever or the F.B.I. must be devilishly full of *dummkopfs*.

The question which rises is: if Hoover knows that enemy spy rings are working here so intensively, why doesn't he break them up? Either the director of the F.B.I. is talking through his hat or – as the Republicans would say of any other holdover from the last Administration – it is time for a change.

11 April 1953, vol. I, no. 13

McCarthy's Bluff, and Two Who Called It

McCarthy has been engaged in a bluff. Last week two witnesses – Harvey O'Connor and Leo Huberman – called him on it. The bluff is this: Congressional investigating committees are not the possessors of a universal writ. They may not inquire into any and everything. The subjects into which they may inquire are limited to those specified in the rule or resolution establishing the committee.

What is McCarthy authorized to investigate? He is chairman of the Senate Committee on Government Operations, known until last year as the Committee on Expenditures in the Executive Department. The old name indicates the true purpose and authority of this committee. It is a kind of super auditing body,

Its name was changed last year but not its authority. It still operates under subsection (g) of Rule XXV of the Senate. This rule gives McCarthy no authority to inquire into the political beliefs and associations even of persons employed by the government, much less of editors and writers not on the public payroll.

McCarthy's two competitors in the witch-hunt lay claim rightly or wrongly to broad powers of inquisition. Velde is chairman of the House Committee on 'Un-American Activities', a term vague enough to cover any person or idea the committee may consider objectionable. Jenner's subcommittee of the Senate Judiciary Committee operates under as loose and sweeping a standard – its concern is with 'internal security'. But McCarthy's lawful province is with 'budget and accounting measures' and with the effect of executive reorganizations. His broadest grant of investigating power is to study 'the operation of government activities at all levels with a view to determining its economy and efficiency'.

This can be stretched to cover the purchase of books for overseas libraries – to ask who bought them and why, even to inquire into their contents. But it gives him no authority to subpoena writers and editors and question them about their political beliefs and affiliations. James Wechsler of the *New York Post* submitted to a non-existent authority when he allowed himself to be interrogated by McCarthy and gave McCarthy a list of persons Wechsler had known as Communists. Cedric Belfrage and James Aronson of the *National Guardian* let themselves in for the usual smear-by-implication when they pleaded their privilege before McCarthy instead of challenging his authority.

Last week two well-known writers, O'Connor and Huberman, taking their cue from Einstein (see 'Einstein, Oxnam and the Witch Hunt' in the *Weekly* for 20 June) declined to plead self-incrimination and thereby challenged McCarthy to cite them for contempt. This was the first time since the case of the Hollywood Ten that writers have challenged the authority of a Congressional committee to inquire into political beliefs. Like the Hollywood Ten, O'Connor and Huberman pleaded the

First Amendment in their refusals to answer. But the Hollywood Ten were before the House Un-American Activities Committee. These new challenges were to the more limited authority of the McCarthy committee. The two writers refused to answer questions not only on constitutional grounds – the fact that the First Amendment protects freedom of expression from restriction by Congress – but also on the ground that the questions were beyond the scope of the authority conferred by the Senate on McCarthy's committee.

O'Connor declined to answer any questions as to political beliefs and associations. We are reprinting the full text of his testimony on page 3 for its value as news, inspiration and example. The celerity with which McCarthy got the author of *Mellon's Millions* off the witness stand was eloquent.

Huberman in a prepared statement said he had never been a Communist but was a Marxist and Socialist who believed 'in working together with others, including Communists, to the extent that their aims and methods are consistent with mine'. Huberman said he was stating that much under oath 'not because I concede the right of this committee to ask for such information, but because I want to make it crystal clear that Communism is not an issue in this case and to focus attention on what *is* the issue – my right as an author and editor to pursue my occupation without interference from Congress or any of its committees'. (The full text of Huberman's testimony will be published in the August issue of the *Monthly Review*, which he edits with Paul Sweezy.)

Huberman was asked over and over again by Mundt and McCarthy to explain how his views 'deviated' from those of Communism. Huberman declined to answer and declined to invoke the Fifth, declaring himself ready for a judicial test of his right to resist inquisition into his political views. At the end Mundt covered the committee's retreat with a lengthy statement, suggesting that Huberman not be cited for contempt since he had (1) admitted authorship of his books and (2) said that he was not a Communist. This suggests that the committee is unwilling to venture a contempt proceeding against a writer who says he is not a Communist but refuses to answer other questions about his political beliefs or affiliations.

O'Connor's challenge had to be taken up or risk complete collapse of the McCarthy committee's pretensions to indulge in ideological inquisition. The committee has voted to cite him for contempt. A majority vote of the Senate is needed to initiate a prosecution. Should O'Connor be indicted, the stage will be set for a fundamental battle against McCarthy and McCarthyism, in which every American who cares for freedom must support Harvey O'Connor.

25 July 1953, vol. I, no. 27

Scholarly Moment before the Jenner Committee

Writers on Marxism are advised not to quote Marx, Engels and Lenin too often. Palmer Weber many years ago had the temerity to pick 'Three Uses of the Concept of Matter in Dialectical Materialism' as the subject of his master's thesis in philosophy at the University of Virginia. Part 4 of the Jenner Committee hearings on 'Interlocking Subversion in Government Departments' released this week shows how this particular wild oat caught up with him.

When Weber was before the committee, Senator Welker wanted to know why 'starting on page 121 of your thesis, you used Engels forty times and Lenin forty times and Karl Marx twelve times'.

This led to a learned exchange with the Senator. Weber tried to explain that up to page 121 he had been dealing with earlier concepts of matter, while from that point on he was discussing Marxist concepts and had to document his sources. 'That is very true,' Senator Welker conceded, 'which leads me to this question – ninety-nine of your references were Communist. Now at the time you wrote that thesis were you a member of the Communist Party?' Weber took refuge in the Fifth Amendment. It is a pity the witness was unable to reply that he was only studying Marxism as a form of penance while preparing for holy orders on a grant from the U.S. Chamber of Commerce.

10 October 1953, vol. I, no. 36

The Hounded Champions of the Alien Meet in Chicago . . . A First-Hand Full Report from a Lonely Battlefront

Chicago – Walsh's Hall at 1014 Noble Street might have been the scene of the Hunky wedding in Upton Sinclair's *Jungle*. The hall lies in a Polish area, one of those incomparably dreary Chicago working-class districts which sprawl out across the bare plain, miles away from the opulence of Lake Front and Loop. The building is a three-storey walk-up, on the top floor of which is the 'hall', a barn of a place, with a stage at one end and a small, faintly and grotesquely Moorish balcony at the other. High columns intended to be ornamental line the wall on either side; they appear to be ordinary cast-iron waterpipe stood on end by some plumber aspiring in his spare time to architecture. The windows are long and narrow. Through them, even under a cloudless sunny sky, the wintry Chicago landscape managed to look grey and bleak – row on row of ill-matched dirty brick and unpainted façades with gaps of dismal backyard in which there stood a few forlorn trees.

The hall was freshly hung with blue and white banners – 'The Bill of Rights Belongs to All', 'Stop Police State Terror Against Foreign-Born Americans', 'Public Hearings on the Lehman–Celler Bill'. On the stage, against the faded green trees of what appeared to be a set left over from some forgotten performance of *As You Like It*, a big benevolent bear of a woman, six feet tall with grey hair, grandmotherly expression, and one of those round unmistakable Russian Jewish faces, was reading aloud Eisenhower's campaign pledge to revise the McCarran–Walter Act. The woman was Pearl Hart, a Chicago lawyer famous throughout the mid-west for a lifetime of devotion to the least lucrative and most oppressed kind of clients.

This was the opening session of a National Conference to

Repeal the Walter–McCarran Law and Defend Its Victims, sponsored by the American Committee for the Protection of the Foreign Born, one of the last functioning Popular Front organizations.

At that early morning hour the seats beside the long wooden tables set up in the hall were but half filled. That such a meeting should be held at all was something of a miracle. The American Committee for the Protection of the Foreign Born is on the Attorney General's list. It is now involved in proceedings before the Subversive Activities Control Board to compel the committee's registration under the McCarran Act as a Communist front organization. Its devoted executive secretary, Abner Green, a tall, lean man with the kind of long cavernous face Goya liked to paint, served six months in jail after refusing to hand over the organization's records to a Federal grand jury in July 1951. The secretary of the local Los Angeles committee, Rose Chernin, was unable to attend because she is under bond in denaturalization proceedings. The secretary of the Michigan committee, Saul Grossman, who was present in Chicago, goes on trial in Washington this week for contempt of Congress in refusing to hand his records over to the House Un-American Activities Committee.

Despite this, about 300 delegates from sixteen states had arrived, some from as far as Seattle and Los Angeles, and 150 more were to follow. They seemed, considering the circumstances, an extraordinarily cheerful lot. But looking at them during the day one was fascinated by several observations. The first was that the audience was a forest of grey heads, almost entirely made up of elderly folk – those who appeared young in that gathering were, when one looked at them more closely, seen to be middle-aged. This is unfortunately true of most radical meetings in America nowadays; it is as if those with their lives still ahead of them are too cautious or cowed to appear at such affairs. What struck one next about the gathering was the absence of foreign accents – with few exceptions one heard American speech indistinguishable from that of the native born. Assimilation has done its work and relatively few new immigrants are coming in. One also began to notice that though the deportation drive hits the labour unions hard, there were no labour union representatives present, other than men from a few so-called 'progressive' locals. The Left labour leaders were conspicuous by their absence; the Taft–Hartley oath made their appearance at the meeting of a blacklisted organization too hazardous.

Not so many weeks ago the case of an air force officer named Radulovich attracted national attention. He was about to be blacklisted as a security risk because his father and sister were supposed to have Communist views or connections. Edward Murrow put the case into a brilliant TV show and the Secretary for Air finally cleared Radulovich. But this comparative handful of elderly folk in Chicago were fighting a last ditch battle for a thousand and one other Raduloviches arrested – as the elder Radulovich may be – for deportation. This committee, just twenty-one years old, is the only one of its kind.

On the eve of the conference, the American Committee for the Protection of the Foreign Born was given the treatment. The local Hearst paper published a smear attack and telephoned the committee's various sponsors and scheduled speakers in an effort to frighten them off. The campaign failed. Among those who spoke at the banquet in that small hall that night were Professor Louise Pettibone Smith, Professor Emeritus of Biblical History at Wellesley; Professor Robert Morss Lovett, and Professor Anton J. Carlson, the University of Chicago's famous physiologist, who had not intended to speak but changed his mind after a call from the Hearst press. The sight of these three aged academic Gibraltars of liberalism was inspiring, but again it was sad to note that the distinguished speakers – like the audience – were elderly.

An amazingly large proportion of the victims, too, are elderly. In his comprehensive report, Abner Green pointed out that of 300 non-citizens arrested in deportation proceedings, almost one-third – ninety-three in all – are over the age of sixty and have lived in this country an average of forty to fifty years. The kind of sick and aged folk being hauled out of retirement for deportation as a political menace to this country would be ludicrous if it did not entail so much tragedy. Two cardiac patients, Refugio Roman Martinez and Norman Tallentire, died of heart attacks in deportation proceedings. The economist and writer, Lewis Corey, long an anti-Communist, died 16 September at the age of sixty-one in the midst of deportation proceedings begun against him because he was a Communist thirty years ago. In California, a Mrs Mary Baumert of Elsinore, now seventy-six years old, was arrested last month for deportation although she had lived here fifty-one years. In Los Angeles on 4 November, Mr and Mrs Lars Berg, sixty-nine and sixty-seven respectively, were locked up on Terminal Island for deportation to their native Sweden; they have been American residents since 1904. One Finn arrested for deportation has lived here since he was three months old!

As in the days of the Inquisition, the Immigration and Naturalization Service and the F.B.I. are engaged in using fear to recruit informers, even informers against their own kin. A striking case was that of Francesco Costa of Rochester, N.Y., arrested for deportation to Italy at the age of eighty-three because he refused to provide information to the Justice Department that could be used to deport his son, Leonard, to Italy. A triple squeeze play was brought to bear on Clarence Hathaway, once editor of the *Daily Worker*. When he declined to be used as an informer, denaturalization proceedings were brought against his wife, Vera. Her brother, William Sanders, fifty-five, an artist who had never engaged in politics, was himself arrested after he refused to give testimony against his sister. Sophie Gerson, wife of Simon W. Gerson, one of those acquitted in the second Smith Act trial of New York Communist leaders, was arrested for denaturalization to punish her husband.

By a political Freudian slip, no mention was made at the conference of one of the worst cases of this kind. In the fall of 1952, Earl Browder and his wife were indicted for perjury in her original immigration proceedings and in February of this year Mrs Browder was arrested for deportation. These punitive actions followed a warning from Bella Dodd to Earl Browder (see this *Weekly*, no. 7, 7 March 1953) that he had better show some sign of cooperation. Though the ex-Communist leader in lonely poverty has withstood the temptation of the rewards which would be his were he to sell his 'Memoirs' to the F.B.I. and the magazines, little consideration has been shown him. This reflects the savage unfairness with which the Left treats its heretics, however honourably these heretics behave.

The deportations drive cuts across every basic liberty. Fifteen editors associated with the radical and foreign language press have been arrested for deportation or denaturalization, including Cedric Belfrage of the *National Guardian*, Al Richman of the West Coast *People's World*, and John Steuben of the *March of Labour*. The foreign-languages editors arrested are elderly folk editing papers which are dying out as the process of assimilation steadily cuts into the number of Americans who still read the language of 'the old country'. Almost one third of those arrested for deportation are trade-union members or officials. Ever since the Bridges cases began (the government is shamelessly about to launch a fourth try), the use of deportation as a weapon against labour militants has been overt and obvious. Cases are pending against James Matles and James Lustig of the United Electrical Workers and against the wife of William Senter, of St Louis, another U.E. official, now up on Smith Act charges.

One of the leading victims of the current drive, Stanley Nowak, was present in Chicago. After ten years as a Democratic member of the Michigan State Legislature, part of this time as floor leader, he is facing denaturalization proceedings. This Polish-born legislator played a role in the organization of the automobile industry and was first elected to the legislature in 1938 from the West Side area of Detroit, a Ford worker constituency. Similar charges ten years ago ('Communist and anarchist sympathies') were dismissed with an apology by then Attorney General Biddle but have been revived under the McCarran–Walter Act.

The most numerous and widespread abuses have occurred in the treatment of Mexican-Americans. Reports to the conference from Los Angeles pictured terror and lawlessness – the use of roadblocks and sudden raids on areas in which persons of Mexican origin live, the invasion of their homes without warrants, the exile to Mexico of native-born Americans of Mexican parentage. The Mexican-American community is kept steadily 'churned up' to maintain it as a source of cheap labour in constant flux. Green reported that during the first six months of 1953 more than 483,000 persons were deported to Mexico – while almost half a million others were being brought in for low-paid agricultural work.

The government is using 'supervisory parole' to harass and intimidate radicals who cannot be deported because no other country will accept them. Three Communist leaders convicted under the Smith Act, Alexander Bittelman, Betty Gannett and Claudia Jones, out on bail pending appeal, were summoned to Ellis Island recently. They were told that they were being put under supervisory parole, must report once a week, submit to physical and psychiatric examination, abandon all political activity *and give information under oath as to their associations and activities*. They are challenging the order in the courts.

Last 17 March Attorney General Brownell made a particularly vulgar St Patrick's Day speech to the Friendly Sons of St Patrick – their parents once the target of similar anti-alien hysteria. In this he announced that 10,000 citizens were being investigated for denaturalization and 12,000 aliens for deportation as 'subversives'. Action on this scale would dwarf the notorious deportation raids of the early twenties.

The suffering in terms of broken families and disrupted lives is beyond the most sympathetic imagination. As serious is the moral degradation imposed by spreading terror. People are afraid to look lest they be tempted to help, and bring down suspicion on themselves. This is how good folk in Germany walked hurriedly by and shut their ears discreetly to tell-tale screams. The American Committee for Protection of the Foreign Born is fighting to keep America's conscience alive.

21 December 1953, vol. I, no. 46

But It's Not Just Joe McCarthy

Buds are beginning to appear on the forsythia, and welts on Joe McCarthy. The early arrival of spring and a series of humiliations for our would-be Führer have made this a most pleasant week in the capital.

The events of the week are worth savouring. Blunt Charlie Wilson called McCarthy's charges against the army 'tommyrot' and for once Joe had no come-back. Next day came the ignominious announcement that he was dropping that $2,000,000 suit against former Senator Benton for calling McCarthy a crook and a liar; the lame excuse promised to launch a nationwide 'I Believe Benton' movement. Stevenson followed with a speech calculated to impress those decent conservatives who had grown disgusted with the Eisenhower Administration's cowardice in the Zwicker affair.

When McCarthy sought to answer Stevenson, the Republican National Committee turned up in Ike's corner and grabbed the radio and TV time away from him. Nixon was to reply, and McCarthy was out (unless somebody smuggled him into the programme in place of Checkers). While McCarthy fumed and threatened, his own choice for the Federal Communications Commission, Robert E. Lee, ungratefully declared he thought the networks had done enough in making time available to Nixon. Next day a Republican, albeit a liberal Republican, Flanders of Vermont, actually got up on the floor of the Senate and delivered a speech against McCarthy. That same night Ed Murrow telecast a brilliant TV attack on McCarthy.

Under Stevenson's leadership, Eisenhower rallied. At a press conference he endorsed the Flanders attack, said he concurred heartily in the decision to have Nixon reply to Stevenson, asserted that he saw no reason why the networks should also give time to McCarthy. Like an escaped prisoner, flexing cramped muscles in freedom, the President also made it clear he had no intention of turning Indo-China into another Korea and even had the temerity to suggest that it might be a good idea to swop butter and other surplus farm commodities with Russia.

The White House conference was no sooner over than Senator Ferguson as chairman of the Senate Republican Policy Committee released a set of suggested rules for Senate investigating committees which are no great shakes at reform but would, if adopted, make it impossible for McCarthy any longer to operate his subcommittee as a one-man show. These may be small enough gains in the fight against McCarthyism, but they were bitter pills for McCarthy to swallow.

So far McCarthy's colleagues on both sides of the aisle have been lying low. When Flanders attacked McCarthy, the Senate was as silent as it was some weeks earlier when Ellender of Louisiana made a lone onslaught and Fulbright of Arkansas cast the sole vote against his appropriation. Only Lehman of New York and John Sherman Cooper (R.) of Kentucky rose to congratulate Flanders. Nobody defended McCarthy, but nobody joined in with those helpful interjections which usually mark a Senate speech. When the Democratic caucus met in closed session, the Stevenson speech was ignored. Lyndon Johnson of Texas, the Democratic floor leader, is frightened of McCarthy's Texas backers.

Great issues are rarely resolved by frontal assault; for every abolitionist prepared to challenge slavery as a moral wrong, there were dozens of compromising politicians (including Lincoln) who talked as if the real issue were states' rights or the criminal jurisdiction of the Federal courts or the right of the people in a new territory to determine their own future. In the fight against the witch mania in this country and in Europe, there were few enough to defend individual victims but fewer still who were willing to assert publicly that belief in witchcraft was groundless. So today in the fight against 'McCarthyism'. It is sometimes hard to draw a line of principles between McCarthy and his critics. If there is indeed a monstrous and diabolic conspiracy against world peace and stability, then isn't McCarthy right? If 'subversives' are at work like termites here and abroad, are they not likely to be found in the most unlikely places and under the most unlikely disguises? How talk of fair procedure if dealing with a protean and Satanic enemy?

To doubt the power of the devil, to question the existence of witches, is again to read oneself out of respectable society, to brand oneself a heretic, to incur suspicion of being oneself in league with the powers of evil. So all the fighters against McCarthyism are impelled to adopt its premises. This was true even of the Stevenson speech, but was strikingly so of Flanders.

The country is in a bad way indeed when as feeble and hysterical a speech is hailed as an attack on McCarthyism. Flanders talked of 'a crisis in the age-long warfare between God and the Devil for the souls of men'. He spoke of Italy as 'ready to fall into Communist hands', of Britain 'nibbling at the drugged bait of trade profits'. There are passages of sheer fantasy, like this one: 'Let us look to the South. In Latin America there are sturdy strongpoints of freedom. But there are likewise, alas, spreading infections of Communism. Whole countries are being taken over ...' What 'whole countries'? and what 'sturdy strongpoints of freedom'? Flanders pictured the Iron Curtain drawn tight about the U.S. and Canada, the rest of the world captured 'by infiltration and subversion'. Flanders told the Senate, 'We will be left with no place to trade and no place to go except as we are permitted to trade and to go by the Communist masters of the world.'

The centre of gravity in American politics has been pushed so far right that such childish nightmares are welcomed as the expression of liberal statesmanship. Nixon becomes a middle-of-the-road spokesman and conservative papers like the *Washington Star* and *New York Times* find themselves classified more and more as parts of the 'left-wing press'. In this atmosphere the Senate Republican reply to McCarthy's silly 'Communist coddling' charges against the army is to launch a formal investigation of their own through Saltonstall and the Armed Services Committee. This will be the Republican and army analogue of the Tydings inquiry into the charges against the State Department and will be greeted with the same cry of whitewash by the growing lunatic fringe behind McCarthy.

There are some charges which must be laughed off or brushed off. They cannot be disproved. If a man charges that he saw Eisenhower riding a broomstick over the White House, he will never be convinced to the contrary by sworn evidence that the President was in bed reading a Western at the time. Formal investigations like Saltonstall's merely pander to paranoia and reward demagogy. What if McCarthy were next to attack the President and the Supreme Court? Are they, too, to be investigated? Is America to become a country in which any adventurer flanked by two ex-Communist screwballs will put any institution on the defensive?

McCarthy is personally discomfited, but McCarthyism is still on the march. Acheson fought McCarthy, but preached a more literate variation of the Bogeyman Theory of History. Eisenhower fights McCarthy, but his Secretary of State in Caracas is pushing hard for a resolution which would spread McCarthyism throughout the hemisphere, pledging joint action for 'security' and against 'subversion'. Nowhere in American politics is there evidence of any important figure (even Stevenson) prepared to talk in sober, mature and realistic terms of the real problems which arise in a real world where national rivalries, mass aspirations and ideas clash as naturally as the waves of the sea. The premises of free society and of liberalism find no one to voice them, yet McCarthyism will not be ended until someone has the nerve to make this kind of a fundamental attack on it.

What are the fundamentals which need to be recognized? The first is that there can be no firm foundation for freedom in this country unless there is real peace. There can be no real peace without a readiness for live-and-let-live, i.e. for coexistence with Communism. The fear cannot be extirpated without faith in man and freedom. The world is going 'socialist' in one form or another everywhere; Communism is merely the extreme form this movement takes when and where blind and backward rulers seek by terror and force to hold back the tide, as the Tsar did and as Chiang Kai-shek did.

There must be renewed recognition that societies are kept stable and healthy by reform, not by thought police; this means that there must be free play for so-called 'subversive' ideas – every idea 'subverts' the old to make way for the new. To shut off 'subversion' is to shut off peaceful progress and to invite revolution and war. American society has been healthy in the past because there has been a constant renovating 'subversion' of this kind. Had we operated on the Bogeyman Theory of History, America would have destroyed itself long ago. It will destroy itself now unless and until a few men of stature have the nerve to speak again the traditional language of free society.

The business of saying, 'Of course there are witches and their power is dreadfully pervasive and they are all around us, but we must treat suspects fairly . . .' is not good enough. To acquiesce in the delusions which create a panic is no way to stem it.

15 March 1954, vol. II, no. 8

The Last Stand of Low Blow Joe

The first member of the Senate Judiciary Committee to arrive for the Brennan hearing was its chairman, Senator Eastland, resplendent in a new suit of brown Harris tweeds, his strong jaws clamped fiercely on a big 50-cent cigar. Robert Morris, counsel of the Internal Security subcommittee, came along soon after, interrupting the hard casuistical wrestle he had begun the day before to determine whether Eugene Dennis was still a Marxist-Leninist, or had lapsed into Bukharinism. McCarthy, fresh shaven, slipped in a few minutes later, taking a seat low down on the committee table, and grinning with delight as the movie cameras again whirred over him. Room 424, Senate Office Building, the Judiciary Committee hearing room, with chairs for scarcely three score visitors and only two small press tables, was a come-down from the great caucus room on the third floor where McCarthy had battled the army. But Joe looked like an old trouper who had finally got an engagement again; the standees were three rows deep; the room was like a Turkish bath; the fall guy was a U.S. Supreme Court nominee; it looked like Joe's chance for a come-back in the headlines.

Three weeks earlier McCarthy had failed miserably to block the nomination of J. David Zellerbach as Ambassador to Italy by exposing him on the Senate floor as a former director of the Fund for the Republic. McCarthy accused the Fund of trying to 'discredit any committee which attempts to disclose [*sic*] Communists', but the Senate nevertheless confirmed the appointment by vote. Now McCarthy was before a smaller and more favourable forum, or at least so he had reason to believe. With Eastland in the chair and Senators Jenner and Butler on the other side of the table for moral support, McCarthy went into the old act. In that flat remorseless metallic voice 'The Investigator' preserves for posterity, McCarthy said the Supreme Court in a number of cases soon to come before it would decide 'whether Congress will be able to pursue its investigations of Communism'. He thought it important for the American people to know if the judges 'are predisposed against Congressional investigations of Communism'. He said that he wanted to learn if the new appointee to the Supreme Court had referred to Congressional investigations as 'Salem witch hunts' and 'inquisitions' and had accused Congressional committees of 'barbarism'.

All the old tricks were on display. There was the studied discourtesy; he constantly referred to 'Mr' Brennan, though Brennan was sworn in last fall as a U.S. Supreme Court Justice. There was the fake drama. McCarthy had evidence. The evidence 'came from the mouth of Judge Brennan'. The phrasing implied that it had been painfully extracted. It was only the heckling from Senator O'Mahoney which finally deflated this. The 'evidence' consisted of copies furnished McCarthy by Mr Justice Brennan of two speeches he had made. One was a St Patrick's Day address to the Boston Charitable Irish Society in 1954; the other was in February 1955. McCarthy did his best in the familiar style to make it appear that the latter was an address at Fort Monmouth, perhaps to an assembly of those very subversives he was labouring so hard to expose at that time. Mr Justice Brennan, a short, round-faced, pleasant looking man, pointed out with some asperity that the speech was at Red Bank, N.J., not Fort Monmouth, and to a gathering of the Monmouth County Rotary Club.

In the Inquisition the first cause for suspicion was to doubt the need for the Holy Office, the second to seem sceptical of the Devil's all-pervading power. It was to these two questions in their contemporary form that McCarthy addressed himself. 'Mr Brennan,' McCarthy began his interrogation, 'do you approve of Congressional investigation to expose the Communist conspiracy?' Mr Justice Brennan passed this one easily. He not only approved but could think of no more important function. But at the second question, the Justice balked. Would he agree,

McCarthy asked, that the Communist Party was not just a political party but a conspiracy to overthrow the American way of life? The Justice explained, in obvious reference to the pending test of the Internal Security Act in the Communist Party registration case, that his oath of office forbade him to answer questions now before the court. McCarthy felt he had his victim hooked, and proceeded to make him sweat by asking the same question several times more in slightly different forms. Finally McCarthy sneered, 'I'd like to know whether the young man agrees with the *Daily Worker* and all the Communist line papers,' to which the Justice still replied stubbornly, 'I cannot venture any comment on matters before the court.'

Justice Brennan might have held out against frontal assault by McCarthy but began to give way when Senator O'Mahoney, his principal champion on the committee, undermined his resistance. The prospect of defending a nominee for the Supreme Court who refused, on mere legal grounds, to take a firm position against Satan and sin was too much for O'Mahoney. To McCarthy's delight, O'Mahoney began to 'clarify' the question for Mr Justice Brennan. He cited the President's resolution against Communism in the Middle East as if it were authoritative gloss on Holy Writ and told the Justice the question asked by McCarthy had already been settled. 'Do you believe,' Senator O'Mahoney insisted, all but prodding the Justice in the ribs, 'that international Communism is a conspiracy against the United States?' 'That,' the Justice said, taking his cue, 'I can answer.' But then Senator Jenner wanted to know whether he drew any line between international Communism and the Communist Party and Brennan again tried to explain that there were particular cases before the court involving this very issue. Senator Hennings tried to rescue him with a series of questions designed to show that conspiracy prosecutions were peculiarly dependent on the particular facts in each case but this was too subtle to save him. A few minutes later Brennan's shoulders were pinned to the mat. When McCarthy asked him, 'You do agree that Communism constitutes a conspiracy against the United States?', Brennan finally answered 'Yes.'

The retreat had begun, and McCarthy pressed harder. He

wanted to know about those speeches the Justice had made criticizing Congressional committees. He soon had Justice Brennan saying, 'sorry you read them that way' and 'I was not concerned with any particular committee as such' though quite obviously they were aimed squarely at McCarthy. He even said he didn't believe he had called those investigations 'Salem witch hunts' at which McCarthy, in his best inexorable voice, said 'Yes, you did,' and proceeded to quote a passage from the Boston speech about 'practices reminiscent of Salem witch hunts'. McCarthy tightened the screws. He wanted to know what were those 'hopeful signs' Brennan had noted in his Monmouth speech that people were at last 'sickened' of investigatory excesses. McCarthy was having a wonderful time and interjected in a stage whisper while waiting for Brennan to reply, 'I'm giving him a good opening there.' Indeed he was. For the main sign at the time was the discussion beginning in the Senate for a censure motion against McCarthy. It would have been exhilarating if the Justice at that point had said, 'Of course, if you insist on the truth, I was talking of you, Senator McCarthy, and of the rising reaction in this country and the Senate against your abuse of investigatory powers.' But Brennan only mumbled vaguely about reformed rules of procedure. It was painful to watch. Was he really compelled to crawl in order to be sure of reaching the Supreme Court? The new Justice was only saved from further humiliation by the bell. Senator Eastland recessed the hearing. How little unalloyed courage there is.

What happened overnight is a mystery. For with the new Justice on the ropes, McCarthy suddenly threw in the sponge. At 8 a.m. – two and a half hours before the hearing was to resume – the radio already carried McCarthy's letter to Senator Eastland saying he thought further questioning would serve no useful purpose because the record 'now confirms that Justice Brennan harbours an underlying hostility to Congressional attempts to investigate and expose the Communist conspiracy'. It was a pleasure to hear grey-haired Senator Watkins, looking like a stern Grant Wood elder, comment later at the hearing, 'I completely and utterly disagree with what he [McCarthy] has said.' It was even more cheering to have Senator Watkins say to

Mr Justice Brennan, 'Though you have not always been in agreement with the way we did our job, a good many Americans have that same point of view and I don't disagree with that although I am one of the investigators on the Internal Security Committee and have been since it was organized.' Something suddenly had made McCarthy lose his nerve; perhaps the change of atmosphere made him feel his fight was hopeless. The hearing was a reminder of what the country has so recently and narrowly escaped. It looks as if we have just seen the last stand of low blow Joe.

4 March 1957, vol. 5, no. 9

A Proposal of Belated Justice to the Blacklisted Teachers of New York

In view of the teacher shortage, the science race with the Soviet Union and the growing national bad conscience about the Oppenheimer case, the *Weekly* suggests that a committee of public-spirited citizens should be formed in New York to review the cases of the teachers blacklisted for loyalty/security reasons in the schools of that city, to make a full report to the public and to recommend the reinstatement of all but those guilty of some actual misconduct as teachers.

We believe the time has come to crack the icecap which the Cold War spread over the nation's schools and that New York City is the place to begin. We believe that action of this kind is called for not just on utilitarian grounds, because the shortage of teachers is acute, but for profounder reasons of education in the fundamentals of a free society.

Review, amends and reinstatement in America's greatest city would demonstrate to the world that we were recovering in a big way from McCarthyism and it would teach students by example that in preaching freedom of ideas we again meant what we preached. To talk of political freedom and then to blacklist teachers because of their political associations, real or suspected, was to teach a whole generation of children that our talk of democracy was hypocritical.

Above all, a change is called for because the New York City Board of Education, despite a ruling to the contrary by the State Commissioner of Education, is still fighting to apply the rule that a teacher suspected of Communism can only prove his loyalty by informing on others. There could be no more revolting ethical lesson taught in the classrooms of New York.

The dismissal of teachers for real or suspected political association, the insistence that they turn informer to save their own skins, are certainly subversive in the true sense of the word. In this sense the Boards of Education and of Higher Education have been a subversive influence in the school system of New York for close to a decade.

But obviously this is not what the Board of Education meant when in its 'Feinberg law' report this year it said 285 teachers had been severed from the school system since 1951 as a result of its investigations into 'subversive activities'. It is time an independent inquiry was made into this queasy wording.

How many were found guilty of 'subversive activity'? What standard did the board apply? How many were really discharged for 'insubordination and conduct unbecoming a teacher' when they refused to answer questions about their own political beliefs and those of their associates? Is it true that the Feinberg law, bad as it is, has never really been applied but that the board has fallen back on the easiest route of discharge for 'insubordination'?

The New York City Board of Education has not acted with mere cowardly acquiescence in popular hysteria. On the contrary it has gone beyond the call of duty in vindictive zeal. Symptomatic is the case of the five teachers (three of them high-school teachers of science) suspended in September 1955, for refusing to inform. When the State Commissioner of Education ruled in July 1956 that teachers need not be informers to prove their loyalty, the board should have closed the case with that decision. Instead it appealed to the State Supreme Court, where the Commissioner was upheld, and is now appealing again. Do the people of New York really approve the expenditure of tax funds in these appeals, in so repugnant a cause?

Some of New York's best and most needed teachers are

among those purged. Of the 350 or so teachers who have lost their jobs (there are forced resignations not included in the published totals), about 75 were teachers in the so-called 'difficult' and minority-group schools (Negro and Puerto Rican). About 175 were elementary schoolteachers, some of them known as experts in the teaching of arithmetic and elementary science.

A public investigating committee will find, we believe, not one single instance where incompetent teaching, misuse of the classroom for indoctrination or any other violation of professional conduct was alleged much less proven. Instead these were, almost without exception, teachers of competence and integrity.

16 December 1957, vol. 5, no. 48

2: The Cold War

Washington after Stalin

Amid the burst of bad manners and foolish speculation, there was remarkably little jubilation. A sudden chill descended on the capital. If Stalin was the aggressive monster painted in official propaganda, his death should have cheered Washington. Actually the unspoken premise of American policy has been that Stalin was so anxious for peace he would do nothing unless Soviet soil itself were violated. With his death, the baiting of the Russian bear – the favourite sport of American politics – suddenly seemed dangerous. Even Martin Dies rose in the House to say that while Stalin was 'utterly cruel and ruthless, he was more cautious and conservative than the younger Bolsheviks'. Few would have dared a week earlier to dwell on the conservative and cautious temperament of the Soviet ruler, much less imply that this was favourable to world stability and peace. Now this theme leaked from every State Department briefing. There was apprehension that after Stalin there might come someone worse and more difficult to deal with.

The Cold War claque was critical of Nehru for calling Stalin a man of peace, but Washington's own instinctive reactions said the same thing. The stress put by the White House on the fact that its condolences were merely 'official' was small-minded and unworthy of a great power. After all, it is fortunate for America that when Stalin's regime met the ultimate test of war, it did not collapse like the Tsar's. The war against the Axis would have lasted a lot longer and cost a great many more American lives if there had been a second Tannenberg instead of a Stalingrad. Stalin was one of the giant figures of our time, and will rank with Ivan, Peter, Catherine, and Lenin among the builders of that huge edifice which is Russia. Magnanimous salute was called for on such an occasion. Syngman Rhee, ruler of a satellite state precariously engaged in fighting for its life against forces supplied by Russia, demonstrated a sense of fitness in his own condolences which Washington seemed afraid to show.

It is difficult to pursue dignified and rational policy when official propaganda has built up so distorted a picture of Russia. Many Americans fed constantly on the notion that the Soviet Union is a vast slave labour camp must have wondered why the masses did not rise now that the oppressor had vanished. The Bolshevik Revolution is still regarded here as a kind of diabolic accident. The necessities imposed on rulers by the character of the countries they rule is ignored. To understand it would be to put the problem of peaceful relations with Russia in quite a different perspective and to dissipate febrile delusions about 'liberation'. The wisest of the anti-Communist Russian émigrés of our generation, Berdyaev, in his *The Origin of Russian Communism* has touched on the way Bolshevism succeeded because it was so deeply rooted in Russia's character and past. Bolshevism 'made use', Berdyaev wrote,

of the Russian traditions of government by imposition ... It made use of the characteristics of the Russian spirit ... its search after social justice and the Kingdom of God upon earth ... and also of its manifestations of coarseness and cruelty. It made use of Russian messianism ... it fitted in with the absence among the Russian people of the Roman view of property ... It fitted in with Russian collectivism which had its roots in religion.

Every great leader is the reflection of the people he leads and Stalin in this sense was Russia. He was also the leader of something new in world history, a party: a party in a new sense, like nothing the world has known since the Society of Jesus, a party ruling a one-party state. It is this difference which makes nonsense of prediction by analogy based on the principle of legitimacy in monarchy or the later history of the Roman empire. Struggle among the party leaders occurred after the death of Lenin and may occur after the death of Stalin, but the party itself provides a cement strong enough to hold the state together despite such struggles. To regard this as a group of conspirators may prove a fatal error. This is a movement, with a philosophy comparable to the great religions in its capacity to evoke devotion, and based on certain economic realities which give it a

constructive function. It has proved itself capable of indus-
trializing Russia and opening new vistas to its masses, and this is
its appeal to similar areas in Asia. This is a challenge which can
only be met by peaceful competition, for only in peace can the
West preserve what it has to offer, and that is the tradition of
individual liberty and free thought.

The news from Communist China where party cadres had
begun careful study of Malenkov's work weeks before Stalin
died indicates that the succession was arranged in advance.
There is little reason to expect a sudden fight among the leaders,
and no reason to believe such a quarrel would make for world
stability. It is time in the wake of Stalin's death to recognize two
basic facts about the world we live in. One fact is Russia. The
other is the Communist movement. The surest way to wreck
what remains of capitalism and intellectual freedom in the non-
Communist world today is blindly to go on refusing to recognize these facts and refusing to adjust ourselves to coexistence
on the same planet with them. Eisenhower in leaving the door
discreetly ajar to possible negotiations with Stalin's successor
was wise, and the lesser powers should seize on the sobering
moment to urge Washington and Moscow to get together.

14 March 1953, vol. 1, no. 9

Mr Molotov's Time-Bombs

One of the principal comments on the Berlin Conference, repeated parrot fashion in the American press, is that the parley
served to show that nothing has been changed by the death of
Stalin. There could hardly be a sillier observation. For Russia,
the question of German rearmament is fundamental. Were
Malenkov to follow Stalin to the grave, were the entire Communist regime to disappear, were Kerensky or a tsar to return,
Russian reaction to *this* question would be unaffected. No Russian government would relinquish its hold on one half of Germany to permit its reunification and rearmament as part of a
hostile bloc, knowing that the rearmed Reich's first demand

would be revision of its eastern frontiers at the expense of territories now held by Russia and Poland.

The magisterial *Times* of London spoke with more objectivity. 'It is now clear,' it said on 19 February, 'that neither Russia nor the West can agree to German unification on terms compatible with their national interests. The linch-pin of Western defence – West German cooperation – remains the hard core of Russian fears; and the main Western anxiety – Russian armies in the heart of Europe – is, in the Russian view, the indispensable condition of Soviet security. In the state of the world today, neither fear can be discounted as mere propaganda.' Few American newspapers would have the capacity, fewer still the courage, for so impartial a statement. Its expression by Britain's leading newspaper is, however, no accident. On the contrary, the complacent tone and detached analysis reflect Britain's own position, which is to try and make the best of two possible worlds, to enjoy the financial benefits of a close entente with the U.S. while striving to enlarge its trade with the U.S.S.R.

It is this which explains the readiness to fall in with some dubious propositions. The notion that 'the linch-pin of Western defence' is the rearmament of Western Germany panders to the cliché of American politics. It cannot be reconciled with political reality. When Acheson and Adenauer sprang this idea on Bevin and Schuman in the fall of 1950, they had great difficulty in selling it. There was then one good military argument for it. Were the Korean war to expand into a world war, as then seemed possible, it was important to confront Russia in the West with German forces. It was the logic of the Korean war which alone made West German rearmament at all palatable, and it is the ending of the war – and not some magic spell laid on by Moscow – which has done more than anything else to take the steam out of E.D.C.

While the ending of the war has shown that the Soviet bloc is in no mood for risky political or military adventures, the German question bristles with dangers. No peace treaty can be signed without tackling the question of the eastern frontiers; the stronger Germany becomes the greater the demands it will make; a 'united Europe' must either support those demands or break with Germany; to break with Germany would risk another and more dangerous version of the tactic Germany pursued at Rapallo and again with the Nazi-Soviet Pact. Germany would become the arbiter of Europe. Once united, it cannot be kept from rearming. Once rearmed, it cannot be kept by any device from resuming the course natural to a central power, i.e. to play one side against the other. No defence system on either side could have a more treacherous 'linch-pin'. An unnamed French provincial paper quoted by *The* (London) *Times* (20 February) said 'it was chimerical to expect' that either East or West at Berlin 'would seriously envisage abandoning their piece of Germany', and asked, 'Is not our best guarantee of security to be found in this division more than in the juridical precautions of E.D.C.?' A majority of Frenchmen would almost certainly agree.

Beneath the surface of contemporary politics, essentials of geography and strategy – the essentials which drew Tsar and Third Republic together in 1894 – have reasserted themselves. Though Russia and France today belong to hostile blocs, their unspoken cooperation has succeeded for almost four years in blocking German rearmament. From one point of view, the French idea of a European army as a means of rearming the Germans without permitting the rebirth of the German General Staff was a brilliant self-deception; the German General Staff has already been reborn, and once the Germans are rearmed no scrap of paper will inhibit them from marching on their own when they wish to do so. But from another point of view, the E.D.C. idea was an ingenious device for delaying a decision; Acheson was dazzled by it, Adenauer was kept dangling – and the debate in the Chamber of Deputies goes on. It will not be speeded by events at Berlin.

American public opinion is poorly informed on Berlin. This conference was an example, not of secret but of half-truth diplomacy, which is considerably worse. The Big Four met behind closed doors and press officers of each afterwards 'briefed' his own nation's correspondents. This was the system used at Panmunjom. The method encourages each participant to re-arrange the libretto to make himself the hero. What the American people read was not so much the news of the conference as a 'line' handed out each day to the correspondents. The result is propaganda, not news. This is the system used by the State Department and by the Department's officers in the corridors of the U.N., but there and in Washington are other sources of information. In Berlin, there was little but this unnourishing pap – and the bare text of speeches – for hungry correspondents to feed upon.

The American point of view of international questions tends to be as simple-minded and self-righteous as the Russian. All the emphasis on 'Western unity' at the conference gets in the way of understanding what happened, because this must begin with some appreciation of the different approaches to the conference on the part of the British, French, and Germans. The British thought an isolated conference on Germany bound to fail, and were anxious only that it not break up in ill-feeling. The French were chiefly concerned with using Berlin as a means of opening a way to peace in Indo-China. The majority of the Germans wanted some progress towards unification of their country. None of our 'allies' shared the main preoccupation of Mr Dulles, which was to demonstrate as rapidly as possible that agreement could not be reached and thus presumably speed ratification of E.D.C. and West German rearmament. Mr Dulles put through his demonstration in one, two, three order, but the result will not be to speed up his object because British, French and German reactions are as different from his as were their initial expectations.

The rearmament of Germany is Dulles's great passion, but Western Europe feels no urgency about it. The British, on his prodding, will make a new token payment on account towards E.D.C. but their pledge of cooperation will not be enough to satisfy the French. At the moment, in Egypt and Iran particularly, Washington is a greater menace to the Empire than Moscow, and Britain has no desire to sink into the role of a European power, linked uneasily in a European army with the Germans. The improvement in Mr Molotov's manners has been enough to appease the British; if they must haggle with the

Russians they would rather haggle over trade than the Oder-Neisse frontier. As for the Germans, they show no great enthusiasm for rearmament. The Social Democrats, who would be the strongest party in a reunited Reich, thought unification should have been bartered for abandonment of E.D.C. Powerful sections of the British Labour and French Socialist parties agree. The special meeting of the Socialist International at Brussels will see a strong demand from all three countries for postponement of German rearmament until the possibility of such a deal has been fully explored.

In his haste to get the Berlin meeting over with as quickly as possible, Mr Dulles allowed Mr Molotov to plant a whole series of time-bombs. The failure to explore many questions fully will give Soviet propaganda an advantage. At one point the Soviet Foreign Minister offered the idea of a plebiscite in which the Germans could choose between unification and E.D.C. It was quickly hooted down, but this will look like an attractive proposition to many Germans in the wake of a conference which leaves the Reich divided indefinitely. Another example is the unresolved question of the proposed European security pact and N.A.T.O. Molotov attacked N.A.T.O. but only made the abandonment of the E.D.C. (i.e. German rearmament) a condition for the treaty. Unofficial Russian spokesmen said N.A.T.O. would not be incompatible with such a treaty. Whether real or illusory, the prospect of combining a continental security pact with Russia and an Atlantic security pact with the U.S. will attract many West Europeans and seem well worth the abandonment of so dubious a proposition as a rearmed Germany.

Austria is another example. Mr Dulles broke off negotiations just when they began to seem promising. Obviously the Russians will not give up the right to station troops in Austria (and thus their right to keep troops along the supply route across satellite Hungary and Rumania) as long as the West has forward bases of its own in Germany and Trieste. But Molotov showed a readiness to reduce this to token proportions and to give Austria more freedom than before, though less than full sovereignty. Also unexplored was the Molotov proposal for removing foreign troops from German soil, and permitting four-power supervision of the withdrawal and the zonal police forces which would maintain order. At any normal conference such offers would have been the springboard of negotiation. What they reflected was simple. The Russians are unwilling to give up their hold on Austria and East Germany but they are willing to ease the grip of occupation on both countries.

These possibilities were not explored because relaxation of tension suits the interests of the Russians but not of Mr Dulles and Herr Adenauer. For it is only by maintaining some sense of urgency and danger that they can prevail on the West Germans to rearm, on the Americans to finance that rearmament, and on the rest of Western Europe to acquiesce in it. In this sense, the final decision of the conference was a victory for Mr Molotov. The resumption of negotiation on Korea, the opening of talks on Indo-China, the recognition in fact of Communist China's pivotal position in world politics – these must further relax tension and make German rearmament seem all the less urgent.

Why, then, did Mr Dulles agree to it? There seem to be several reasons. One is that the 'liberationist' views which lie behind his anxiety to rearm the Germans have become anachronistic in the Eisenhower Administration; the budget cannot be balanced if tension increases and what matter a few more German divisions in the new A-bomb and H-bomb strategy? Another is that Mr Dulles had no choice. According to the French press, Mr Molotov in his private conversations with M. Bidault had offered to mediate directly between Ho Chi-Minh and France. In the Chamber of Deputies, M. Mendès-France has been arguing cogently that France would be better off to negotiate directly than to involve Indo-China in the insoluble Korean problem and the political idiocy fomented in Washington by the China lobby. The alternative to Geneva, where Mr Dulles may still exercise some veto power over an Indo-China settlement, were separate negotiations between Paris and Peking. It is this which must make Senator Knowland's tantrums seem so ungrateful to the Secretary of State.

1 March 1954, vol. 2, nos. 5 and 6

The Meaning of Khrushchev's Revisions in Communist Doctrine

The striking thing about the Khrushchev speech to the Soviet Communist Party Congress is that he begins to admit that the danger of thermonuclear war and the consequent necessity of peaceful coexistence are incompatible with the older Marxist-Leninist view of violent revolution. For violent revolution – and this means civil war – in almost any important country between the two rival great powers would bring on intervention and make world war very difficult to avoid. One need only imagine what would happen were revolution to break out in India or Italy, threatening to overturn the world balance of power, to see that if the Russians seriously want peace they must at the same time change the tactics of the world Communist parties for whom Moscow is the new Rome.

So those who want world peace, and see mankind's destruction in a new war, must welcome the signs of a shift in Muscovite doctrine. Khrushchev departed from Lenin, though not necessarily from Marx's later thinking, when he denied that force and civil war were the only paths to socialism, when he continued the new policy of friendliness to the once reviled Social Democrats, and when he even suggested (a real heresy) that 'the parliamentary form' might be used (Lenin said it had to be smashed) and converted from 'an organ of bourgeois democracy into an instrument of genuine popular will'. This until yesterday was 'rightist opportunism'.

In this context perhaps the most interesting observation made by Khrushchev came when he spoke of the possibility of using parliamentary forms 'for the transition to socialism' and then added, 'For the Russian Bolsheviks, who were the first to accomplish the transition to socialism, this way was excluded.' This begins to recognize that the conclusions drawn by Lenin from Russian experience where parliamentary forms under the tsars were delusive, do not necessarily fit other countries where parliamentary forms and democratic government have often been the vehicles of peaceful social change and reform. The reader should also notice in this connection that Khrushchev speaks of 'the right-wing bourgeois parties' as being bankrupt, which implies that left-wing 'bourgeois' parties may be allies in 'the peaceful transition to socialism'.

The Khrushchev speech is not to be read merely as a new encyclical in Communist political theology. At this very moment the future of France and Italy may well depend on the attitude taken by their Communist parties; they hold the balance of power in the former, and may soon do so in the latter. Despite socialist fears of Communist duplicity, a new Popular Front may be necessary in France to meet the North African crisis and the new Fascist threat visible in Poujade. In Italy the pro-Soviet Left Socialists of Nenni have been seeking alliance with the left wing of the Christian Democrats. Some such coalition may be necessary to unite all those in Italy who want social reform against tomorrow's danger of a new Italian Fascism.

Such coalitions could only be stabilizing influences if the Communists in France and Italy can provide some assurance that their support would be something more than a Trojan horse from which first to capture and then liquidate (as happened in the 'popular democracies') their non-Communist liberal and socialist allies. Socialist fears of a Communist alliance are all too well founded in recent East European experience. Add the sudden shifts to which the Communist line is subject and the slavishly abject dependence of the Communists on Moscow and you begin to see the real dimensions of the problem. Yet unless there is some way to unite the various kinds of people in Italy who want social reform, whether Catholic, Republican, anti-clerical, Socialist or Communist, Fascism may easily revive since fundamentally nothing in poverty-stricken Italy has happened since the war except to shore up the rotten foundations.

The French situation is not the same but just as critical. The North African revolution deeply touches French national pride; without North Africa, she sinks into a third-rate power, facing a resurgent Germany. The white colonists see the fruits of a generation's labour endangered by a primitive and barbaric tide. To get them to give up what they have, to conciliate the miserable Arab masses, and to reconcile them if possible to a new equal life with and within France, is the greatest task which has faced French statesmanship since Napoleon. In the national bitterness of failure, a new Fascism may make its thrust. But can Frenchmen unite to fight it, if they must fear that part of their ranks may break away at any time on orders from a foreign source? This is the question which haunts Mollet and Mendès-France.

The international perspective is as difficult. A growing instability in France and Italy, coupled with an increase in Communist power in both countries, would make relaxation of tension between East and West impossible. Khrushchev admits that if good relations are not established between Moscow and Washington, there is no way to cut down the arms race and a tension that must grow more warlike. Yet such good relations will be impossible to achieve if there are crises in France and Italy. This is what makes Communist policy in both countries so important to peace, and this is what makes Khrushchev's revisions of Communist doctrine in the direction of peaceful change and social democracy so important.

The question which the Khrushchev speech does not deal with is how he can reconcile this responsible attitude towards West European problems with a Middle Eastern policy which rests on arms shipments into so tense an area. The policy of peace cannot be reconciled morally or politically with the kind of dangerous fishing in troubled waters which Moscow pursues in the Middle East. There Russian policy encourages war, and discourages those who would like to see stability created by removing the area from great power rivalry.

Finally Khrushchev's discussion of the Beria affair and liberty within the Soviet state must put liberals and Socialists on warning against too close a Communist embrace. The Communists still have a lot to learn. Khrushchev is still talking the kind of coarse demonological rubbish in which he engaged at Belgrade on meeting Tito. If Beria, the highest G-man of the Soviet state, was an imperialist agent – and we leave this kind of poppycock to party stomachs – then the whole secret police system stands condemned and a first essential under Communism as under any other society is to give the individual *rights he can enforce against the police and the state*. The injustices Khrushchev so conveniently blames on Beria are the same ones which Beria blamed in the same terms on *his* predecessors. Yet when Khrushchev says that 'experience has shown that enemies of the Soviet state attempt to use the slightest weakening of Socialist law for their foul subversive activities' he is talking the same witch-hunt language we know so well in America and opposing fundamental reforms to make new Berias impossible. All the reforms Khrushchev mentions are mere purges from the top in the secret police apparatus – not the basic reforms in criminal procedure promised after Stalin's death and the exposure of the doctors' frame-up. The demonology still reflected in Khrushchev's speech must be got rid of if a decent society is to be created. Here, too, the Communists must learn from the best traditions of the West if there is to be progress towards world peace and stability. In this respect, too, revision of 'Marxism-Leninism' is overdue.

20 February 1956, vol. 4, no. 7

The Hungarian Rebels Have Destroyed the Last Illusions of an Era

It is not easy to see the really momentous events of one's time while they are happening. Budapest is the biggest. Abandoned by the West, shunned fearfully by their Eastern neighbours (even the Polish press is afraid to let go and show its sympathy), fighting the world's biggest army with home-made weapons, the Hungarians seemed doomed and in one sense perhaps are. But in another sense, they – alone – have brought the new Russian empire low in a literal sense, low in the minds of men everywhere.

The world will never be the same again when this prolonged battle and general strike is over. An era is dying, the era in which many of us intellectuals grew up, the era of the Russian Revolution, the era in which – for all its faults and evils – defence of that revolution was somehow the moral duty of all progressive-minded men. That is over, and with it the companion notion – especially powerful in the East – that Russia was not an imperialist power.

What emerges from the ruins in Budapest is the old Ivan, the bewildered peasant soldier of a bureaucratic despotism, heavy-handed, cruel in a slovenly way, and not too sure of itself, weakly reforming and brutally repressing in fits and starts.

The full flavour of the change can be sampled in the statement made by the Dean of Canterbury. 'The danger of a relapse into Fascism,' said the Dean, 'was something that no eastern workers' state could tolerate.' This is an archaic survival from a world which has vanished in the Budapest fighting.

The reality appears in the dispatches of the past few months from Poland and Hungary. There is the item from Warsaw (London, *The Times*, 19 October) that the Warsaw branch of the Communist-run youth movement had put forward among its demands 'the closing of exclusive shops for officials'. What kind of a workers' state is it in which the better things of life are reserved for officials?

There is the item in the demands put to Nagy by the workers of the Borsod district (London, *The Times*, 27 October) demanding not only better wages and working conditions, and a Parliament no longer to be a rubber stamp but also (curiously) 'the publication of the Hungarian-Soviet trade agreement'.

Everywhere in Eastern Europe the Russians are accused of using their power to buy cheap and sell dear to their satellites; the Poles claim they have been forced to sell their coal to Russia at half the price it could bring in Scandinavia or England. This is what capitalist countries do (when they can get away with it) in their colonies.

One of the grievances in Hungary (on which there is an illuminating item in Claude Bourdet's *France-Observateur* for 1 November) is Russian control of Hungary's uranium mines. Hungary is poor in power for its industries, looks to civilian atomic use, and believes Rakosi 'sold out' exclusive control of its uranium to Russia.

Then there is that item from Radio Budapest as we go to press which admits, 'according to the latest reports prisoners have been transported to the east in locked railway cars and for that reason the railwaymen started to strike again'. What a world of terror in one banal sentence! For the nineteenth century, to be 'transported' meant in Russia transported to Siberia. Post-Stalin amnesty and revelation have since confirmed what dismal hells the secret police operated in Siberia for political prisoners in the mines and timber stations of the icy North; the ride there in locked cars like cattle was the prologue of the ordeal.

It is easy to understand why the sight of those locked cars going east drove the Hungarian railwaymen to strike again and saboteurs to blow up stretches of track ... If there is a danger of a relapse into reaction in Eastern Europe, the Russians and the Stalinist Communists have created that danger. They will never live this down. Budapest is worse than the Khrushchev speech because the speech, for all its revealed horrors, bore the implied promise of real change for the better. Budapest months later demonstrates how unwilling the Stalinist bureaucracy is to make real changes at home and abroad. What happened in Budapest will some day happen in Moscow.

19 November 1956, vol. 4, no. 44

The Secret of All That Enthusiasm about the Geophysical Year

When the Russians last August announced that they had fired off an intercontinental ballistic missile, a tantalizing observation was made by the Military Correspondent of *The* (London) *Times*. He pointed out (28 August) that an I.C.B.M. with a 10-megaton thermonuclear warhead would cause total or severe damage within a radius of seven miles. 'To guarantee the destruction of an airfield,' he wrote, 'the missile would have to land within seven miles of it.' But with a missile travelling 5,000 miles, he went on to say 'an error of less than one-tenth of a degree in the aim of it would subtend an error of seven miles at the target.' A successful shot by intercontinental missile would require maps far more exact than those we now possess. 'It may be doubted,' he said significantly, 'whether anyone knows with certainty precisely where Moscow and New York lie in relation to each other.'

Despite the talk on both sides about pure science, the secret of why the military of the U.S. and the U.S.S.R. are so interested in the Geophysical Year and in an artificial satellite is because they must have far more precise maps if they are to use the I.C.B.M. effectively.

With that London *Times* story as a background, it is interesting to read the testimony taken by the House Appropriations Committee earlier this year on the earth satellite programme during its hearings on the 1958 Defence Department Budget. (This begins at page 881 of Part 1.) Dr John P. Hagen, director of Project Vanguard, the code name for this programme, did his best to create the impression that the satellite programme was of no particular military importance. But he did say it would provide a much more exact knowledge than map-makers now have.

The satellite, Dr Hagen explained, would be fairly close to earth, 'and we will know its velocity to a high degree of precision. If we then measure the time it passes over two different points, we can get the linear distance between those points.' Where there could be no actual surveying, he went on, as between Hawaii and the West Coast, 'we really do not know the precise distance. There is no good way presently to measure over water distances because of the deflection of the vertical. That is another kind of thing that will come out of the satellite experiment if and when it is successful.'

An Associated Press dispatch from Paris on 7 October quoted a General Pierre Gallois along the same lines. 'For example,' he was quoted as saying, 'everbody knows the Dniepr dam. But Soviet maps are very imprecise. To plot the topography precisely it would have been necessary to go there with a sextant and plot its coordinates. To direct an intercontinental bomb with precision, the photos and the maps supplied by the satellite will be of considerable utility.'

The race for the satellite is a race to give the new ultimate weapon, the I.C.B.M., the precise maps it requires.

How John Foster Mitty Triumphed at Versailles

The advance billings contained a curious comparison. The word passed out at those private briefings to which only Grade A homogenized Washington correspondents are invited was that the N.A.T.O. conference would be the greatest since Versailles. Subconsciously someone seemed to think that the war had already been fought to a successful conclusion. In Walter Mitty-like moments of euphoria, the State Department may have pictured the conference as another Versailles at which it would dictate unconditional surrender to an enemy laid low so swiftly by long-distance pushbutton that there was no need to disturb Detroit's plans to put higher tail fins on next year's models. (How Mr Dulles must dream of that moment, when, atheistical materialism having bit the dust, he can lead an abject Khrushchev to the baptismal font while Mme Furtseva hies her to a newly reopened nunnery!) Such are the pleasant visions which forty winks after lunch bring elder statesmen.

As it turned out, we had difficulty in imposing terms even on our allies. In a sense the Russians turned up at this new Versailles but only to take their seats almost as full members of N.A.T.O. Mr Dulles must have felt surrounded at the conference table by that indefatigable letter-writer, Marshal Bulganin, who might now be described as the inventor of the intercontinental missive. The success of this new form of bombardment may be measured by the fact that for the first time it severed Mr Dulles from his diplomatic Siamese twin, Dr Adenauer. The Paris meeting might be summed up by saying that the Secretary of State came to conquer, and stayed to correspond – or at least promise to.

There was an exchange of promises. Our N.A.T.O. allies promised *in principle* to take our missiles while we promised *in principle* to reopen negotiations with the Russians. Both promises closely examined confirm Mr Dulles's astringent remarks at his last press conference before Paris about the value of agreements in principle. The vague nature of the missiles agreement was revealed by the evasiveness of General Laurie Norstad's interview on *Meet the Press* in Paris after the conference adjourned. When Marquis Childs asked the N.A.T.O. commander what he could do if an allied country refused to take missile bases, General Norstad replied that it was not necessary for every N.A.T.O. member to have missiles. When William H. Lawrence followed this up by asking whether N.A.T.O. agreement represented a moral commitment to take missiles, General Norstad answered, 'I'm afraid that question isn't susceptible to a yes or no answer.'

Unfortunately, both sides managed to exchange cheques calculated to bounce. The nature of the agreement to reopen negotiations with the Russians is equally obscure, as is the question of whether West European statesmen were serious about peace in exacting that promise or merely going through the motions to satisfy a public opinion less numb than our own. The so-called European revolt against American domination of N.A.T.O. may easily be exaggerated. Paul Johnson reported from Paris in the London *New Statesman* of 28 December that Macmillan 'held a confidential briefing of top U.S. journalists. America was not to worry, he told them, because Britain had endorsed the demand for East-West talks; he only did it to satisfy public opinion at home . . .'

Dr Adenauer's conversion to negotiation may be similarly suspect. As the conference closed, a dispatch from Bonn (*New York Times*, 21 December) said both Herr Ollenhauer, leader of the Social Democrats, and the leadership of the Free Democrats were suspicious that the West 'would make only a perfunctory effort at a political solution to the East-West tension and then push on with the armaments race'.

Neither the widespread West European hostility to missile bases nor the inane quality of that TV report by Eisenhower and Dulles on the Paris conference should blind one to the shrewd plans and powerful influences moving towards an intensified arms race. The game was lost at Paris when the N.A.T.O. Council rejected the Norwegian resolution to defer a decision on missiles 'until all efforts to come to terms with the Soviet Union had been exhausted'. Pineau's formula to 'establish the principle of stationing missiles and warheads in the countries desiring them while expressing a continuing willingness to explore settlement of political and disarmament problems with the Soviet Union' was made to order for the State Department and the Pentagon.

This flabby formula might still be the framework for effective pressure if earlier proposals from Canada and Western Europe for closer N.A.T.O. political consultation had been adopted. But Mr Dulles is as unwilling to negotiate with our allies as with the Russians. A year ago the so-called report of the three wise men of N.A.T.O. – Italy's Martino, Norway's Lange and Canada's Pearson – proposed machinery for joint consultation, for 'the discussion of problems collectively, in the early stages of policy formation, and before national positions became fixed'. Such consultation might provide a brake on the arms race and a prod towards negotiation. Instead of establishing such machinery, however, the N.A.T.O. Council could agree only that 'our permanent representatives will be kept informed of all governmental policies which materially affect the alliance and its members'. This is a promise to consult, if at all, only with our own representatives on N.A.T.O. To keep them informed is hardly the same as to discuss problems collectively in advance of taking up fixed positions of policy.

Mr Dulles's conception of 'interdependence' has always been that of a one-way street, and he has hit on an ingenious programme for tying Western Europe economically and politically to the arms race. Not enough attention has been paid to the full implications of the programme he advanced the first day of the council meeting for a coordinated West European arms production industry to be supported by 'procurement for our own forces as well as for our military assistance programmes'. This is the germ of a new Marshall plan, but a Marshall plan tied to armament rather than reconstruction. Europe would be given a chance to earn dollars by turning out munitions for the American market. This would have several consequences. It would make larger sections of European industry dependent on a continued arms race, and therefore a political factor against negotiation and relaxation of tension. By stepping up the arms race through wider West European participation, we would force similar diversions of industrial capacity in the Soviet bloc from consumer goods to arms production, a move the Poles especially fear. The belief here is that by stepping up the pace and reducing consumer goods supply in the Soviet bloc we can increase tension and repression within the Soviet Union and its satellites. It is also calculated that if West European countries begin to produce missiles, it will increase the demand for the nuclear warheads with which to arm them. This is a programme for creating abroad the kind of vested interests in tension which already exist at home.

The motivations and the strategy of this course may be read between the lines of the 'leak' to the *Washington Post* (20 December) of the so-called Gaither report. Its conclusion according to the *Post*'s account, was that the recommended additional expenditures on arms and shelters 'would come at a fortuitous moment in the American economy ... with benefit both to the economy and to the national defence'. The committee which worked on the Gaither report, the *Post* account says, 'started on the premise of a recession, not of further inflation'. A heightened arms race is advocated as a means of stopping the slump in business and the stock market.

At the same time the Gaither report envisages stepped-up arms output as a means of economic warfare against the Soviets. The *Washington Post* said the Gaither committee was 'unfavourably' impressed with the long term rate of Soviet industrial growth which it estimates to be about twice our own. 'This growth, admittedly based on a less "mature" industrial economy and apparently beginning to slow down,' the *Washington Post* said, 'permits the Kremlin to devote about 25 per cent of its production to the military compared to only about 8.7 per cent of American production so committed. The Soviet gross product is only one third that of America. In another ten years it is estimated to reach about one-half the American figure, because of a faster rate of growth.' The Gaither report calculates, according to the *Post* that if the U.S. added about ten per cent to its defence commitment in terms of gross product, 'the Soviets would have to raise theirs by one third and do so in a nation already on the meagrest ration of consumer goods'.

So we emerge from the N.A.T.O. Paris conference with no real change of position. We still regard the arms race as a means of maintaining prosperity at home and poverty in the Soviet bloc. We believe that if the heat is only kept on long enough the Russians will be so eager for disarmament that they may even surrender on Germany. In this perspective, it is strange to have the President questioning Russian sincerity about disarmament since the foundation of this whole policy is a belief that Moscow wants and needs arms reduction so desperately it will some day pay a huge price for it.

This is, it goes without question, a most dangerous game but there is no sign of real opposition to it. The Democrats are on the whole more devoted to the arms race even than the Republicans. No Democrat says what Kennan or Lester Pearson or Hugh Gaitskell has been saying; none of them questions the arms race, as General Bradley did.

A sampling of opinion expressed by the more intelligent Democrats in Congress is cause for despair. Green of Rhode Island returns from Europe to say that its prosperity shows it can easily afford a larger arms budget. Mansfield of Montana, the party whip in the Senate, supported the Eisenhower–Dulles missile-bases policy in an extraordinary vapid TV interview on *Face the Nation*, 15 December. The 'radicals' of the House, a group of twelve Democrats which includes Reuss of Wisconsin and Jimmy Roosevelt, issued a statement criticizing Dulles's no-negotiation article in *Life* but declaring themselves 'pleased with the decision of the N.A.T.O. countries to work out ways for sharing missiles and nuclear weapons with our European allies' and pledging themselves 'to support any changes in law necessary to accomplish this'. The very Democrats who make Dulles their whipping boy do not have the imagination, insight or courage to do other than follow dutifully in the path of his policies. No one questions the wisdom of an arms race, no one speaks of the need to provide an economic substitute for arms orders, no one speaks the language of peace.

The conservative *Washington Star* has been advocating negotiation and coexistence but without finding an echo among the Democrats. The *Washington Post* in a striking editorial 13 December, suggested that the U.S. accept Bulganin's proposal for a cessation of nuclear testing and propose on its own a ban, with inspection, against I.C.B.M.s and I.R.B.M.s. No Democrat takes it up. No one with any knowledge of Poland can doubt the desperate sincerity of Rapacki's proposal to make Central Europe an area clear of nuclear weapons, but no one here even discusses it. The truth is that Washington, whether Republican or Democratic, just is not interested in disarmament and does not want relaxation of tension.

A striking example of Democratic bankruptcy on foreign policy was provided by Pennsylvania Senator Joseph Clark's reaction to the Gaither report leak in the *Washington Post*. On domestic policy, Clark is a veritable second George Norris. On foreign policy, he faithfully regurgitates the nonsensical cud of those two bloodthirsty idiots, Symington and Jackson. Clark took the Gaither report hook, line and sinker, its 'horrifying facts' and the 'desperate need' it supposedly discloses. But on a domestic matter Senator Clark would never think of accepting without question the one-sided views of an Administration committee, briefed in private by the very agencies they were supposed objectively to study. Policy ought to be formed in the open, on the basis of public hearings, in which all points of view are explored, not determined by a small elite in secret sessions on the basis of secret evidence. What was the evidence here? The self evaluations of the military and of Central Intelligence. The Gaither committee under these circumstances necessarily became the sounding board of military desire for larger appropriations. It was not a Royal Commission, studying the arms race afresh, but another small group of hand-picked worthies given the full treatment at Pentagon and C.I.A. Yet there is not a single voice in the Senate or the country to question this way of coming to conclusions on life-and-death issues.

It will take a bigger revolt than Western Europe has yet staged to change this drift and make a dent on the leaden bipartisanship of American foreign policy. We are wedded to the arms race, no matter to what abyss it may lead. Washington may not want war, but it certainly doesn't want peace. It is thus no mere error of tactics or consequence of better propaganda which has given the peace banner to Moscow. When Khrushchev even writes a letter to the London *New Statesman* (21 December) respectfully answering Bertrand Russell's open letter to Eisenhower and Khrushchev in the same publication (23 November), he establishes something of a new mark in urgent unconventional effort. We can only hope that if Jim Hagerty hears of this and decides that Ike, too, ought to answer Lord Russell (aren't we supposed to be respectful in this post-sputnik era to intellectuals?), somebody will head him off before he gets one of those State Department drafts explaining that we cannot negotiate with Moscow because the Communists don't believe in God. Neither – someone had better tell Hagerty – does Russell.

6 January 1958, vol. 6, no. 1

What the Berlin Crisis Really Shows

No one asks us whether we want to die for Berlin, and no one asks the Russians whether *they* want to die for Berlin, though we are presumed to be free and they are supposed to be slaves. And of course neither side, though each considers itself morally superior, ours as the Bearer of the Cross against Atheistic Communism, and theirs as the Champion of the Oppressed against Capitalist Imperialism, thinks of consulting the millions of other people on the earth a conflict between us might destroy. Though the devices in readiness may poison the air and pollute the soil, the leaders on both sides talk as calmly of resorting to war over Berlin as if the conflict were to be fought with muskets. The Berlin crisis lights up the criminal anarchy to which the world is exposed by a system of national states which recognize no law but their own will and share a common belief in their sacred right to consign millions to death if they so choose.

The differences in our forms of government are said to be the source of inescapable conflict between us. Every government is a device by which a few control the actions of many. The governors may be chosen by birth, ballot or intrigue, but in any case a few govern, the rest obey. On both sides at the moment complex human societies depend for the final decisions of war and peace on a group of elderly men any sensible plant personnel manager, whether under capitalism or Communism, would hesitate to hire.

Here we have at the top a cardiac case whose chief interest is in getting away from his job as often as possible for golf and bridge; his no. 2 man is in a hospital with cancer; the next highest-ranking foreign-policy official is an arthritic on crutches. On the other side, there is an ebullient dictator in his mid-sixties, eager after long years of humiliating subservience to a brutal predecessor to enjoy the pleasures of power in the few years left him; a clever man, but much too fond of his own wit; a man who may not drink too much but certainly talks too much; above all, a man with the unsureness of the newly arrived, anxious to make more legitimate rulers recognize and confer with him and thus give him more solid status, ready to create a crisis and risk a war to get himself a Summit. Who appointed these senescent fumblers? Who are they that the fate of the species should be in their hands?

It is plain to see that deterrence does not deter. We have been living on the comfortable calculation that the new weapons are so terrible that only a madman would use them. Now we can see that the conventional minded may be fully as dangerous as the mad. The closer we come to a showdown, the more men forget all they have been saying about war now being obsolete. In Congress even the faltering voices of conciliation say that of course on Berlin we cannot compromise and of course if the top men give the signal we will all march as one into the fire. No one says it would be as insane to risk a world conflagration over one city as it would be to allow two quarrelling home-owners to burn down a whole town in their readiness to spite each other. Such thoughts, on both sides, are suspect. The issue, we are told, is not Berlin. Berlin is a symbol. The issue is that neither side wishes to lose face; neither wishes to back down; both fear irreparable damage to their prestige; both see allies drifting away if they do not stand firm; both fear other nations will think less of them if they do not show a readiness to fight for their rights. In short, the motivations of the duel and the momentum of the bar-room brawl, first the bluff and then the fight, are the determinants of national policy on both sides.

All this immemorial puerility of the human species is covered over with an equally ancient self-righteousness. The old mouldy nonsense is reappearing in the pulpit, the newspaper columns and the halls of Congress. This (like every war known to history) is a conflict between freedom and slavery, right and wrong, good and evil. Compromise would therefore be wicked and only the slaughter of millions devout. The other fellow is No Good; he eats pig; he does not worship the walrus; he defiles our totem pole; he knows not Allah; he is not godly like us. To kill him is a virtue which will earn us Paradise.

9 March 1959, vol. 7, no. 10

Patriotic Reflections on the Eve of a Foreign Invasion

One gets the impression, on plunging again into the overheated atmosphere of Washington after a blissful two weeks away, that the United States is in a panic, on the verge of an invasion, in imminent peril from the expected arrival of a man named Khrushchev. Full-page newspaper advertisements, speeches in Congress, letters to the editor, debate the best way of meeting the menace. Some would have us greet his arrival by staying home behind closed shutters. Others want to organize public meetings of protest. A retired admiral suggests a nation-wide day of prayer, perhaps to ask God to reward us righteous with a new ultimate weapon. Russian intelligence, studying the press clippings from America on the eve of the visit, may reasonably conclude that we Americans are a highly nervous people.

We hope Khrushchev will not be taken in by all this flattery. It implies that he is a foreign wizard in whose subversive wake our drug stores may begin to sell paper-backed editions of *Das Kapital* and our bewitched women's clubs to schedule lectures on dialectical materialism. We suspect that the Russians would be behaving as neurotically as we are if they, too, enjoyed a free press. We can see a syndicated series by Molotov (like

Truman's) warning against the danger of visits to the perfidious capitalists, and insinuating that Khrushchev (like Eisenhower) is about to relinquish Russia's most prized possession, perpetual Cold War. We can visualize an opposition paper in Moscow demanding that Khrushchev agree to no relaxation of tension until Eisenhower has set free the captive Eskimos and restored Alaska's rightful place as the 49th State in the Union of Soviet Socialist Republics. We can hear a Soviet general warning that the exchange of visits must not beguile Russia into lowering its guard (and its air force expenditures) because America was still intent on spreading its philosophy of free enterprise to the whole world. We can even imagine the obliging Orthodox Patriarch urging a day of prayer for the peaceful conversion of the American to Marxism-Leninism. In short we believe that the great Russian people, freed from the shackles of despotism, could be as screwy as we are.

31 August 1959, vol. 7, no. 32

Getting Ready to Detect 'Moonquakes'

In those areas of seismic detection which do not involve disarmament, the government's experts seem confident of developing devices which can detect at distances considerably greater than Irkutsk or Omsk. It is only in the seismology which might lead to an arms agreement that stress is on the negative, on what can't be done. A scientist friend, for example, told us he heard we were developing means to monitor seismic shocks – 'moonquakes' – on the moon, which even the A.E.C. might admit is somewhat less accessible than the Soviet Union.

We checked around the capital for confirmation and found it at the National Aeronautics and Space Administration. We were told by its press officer that N.A.S.A. has parallel contracts with Caltech and Lamont Observatory at Columbia for the development of a 'missile transportable, hard landing' instrument for the detection of seismic disturbances. This is to be dropped on the moon and telemeter its reports back to earth. Each contract is for $130,000. The device is to be ready by 1963. Since the principles of seismic detection and telemetry are well understood, this is not considered too difficult an assignment.

Of course, if it became necessary to make a moon monitoring agreement with the Soviet Union, we would expect to be warned by Dr Teller that moonquakes might be muffled in moonbeams and sublunatic nuclear explosions hidden in large holes of green cheese.

4 April 1960, vol. 8, no. 13

The Q. and A. of a World Crisis

What wrecked the summit?
Eisenhower's avowal of responsibility for aerial reconnaissance and his declared intention to continue it.

Did Khrushchev go to Paris intending to blow up the conference?
Yes. His terms, by including a public apology and punishment for those responsible, were impossibly humiliating and he knew it. Eisenhower was responsible.

Why did Khrushchev take so drastic a position?
I believe he was offended and angered, that he really liked Eisenhower and felt personally let down. He had given the President an out in his speech of 7 May in which he said that perhaps Eisenhower had known nothing about the U-2 flight and it had been the independent work of 'madmen in the Pentagon'. This accorded with Herter's statement that same day, 'Specific missions of these unarmed civilian aircraft have not been subject to presidential authorization.'

Could the summit conference still have been saved?
At that point yes. On 8 May the President met with Herter to prevent the incident from wrecking the summit meeting and though no announcement was made James Reston reported in the *New York Times* next morning, 'elsewhere it was stated on responsible authority that the President had ordered a halt to all

flights over or near Communist frontiers pending an executive investigation of the entire intelligence apparatus of the government.' Had the Administration allowed this report to stand uncontradicted, it would have satisfied our alarmed allies about the U-2 flights and provided a face-saver for Khrushchev with his own people.

Why did Herter next day indicate instead that the flights would go on?

This is the key point at which a future Congressional investigation, as foreshadowed by Mansfield in the Senate last Tuesday, ought to begin. Reston is a responsible and able newspaperman, bureau chief for our leading paper, with more access than any other publication to official channels. Who was the 'responsible authority' who assured Reston the evening of 8 May after the Eisenhower–Herter meeting that overflights had been halted? Why was it decided instead to have Herter next day issue a statement which invited the belief that overflights would continue? It was the President's affirmation of Herter's statement on 11 May that was followed by Khrushchev's angry remark in Moscow that Eisenhower would no longer be welcome.

What led the Administration to take so tough a line?

Perhaps two factors played a part. One could have been a typical press relations gimmick; we turn a liability into an asset by taking our admission of aerial espionage, which leaves us in the wrong, and put Russia in the wrong instead by claiming that its secrecy made such surveillance necessary, a service to the world, a form of 'open sky' operation designed to bring about an 'open society'. Thus we become the champions of 'openness' a good word against 'secrecy' a bad. This is the kind of slick Madison Avenue operation to which this Administration has always been prone. A second argument discernible in the line being leaked out by the Pentagon is: we do a switch, say that the ease of the U-2 operation shows how open the Russians are to attack, we still have more bombers than they do, they still don't have the advantage in missiles they'll have a few years hence, this is the 'deterrent gap' when we can still smash them and they know it, let's get tough while we can. This, we suspect, is how the military argues.

How do you reconcile this speculation with Eisenhower's statement at Paris on 16 May that on 12 May he had ordered all overflights permanently ended?
Judging by the surprised reaction in Washington, that order of 12 May was so secret that it must have been a soliloquy. The Vice-President's explanation at Auburn, N.Y., 17 May, only adds to reasons for scepticism. Nixon said Eisenhower went to Paris prepared to give up aerial surveillance but only if East and West agreed to substitute a United Nations 'open skies' programme (*New York Times*, 18 May, p. 14, col. 6, City Edition). I believe this was another in the series of 'little white lies' which have marked this U-2 affair from the beginning. The impression is strengthened by the curious evasiveness of 'Chip' Bohlen's discussion of it at the Paris press briefing.

What is the meaning of the 'secret' world-wide combat alert ordered by Secretary of Defense Gates from Paris which took place during the night and early morning preceding the meeting of the Big Four?
This seems further evidence that Eisenhower had been sold a tough line by the military. Obviously a world-wide alert, especially at our bases abroad, could not be kept a secret from the Russians even if it hadn't been conveniently leaked at Denver and San Diego. This was a bit of muscle-flexing intended to throw a scare into the Russians. It was a most irresponsible and dangerous kind of manoeuvre. It might easily have led the Russians to believe that a major surprise attack on them was in the making, and led them to try a pre-emptive blow to ward it off. In my opinion a show of this kind, even more than the U-2 flight, forced Khrushchev to take a hard position lest he be suspected at home and abroad of weakness.

Do you believe that the U-2 affair alone was enough to make the Russians decide to scuttle the summit meeting?
No. I believe it was only the final straw. The Russians had

ample reason to doubt our sincerity in talks on disarmament, nuclear testing and Berlin. Our attitude towards the summit was frivolous; the idea was that if the Russians had any more concessions to make, we would be glad to receive them. There was no real preparation for negotiation. On disarmament, as Gaitskell noted in the House of Commons, 13 May, the Western plan emphasized control and inspection, leaving actual disarmament to the distant future. Our announcement of resumed testing, 7 May, was an affront after the Russians a few days earlier at Geneva had made fresh concessions. Then there was Eisenhower's remark to George Meany, 6 May, about his projected Moscow trip, 'If I go.' It requires no esoteric theories about pressure from Stalinists and Peking to explain Khrushchev's anger. I think he decided that nothing was to be gained from the summit meeting with Eisenhower, that he would only be giving him the mantle of peace with which to elect Nixon in November, and that it would be better to exploit the U-2 affair and call off the talks until after a new President had been elected.

Who's your candidate for President?
Adlai Stevenson.

Do you think the collapse of the summit has improved his chances?
Yes and no. Some people will feel that the country needs a really big man in the White House for a change now that we may be in a crisis. Others will feel that we need somebody who can talk tough to the Russians.

What about Kennedy?
His youth will hurt him now.

Do you think Kennedy's a man of peace?
He moved leftward to defeat Humphrey, and until the summit collapsed he had to stay that way to cut the ground from under Stevenson. But if he's really that much of a liberal, why has he been such a favourite of Henry Luce?

Do you think the collapse of the summit will help or hurt the Republicans?

Hurt them. Not just because they've lost the peace issue but because they have no commanding figure left in whom the people have confidence. If they had a new glamorous soldier candidate, they might do well on a brink-of-war campaign. Nixon looks too young, shallow, tricky.

What does the summit collapse do for the Democrats?

Puts them on a very difficult spot. To campaign as the peace party when the Russians are acting tough opens them to the charge of appeasement. The Democrats are split wide open between those who believe there is no alternative to peace and those who think we ought to have a super arms race and then 'negotiate from strength', i.e. threaten Russian extinction if they don't surrender on U.S. terms. The convention will be a bitter one.

Do you think the Republicans might turn to Rockefeller?

Possibly. Because the collapse of the summit is a defeat for the conservatives of the party. Rockefeller favours a radical increase in arms spending, and a radical reorganization of the armed services, at one and the same time for thermonuclear preventive war power and mobile limited nuclear war to defend American interests (especially oil interests) in the hot spots of the world. He's willing to rally popular support by combining a garrison state with a social welfare state. He's made to order for the George Meany mentality in labour.

Can a peace candidate be elected?

Only if the Russians do not create a new crisis over Berlin. The signing of a separate treaty before the election, especially if followed by trouble between the East Germans and our military, will play into the hands of the war party here. The Russians cannot force the U.S. into a humiliating backdown at Berlin and expect peaceful negotiations no matter who is elected.

Is it possible to put Russo-American relations into a sort of deep-freeze until after the elections?
Possible but not probable. Given the realities of mankind and its easy descent into mutual recrimination and suspicion, no such happy solution is likely. It is more likely that the collapse of the summit is the opening of a new and dangerous era in world history, and one which could easily be the last.

Can the nuclear testing and disarmament negotiations go on after the summit has collapsed?
Theoretically, yes. Practically, no. In so far as foreign policy is concerned, all countries have a two-party system – the 'hards' and the 'softs'. We are moving into a period in which the 'hards' will probably be dominant in both the U.S. and the U.S.S.R. The Soviet leaders in their new mood are less likely than ever to allow foreign monitors and on-site inspections on their soil.

What do you see as the most important lesson for the American people in the last few days?
The extent to which our fate is at the mercy of a huge military and intelligence machine which can create incidents and manipulate events; the extent to which, through the press, they can brainwash the country. They easily sold papers as enlightened as the *New York Times* and the *Washington Post* the fantastic line that aerial overflights in violation of international law in a trigger-tense thermonuclear age are a form of public service. If they can sell this line, can one be sure they can't sell the idea of preventive war?

Do you see a step-up in the arms race?
Yes, and we are only a few years away from the stage of technology in which we may see garrison states rise on both sides, digging deep into the earth to give their citizens shelter and reaching high into the skies with space stations from which to aim missiles at each other. The black day of 17 May 1960 may bring nearer the vision of Orwell's *1984*. Coming developments can be a bonanza for the secret police business and the paranoids of both sides. Stalinism and McCarthyism may have their

recrudescence together. World rivalry and many basic similarities have made Siamese twins of the U.S. and the U.S.S.R. If poison runs in the veins of one, it flows in the veins of the other.

Can Krushchev survive a sharp turn of events?
Just as it was a political asset during the period of thaw for ambitious leaders to demonstrate by visits and talks that they could get along with their opposite numbers, so in the coming months it may become an asset on both sides to demonstrate that one can 'talk tough' with the other. Eisenhower's tragedy stems from his weaknesses of character, his essential laziness of mind; Krushchev in anger has destroyed Eisenhower; Ike ends a failure. But Krushchev may go down with him if there is a turn for the worse. It will not be easy for Nikita 'Kukuruchik', the expansive extrovert, contemptuous of stuffed shirts and bureaucratic hacks, to become a Stalinist-style wooden Indian. We suspect neither man will long survive the collapse of their mutual hope. They have ruined each other.

23 May 1960, vol. 8, no. 20

Those Who Can't Afford Bomb Shelters – Do They Deserve to Die?

Adjoining Washington, in suburban Montgomery County, Maryland, a group of junior executive types led by a Princeton graduate named David Scull some years ago ran a successful revolt inside the Republican Party and took over from the old court-house crowd. Mr Scull writes a column in the *Montgomery County Sentinel*. The one in the issue of 21 September was headed 'Darwin Was Right'. It discussed the recent issue of *Life* which assured the country that ninety-seven per cent of all Americans could survive a nuclear war. 'Of course,' Mr Scull wrote,

the President and the editors of *Life* know that millions will die unnecessarily in the event of such a war, but ... From a purely Darwinian point of view, it probably will not be calamitous ... if ten million or so of our sloppier citizens disappear as a result of their own lack of ability or will to survive. Many of these second-class human beings are the ones who are right now asking what the fuss is all about in Berlin. They haven't the wit to understand that Western Civilization, human freedom and the dignity of man are on trial at the Brandenburg Gate.

We suspect such views are all too common in the country-club set. The premise of the private-shelter programme, as begun under Eisenhower and taken over by Kennedy, is that in the event of thermonuclear war each citizen must provide his own protection and be his own Secretary of Defence; the Defence Department, so-called, turns out to be for Offence only. This approach is favoured by the generals, who fear diversion of appropriations to civil defence, and by higher bracket tax-payers, who can afford to build their own shelters and do not see why they should be taxed to provide them for those who can't. This is the same 'rugged individualist' philosophy advocated thirty years ago in the Great Depression. It is smugly assumed that the country would be better off if the 'unfit' die. Then it was by hunger, now it will be by thermonuclear war. This application of a pseudo-Darwinianism to oppose welfare measures is as old as Victorianism, and its use to justify war at least as old as Kaiser Germany. We would be grateful to this obscure surburban Bismarck for bringing into the open an idea not quite suitable for presentation in full-colour photographs by mass-circulation picture weeklies. He makes us feel it will be a positive misfortune if war does not break out after all.

Mr Scull's disapproval extends beyond the poor and shiftless. He suggests that the 'second-class human beings' we could do without also include those who doubt that Berlin is worth a thermonuclear war. To deal with this group requires another order of sacrifice. A mimeographed form being distributed by Montgomery County Defence at P.T.A. meetings lists Mr Scull's real estate firm, Sterling & Scull, as builders of fallout shelters and suppliers of energy foods to stock them. Would Mr Scull be willing to set an example, to launch a new patriotic campaign, to open a Second Front in the battle of civil defence, by rejecting orders from customers whose views on Berlin have not first been certified as upstanding?

16 October 1961, vol. 9, no. 38

Requiescat in Monte

We are less reluctant to invest in the better-grade stocks and bonds now that the *Wall Street Journal* discloses (12 January) that almost all of our top 500 corporations have some sort of underground alternate headquarters for use in the event of thermonuclear war. The bigger the company the deeper the hole. Standard Oil (New Jersey), Manufacturers Hanover Trust and Shell Oil are among those most deeply dug in. They have quarters in the hollowed-out core of Iron Mountain near Hudson, N.Y., 'protected from blast, heat and radiation by countless tons of rock, soil and iron ore'. New York City, 115 miles south, could be incinerated but Iron Mountain would escape unscathed. Only a near direct hit by a multi-megaton weapon could smash this privileged sanctuary. There, when 'a 28-ton steel door in the mountainside swings open' the visitor 'wanders through offices, kitchens, dormitories'. Here the selected few, like the animals on Noah's Ark, would ride out the storm. Among Jersey Standard's 'chosen people' (as the *Wall Street Journal* reverently calls them) are the president, the chairman and the entire board of directors for whom double bedrooms with semi-private baths are assigned. Enough clerks and secretaries to serve them would live in dormitories the construction crew cynically termed 'the slave quarters'. The living rooms are brightly coloured and hung with vivid prints; there is even a music room for piped-in concerts. We found ourselves wishing we believed in immortality. We could almost look forward to a Third World War, knowing we could amuse ourselves by looking down on the Jersey Standard board of directors meeting in cosy imperturbability under Iron Mountain after the rest of us had been pulverized, cannily debating whether to declare an extra dividend, just to improve the tone of the stock market.

24 January 1966, vol. 14, no. 3

The First Military Dictatorship with a Free (But Suspended) Constitution

It is easy to imagine what the U.S. would be saying if the military had seized power in Czechoslovakia, written a Constitution allowing the military junta to suspend indefinitely all basic freedoms, asked the Czechs to vote on that Constitution in an election campaign which allowed no opposition voice, held the plebiscite under martial law, and announced that 99.2 per cent of the people had voted approval.

How the Kremlin must envy U.S. technological superiority in arranging such affairs! How clumsy the Kremlin's manoeuvres in Czechoslovakia appear beside the smooth operations of the colonels in Greece! The Pentagon's excuse for this extinction of liberty in Greece with U.S. arms is strategic – the need to prevent the rise of a possibly neutralist government on N.A.T.O.'s southern flank. The Kremlin's excuse for the Czech operation is strategic – to prevent the rise of a possibly neutralist regime, outflanking Poland to the north and Hungary to the south. But how few Americans will compare them. The remains of our Old Left is as ready to justify the extinction of liberty in Czechoslovakia as the military and cold warriors are to justify it in Greece.

The Greek colonels must be given high marks for virtuosity. The new Constitution contains all kinds of democratic guarantees – but leaves it up to the colonels to decide when, if ever, they are to become effective. In the voting, 'yes' slips were blue, 'no' slips black; there was psychological conditioning in the choice of colours. The voter by dropping or refusing the blank ballots could ingratiate himself with the police and military. The two correspondents of *Le Figaro* reported (30 September) they found piles of 'no' ballots strewn all over the floor of the balloting places they visited. Many feared reprisals if suspected of voting wrongly.

The early returns were too good. *The Times* (30 September) carried a French Agency dispatch saying the first returns from the north of the country 'showed 100 per cent in favour'. Alfred

Friendly in the *Washington Post* (1 October) indicated that the government was embarrassed and holding back early returns which 'smacked too much of those traditional to dictatorship'. The results from Athens were finally given at 75 per cent in favour 'compared with 99.8 per cent in most rural areas' (*New York Times*, 1 October). This reduced the national average to 92.2 per cent. It is hard to know how to assess these final figures since the regime did the counting.

The colonels must be spending a fortune on propaganda. 'Thirty-five foreign writers, of which five were American,' the *Washington Post* reported from Athens (29 September) 'have been brought here as guests of the regime with transportation expenses and hotel bills of them and their wives fully paid.' Kingsbury Smith of the Hearst press, Wm F. Buckley and Erwin D. Canham, editor-in-chief of the *Christian Science Monitor* were among the five. 'So confident was the government in the purity of its electoral process,' was the way Mr Canham admitted this in a 1 October dispatch, 'that it invited half a hundred news observers, myself included, to be their guests at the voting.' With guest-like politeness, Mr Canham went on to say that he had talked with leading members of the government. 'They give the impression,' he wrote, 'of being dedicated, zealous men.'

Similar V.I.P. tours have produced similar compliments from West European parliamentarians. Two British Conservatives issued a statement on their return (London, *The Times*, 19 September) calling the military 'dedicated and able' and the people, 'in spite of what had been written by hostile writers, happy and relaxed'. Six French deputies returned equally euphoric, according to this same story, and declared the Greek economy 'wide open to foreign investments'.

These happy tidings were interrupted on 21 September when a British public relations man, Maurice Fraser, obtained an injunction forbidding the London *Sunday Times* to print a document which had come into its possession. This was a report by Fraser to his employers in the military junta boasting that a British Member of Parliament was on his payroll 'with the object of influencing other British M.P.s'. A week later, while the injunction was still on appeal, the *Sunday Times* said another British M.P. was ready to raise the issue in the House of Commons as a breach of parliamentary privilege. The *Sunday Telegraph* the same day named ten M.P.s Fraser had flown to Athens with their wives on V.I.P. tours. 'During the year,' the *Telegraph* added, 'six German and six French M.P.s have also been flown to Athens, as well as numerous journalists, bankers and businessmen.'

Freedom's frontier in the Balkans is now the world's first military dictatorship with a free constitution, and the first free constitution which provides indefinite suspension by the military dictators. To the creation of this paradox the U.S. has made no small contribution. Richard J. Barnet has just published a new book, *Intervention and Revolution*. In a chapter on 'The Subversion of Undesirable Governments' he quotes a lovely remark by Hubert Humphrey in a happier day during a Senate investigation of the Iranian aid programme in 1957. 'Do you know what the head of the Iranian army told one of our people?' Humphrey asked. 'He said the army was in good shape, thanks to U.S. aid – it was now capable of coping with the civilian population.' The same prowess, due to the same aid, is now on display in Greece.

7 October 1968, vol. 16, no. 20

N.A.T.O., the Poor Czechs and the Arms Race

The first question to ask is: is the U.S.S.R. stronger or weaker because of the Czech takeover? It is weaker. In the first place, in a political crisis, the Czech army proved to be unreliable, and the takeover had to be by Soviet troops. This must cast a shadow over the rest of the Warsaw pact. How reliable would be the Polish army in a similar crisis? In the murky Polish situation, Soviet interests seems to be threatened from two sides. Those who want liberalization are anti-Moscow. But so, Moscow fears, are the die-hards under Moczar; the same extreme Polish nationalism among these Communist right-wingers which expresses itself in anti-Semitism also expresses itself though more covertly in anti-Russianism. No one knows about the East German army, but Germans are even more anti-Russian than Poles. The Czech takeover, like a flash of lightning, suddenly illuminated the rifts in the Warsaw pact. Nationalism is a stronger force than Communism even where Communists are in power. Soviet military 'efficiency' – against deep but passive resistance – is not as important as the political weakness revealed.

The basic imbalance between East and West is not military but technological. Here, too, the Czech takeover weakened the Soviet bloc. Of all the Slav peoples, the Czechs have the most skilled labour force. Their economy has stagnated because they need the kind of machinery only the West can supply and because too many party hacks have been in control of the factories. Had the Czechs been allowed to go through with their plans for a half-billion dollar Western credit for machinery and with the establishment of workers' councils in the factories both these problems could have been solved. If the Russians want all the Western machine tools they can get, why not the Czechs? The changes would have given the Soviet bloc an increase in industrial efficiency and labour morale. It would have made the Czechs and Slovaks more rather than less loyal, as would the political liberalization. The Russian bureaucracy is too fearful to take this route. The route they have chosen means more unrest not only in alienation of the Western Communist parties.

The second question is: what could N.A.T.O. have done to 'save' the Czechs? The answer is nothing. I do not believe the Western powers were taken by surprise. Enough has been leaked by intelligence agencies in their own defence to indicate that they knew what was coming. It is hard to believe that Washington was not explicitly informed in advance by Moscow to avoid the risk of a great power confrontation. The State Department and the White House have been distinctly unfriendly to the Czechs because they have aided the other side in Johnson's war; there was a smug satisfaction in some quarters here that the Czechs had got what they deserved. It is only after the fact that Washington has made a great to-do about the Czech takeover, not because it has any sympathy for Prague but because it sees this as a means of pushing the other N.A.T.O.

powers into spending more on arms and relieving some of the burden on the U.S. in manning the front lines in West Europe.

Even with this pressure, the Brussels meeting of the N.A.T.O. powers only elicited pledges of an increase in arms spending of perhaps one per cent. The reason is twofold. The first is that the N.A.T.O. powers already have an enormous edge in military power. The report prepared for Senator John Cooper by Alain Enthoven, assistant secretary of defence, in October for Cooper's meeting with N.A.T.O. parliamentarians, did argue for some improvement in conventional forces, though it also got Enthoven into trouble with the military. The report showed that, aside from the Vietnam war, the N.A.T.O. forces were already spending $75 billion a year on arms against the Warsaw pact's $50 billion and had 5,470,000 men under arms as against the Warsaw pact's 4,200,000, including naval forces almost twice as big, air forces a third larger and even 105,000 more men in the army and marines. The disparity in nuclear power is even greater. The U.S. alone has 4,206 deliverable nuclear weapons against the U.S.S.R.'s 1,200.

The second reason for the reluctance to build up even more power arises from the West European conviction that a war for Western Europe, the biggest industrial prize in the world, could not be limited to conventional arms so there is no point in buying more of them. As for the nuclear arms, these have long passed the point of diminishing returns. 'What is the meaning of "superiority",' Wm C. Foster of the U.S. Arms Control and Disarmament Agency asked the Business Council in Hot Springs, Va., 10 October, 'when both sides can, under any circumstances, inflict 100 million casualties.' A nuclear war for Europe would destroy Europe and be the mutual suicide of the two great powers. Therefore each tacitly shuts its eyes to what the other does in its own sphere of influence. The U.S. is not going to plunge into a holocaust for Czechoslovakia, Rumania or Yugoslavia.

Detente is still the only path to Europe's salvation. Europe would be better off without the N.A.T.O. and the Warsaw pacts. What Moscow does in East Europe under cover of the Warsaw pact is what we do in Latin America under cover of the

Monroe Doctrine; the latter is our equivalent of Moscow's new 'Socialist commonwealth' doctrine, as so many Latins from Fidel Castro to Juan Bosch have learned. The Russians want to negotiate before the nuclear arms race sets off on a new spiral with the A.B.M. and the multiple warhead; we should negotiate. The higher the level of these arms the more terrible the devastation to both and all sides. Even Tito, the most menaced by the new Moscow hard line, told *Paris-Match* in an interview (16 November), 'The Cold War leads to the hot war' and suggested that he would like to see both the American and Soviet fleets out of the Mediterranean (as has the Foreign Minister of Spain). 'I fear,' Tito said, 'that one day they will clash.' Even if such a clash were kept limited, it might devastate the Mediterranean lands for both navies have nuclear arms. The 'ultimate solution of the problems of the world', Defence Secretary Clifford said on A.B.C.'s *Issues and Answers* (24 November) when he advocated arms control talks with Moscow despite the Czech affair, 'does not lie in larger armaments'. We agree.

2 December 1968, vol. 16, no. 24

Sorry, It's the Same Old Tricky D—y

I have often said that I felt that the first country to deploy an effective A.B.M. system and an effective A.S.W. [anti-submarine] system is going to control this world militarily.*

Senator Russell, who gave instant approval to Nixon's A.B.M. decision, speaking during last year's military appropriation hearings, as quoted by Mansfield, 7 March in a speech against the A.B.M. and its supposedly 'defensive' purpose.

* Just what the August Georgian meant by controlling the world was not explained. In the secret Senate debate on the A.B.M. last 14 October, he voted for the Sentinel programme to make sure (he said) that in the event of a nuclear holocaust, any survivors would be Americans. 'If we have to start over again with another Adam and Eve,' Russell said, 'then I want them to be Americans.' The new pair would we suppose 'control this world militarily', thus presumably giving posthumous satisfaction to the Joint Chiefs of Staff.

Mr Nixon was too clever for his own good at his press conference of 14 March. The very slickness of his performance will deepen distrust as the truth begins to trickle out. He was dishonest about the anti-ballistic missile as he was dishonest about the war in Vietnam. He has stepped into the same credibility gap where Lyndon Johnson destroyed himself. His soft sell and our hopes led us into deception. This is the same old tricky operator.

The impression he created is that he had whittled the A.B.M. down to a minimal system which would cost $1 billion less in the coming fiscal year than Johnson's. But it turns out that his Safeguard will be bigger and cost more than Johnson's Sentinel. This came out in the briefing that same day at the Pentagon when Deputy Secretary of Defense David Packard was asked (we quote p. 14 of the official transcript), 'Can you explain why the cost of your system is nearly a billion and a half more than the previous system yet it has possibly a half dozen complexes fewer?' Packard replied, 'In order to do the job that we believe needs to be done we found it necessary to provide additional capability in the system.' He explained that the new plan would require more radars and more Sprint missiles than Sentinel; 'more faces on the P.A.R. radars' and 'additional P.A.R. and that is a fairly extensive installation'. 'But in general,' he concluded, 'we are providing additional capability for the money.' So the headlines, if Nixon had been frank, would have said that he had opted for a bigger, more costly system.

The impression Nixon and Laird have conveyed is that since the Russians had deployed an A.B.M. we had to deploy one too. But Nixon is preparing to deploy a system many times greater than the already obsolete Galosh around Moscow. Their system, a system on which work halted some time ago, protects only the metropolitan area of Moscow. Nixon's will provide a city defence for Washington, a 'thin' Spartan cover for the entire country, a thick defence for two air-force missile bases in Montana and North Dakota, and site acquisition for Spartan and Sprint installations at nine other sites around the country. This escalates the arms race in response to a spurious *anti-*

missile gap just as Kennedy eight years ago escalated the arms race in response to a non-existent missile gap.

The dimensions of that escalation, when the full truth is known, will prove enormous. Mr Nixon, perhaps inadvertently, let slip a figure which has hitherto been classified. He said the Russians had deployed sixty-seven anti-missiles around Moscow. How many will we deploy? The question came up at Packard's briefing:

Q.: Can you tell us how many Spartan missiles and how many Sprint missiles in total would be in this?

MR PACKARD: Yes I think so.

MR ERYKLUND (information officer): No. You can't.

MR PACKARD: No, I can't. That is classified.

Q.: Can you tell us how many will be at each site?

MR PACKARD: No, we can't tell you that.

Some estimates were provided by the physicist Dr Ralph E. Lapp, 20 March, at Washington State University. Dr Lapp said the number of Spartans deployed for a 'thin' area defence across the country would probably be calculated 'to deal with no more than 100 attacking missiles' and the Spartans would number in the 'low hundreds', i.e. perhaps two or three for each incoming missile. That will already be several times the sixty-seven the Russians have deployed.

What about Sprints? Here we come to another of Mr Nixon's deceptions. He spoke of 'protecting two Minuteman sites'. That sounded very minimal indeed. It turns out, as Dr Lapp explained (20 March) that the 'two *sites*' are really 'two Minuteman wings with a total of thirty-five flights'. Each 'flight', in air force parlance, is made up of ten missiles. So this is a total of 350 missiles, each in a separate silo, or fifty more than one-third of our total Minuteman force of 1,000. If Nixon had been candid, the headlines would have said that the *initial* deployment would safeguard a third of our Minutemen.

How many Sprints would be required to protect 350 Minutemen? Dr Lapp gave a range of estimates, depending on the size and accuracy of the attacking missile. He estimated that even if the Russians achieved one-quarter of a mile accuracy (i.e. if they were able to hit within 500 yards of an object 5,000 miles away!) they would need three 1-megaton weapons for each silo (allowing for 20 per cent system losses and 95 per cent kill probability). That would require 1,000 attacking missiles. The defence, in turn, would probably have to assign three or more Sprint missiles to each hostile object. That is a total of more than 3,000 Sprints! Our *total* Minuteman force of 1,000 would require, by that calculation, 9,000 anti-missiles to protect them. This does not count the Sprints for the city of Washington or the other sites. Let us put the grand total at 10,000 as compared with the Soviet's sixty-seven. That is raising the ante sharply, and they must be expected to reply in kind.

If you figure the missiles at half a million each, that is $5 billion. At $1 million each, it would be $10 billion. The cost figures are not only classified but not really known since production has hardly started. But this provides some idea of the business which A.T. & T.'s Western Electric, the prime contractor, and the 5,000 odd subcontractors can expect from this, the largest procurement contract in military history.

Now we come to a natural question and another deception. Laird has said we needed an A.B.M. as a bargaining card in the coming arms negotiations with the Soviet Union. Nixon, too, talked in his prepared statement as if this A.B.M. programme might be scaled down in future arms talks. But when the question was put to him directly, his answer – slippery as it was – indicated that the A.B.M. was not to be abandoned, *that it was not negotiable within the limits he is already setting for the talks.* 'In any talks with the Soviet Union,' he was asked, 'would you be willing to consider abandoning the A.B.M. programme altogether if the Soviets showed a similar willingness or indeed, if they showed a readiness to place limitations on offensive weapons?' Mr Nixon replied that while he was ready to consider both offensive and defensive weapons, 'the arms talks, that at least preliminarily have been discussed, *do not involve limitations or reductions.* [Our emphasis.] They involve only freezing where we are.' If 'where we are' includes this A.B.M. and the M.I.R.V.s and the rest of the huge expansion we have in the works, what is there to negotiate?

In the light of this reply, the A.B.M. is not a bargaining card at all but an attempt to commit the country to an A.B.M. system in advance of talks, 'The abandoning of the entire system,' Mr Nixon went on to say, 'particularly as long as the Chinese threat is there, I think neither country would look upon with much favour.' If the A.B.M. is to go on 'as long as the Chinese threat is there' then it will go on for a long time indeed. For our military, the mere existence of China is a threat. Mr Nixon went on to make another tricky assertion. Mr Nixon said the Soviet A.B.M. had been deployed originally against the U.S. but 'today their radars, from our intelligence, are also directed towards Communist China.' When Senator Gore opened his hearings on the A.B.M. (6 March) he said that some officials had declared that the Soviet A.B.M. was aimed at China as well as the U.S. but 'this statement flatly contradicts what the Foreign Relations Committee was told by another equally responsible source just a few days ago.' That witness, it has since leaked out, was none other than Richard Helms, head of the C.I.A.

These are only a few of the strands in this thick woven web of deception. Let us take another. If the Chinese threat is the essential factor, as the words we have just quoted indicate, then why is Nixon putting his first A.B.M.s around the Minutemen instead of the cities? The Chinese would have to be twice as crazy as our Joint Chiefs of Staff would like us to think they are to justify that deployment. The latest estimates are that they may have eighteen or twenty I.C.B.M.s in a few years. It would be insane for them to attack the U.S. which can deliver 4,200 warheads, with their puny eighteen or twenty. They would have to be many times crazier to use their handful against our 1,000 Minutemen. China's puny handful have only one possible military significance. Our military wants an A.B.M. against them so it can threaten or make a first strike against China without fear of retaliation. That handful might be used in one last dying attempt to hit back at some American city. If these military lunatics of ours are thinking of a Chinese attack, the only attack remotely conceivable would be a retaliatory attempt against one or two of our cities if we were destroying China in a first strike. (Even this is highly improbable because our first target would be their missiles.) To safeguard against such a contingency a city defence is needed. But Mr Nixon now says no city defence is possible. So how does his A.B.M. protect us from China?

The contradictions are as great if the real enemy is the Soviet Union. At one point in his press conference Mr Nixon said, quite correctly, of the Russians, 'They have always thought in defensive terms, and if you read not only their political leaders, but their military leaders, the emphasis is on defence.' If they think in terms of defence, why make our plans on the assumption that they might make a first strike? An attempt at a first strike would be as certain suicide for them as it would be for the Chinese. Do we think the Russians, too, are irrational? Mr Nixon said we had to deploy A.B.M.s around our Minutemen to make our 'deterrent capability credible'. He talked as if we had no other deterrent but these land-based I.C.B.M.s. But what of our Polaris submarines, on which billions have been spent, to give us an invulnerable second-strike capacity? Even if an enemy could wipe out every U.S. I.C.B.M. in one swift blow, it would face certain destruction from these submarines, always on the prowl, hidden in the seas and much closer to the borders of the Soviet Union.

We can deliver 4,200 warheads averaging one megaton each, more than four times their total capacity. Our land-based missiles can deliver 1,700. Our Polaris submarines can deliver 656. Our third deterrent force, the Strategic Air Command, can deliver the rest, about 1,800 warheads. These are the officially published U.S. figures.

If an enemy destroyed two of these deterrents, he would still face destruction at the hands of the third. If only 100 of our 4,200 warheads survived a first attack, that would be enough (according to McNamara's final posture statement last year) to destroy fifty-nine per cent of Soviet industry and 37 million people in one swift counter-blow. That is half again as many Soviet people who died in the Second World War, and it does not include those who would die after the first twenty-four hours from wounds, radiation, hunger and despair in the atomic ruins. The idea that the defence-minded Russians would try a first strike against such odds is a nightmare dreamt up by the

Strangeloves of the military-industrial complex to create a market for its fantastic wares. Mr Nixon has used the highest office in the land to support their preposterous and enormously expensive nonsense.

To understand the folly of the A.B.M. one need only keep in mind five general propositions. The first is that in the game of nuclear 'cops and robbers' the offence can think up an endless number of relatively inexpensive gimmicks – from penetration aids and M.I.R.V.s and changes in trajectory – each of which forces the defence into complex and costly counter-measures. The A.B.M. defence is like a whole series of Maginot lines, each of which can easily be outflanked and rendered useless. The second is that the offence can concentrate its forces while the defence must spread itself thin. An enemy can concentrate all his missiles on one or two cities for a retaliatory blow. The A.B.M. defence has to have enough protection for *every* city and *every* major industrial and military area sufficiently large to match any such concentration of forces. If an enemy only has ten missiles we have to put three times as many anti-missiles at *every* point we have to defend. The odds are with the attacker. If one warhead gets through, that is the end of the area defended. The attacker only needs one more missile to overwhelm the defence in this game of one-upmanship.

The third proposition is that, contrary to Mr Nixon, it is more, not less, difficult to defend Minuteman bases than it is to defend cities. The firing of our A.B.M.s would, as Dr Lapp explained in a speech at Kansas State University (12 March) foul up the electronic circuitry of the computers and guidance controls on which Minuteman depends. We may 'black-out' our own missile forces and computers in the effort to defend them. The fourth proposition is that if we saw a first strike coming – and a first strike would be a mass of weapons – we would hardly leave our Minutemen in their silos to wait and see how our A.B.M.s would work. We would fire them off at the enemy in the fifteen or twenty minutes of warning time that would allow. The enemy would only hit empty holes and we would only be defending empty holes. The fifth and final proposition is that we still do not know how much damage these defences would do to ourselves. The Spartans could blind hundreds of thousands of our own people in the area defended. The Sprints would create harmful blast and radiation effects if they hit the oncoming missiles below a certain level, let us say ten miles. In a nuclear bombardment, offence and defence would mingle and the defence might only stoke the fires of the very hell the offence had ignited.

In deciding to go ahead with the A.B.M. Mr Nixon has entered the country in a nuclear rat race which must prove ever more expensive as we seek constantly to 'improve' it in response to enemy counter-measures. Mr Nixon tried to give the impression that these measures were purely defensive. But the Russians have said all along that their A.B.M.s around Moscow are purely defensive too; a system around their capital is certainly not a preparation for a first strike. Yet we are responding with this huge A.B.M. programme on the ground that our deterrent is threatened by the Moscow A.B.M. and by the build-up in the number of Russian I.C.B.M.s which is their response to our decision in September 1967 to deploy Sentinel. Mr Nixon spoke as if his A.B.M. system was tentative. So it is, but only in the sense that the Pentagon knows it is inadequate. 'Each phase of the deployment', Mr Nixon said in his prepared statement on 14 March, 'will be reviewed to ensure that we are doing as much as necessary' and to 'take maximum advantage of the information gathered from the initial deployment in designing the later phases of the programme'. This signals annual expansion and 'improvement'. There is no end to the billions this monstrous folly can eat up. Its worst aspect is that our military, as the Russell remark we quoted at the beginning of this article shows, still dream of the perfect missile defence. This would enable them to threaten a first strike with impunity and thus dictate to the world. This is what Laird was hoping for when he wrote of a 'strategy gap'.

We have only scratched the surface of the tricky presentation by Mr Nixon and Defence Secretary Packard. The latter turns out to be another devious character out of the electronics business in which he made his $300,000,000 fortune; his liberal sentiments on arms reduction and social welfare turn out to be eyewash. But we have shown enough to enable the reader to understand why Eisenhower and Kennedy declined to approve the A.B.M. and why *every* science adviser of Eisenhower, Kennedy and Johnson has consistently opposed it. It must be defeated or it will set off a major new spiral in the arms race and divert to the military and the arms industry not only the money but the technological ingenuity so desperately needed at home. It can be defeated if the Senate opposition holds firm and exposes the whole imposture as the Gore subcommittee of Senate Foreign Relations has begun to do. The leaders of the fight against the A.B.M., Cooper and Fulbright, Mansfield and Kennedy, must call halt before it is too late. The peace movement must mobilize as never before to counteract the contractor and military lobbyists for this billion-dollar boon-doggle now swarming into almost every office on Capitol Hill. Not the least of the matters at stake is the future of our best youth. How end alienation from democratic processes and peaceful change when they see a President opt for such terrible waste against near unanimous scientific advice and in the face of social needs so urgent they threaten the future of our society?

24 March 1969, vol. 17, no. 6

Part Three:
The American
Nightmare

1: The Race War

The Negro Strides towards Full Emancipation

For weeks on Mondays, when opinions are handed down, the Supreme Court press room had drawn a full house, including an unusually large number of Negro reporters. Last Monday, after we had all begun to give up hope of a school segregation decision that day, an unusual event occurred. Ordinarily opinions are given out in the press room after word comes down the pneumatic chute that they have been read in the courtroom above. This time the light flashed and there was a different kind of message. The press aide put on his coat and we were all shepherded into the court chamber to hear the opinion read and receive our copies there.

In that tense and crowded marble hall, the Chief Justice was already reading the opinion in *Brown et al.* v. *U.S.* He read in a firm, clear voice and with expression. As the Chief Justice launched into the opinion's lengthy discussion of the Fourteenth Amendment, the reporters, white and Negro, edged forward in the press boxes, alert for indications of which way the decision was going. 'We come then,' the Chief Justice read, 'to the question presented: does segregation of children in public schools solely on the basis of race, even though the physical facilities and other "tangible" factors may be equal, deprive the children of the minority group of equal educational opportunities?' In the moment of suspense which followed we could hear the Chief Justice replying firmly, 'We believe that it does.' It was all one could do to keep from cheering, and a few of us were moved to tears.

There was one quite simple but terribly evocative sentence in the opinion. To Negroes and other sympathetic persons this packed the quintessence of the quieter misery imposed on members of a submerged race. 'To separate them,' the Chief Justice said of Negro children, 'from others of a similar age and qualifications solely because of their race generates a feeling of inferiority as to their status in the community that may affect their hearts and minds in a way unlikely ever to be undone.' So the fifty-eight-year-old ruling of *Blessy* v. *Ferguson* was reversed and the court ruled 'Separate educational facilities are inherently unequal ... segregation is a denial of the equal protection of the laws.'

Among the audience streaming out of the chamber when the Chief Justice had ended, the lawyers of the N.A.A.C.P. suddenly began to embrace each other outside the doors. They had achieved a giant stride towards the full emancipation of their people. The growing political power of the Negro had prevailed over the growing wealth of the Republican Party's newest recruits, the Texas oil millionaires. In a showdown, American democracy had proved itself real. It was the votes which counted.

The unanimous ruling seemed too explicit to be whittled away in the enforcing decree. The rehearing next fall on the form of that decree, the invitation to the Southern States to be heard, offer a period in which tempers may cool and bigots be allowed second thoughts. At the best, Jim Crow will not be ended overnight. The clue to what is likely to happen in most cities, North and South, may be found in a clause of the questions on which the court will hear arguments in the fall.

The court is to consider whether 'within the limits set by normal geographic school districting' Negro children shall 'forthwith be admitted to schools of their choice' or a gradual changeover be arranged. Since most Negroes in most cities already lived in more or less segregated Negro sections, these will still have largely Negro schools. It is on the borderlines that mixing will begin; ultimately the pattern of segregated schools will break down with the pattern of segregated Negro housing areas. The ultimate impact must revolutionize race relations and end the system of inferior status and inferior education which has kept the ex-slave a menial.

The decision may be enough to ensure a Republican victory in the fall elections. If we have not blundered into war, if there is not serious unemployment, the reaction of the Negro to the segregation case may be decisive in many industrial areas. This is especially so if there is a prolonged outburst of bitterness in the South. Were the Democratic party not irremediably split on the race question, the issue of Federal aid to education and a Federal school-building programme might give the Democrats a chance to steal the G.O.P.s laurels and make inroads among the building trades. But of such a strategy there is little prospect.

24 May 1954, vol. 2, no. 18

The South is Sick – That is the Meaning of the Till Murder

Next to the President's collapse, the worst news of the week was from Mississippi. The jury at Sumner brought in two verdicts, not one. The immediate and visible decision was that J. W. Milam and Roy Bryant were not guilty of killing a fourteen-year-old coloured boy. The other, unspoken, unintended, unconscious but indelible was a verdict of guilty against all the rest of us and our country.

There are scenes at the murder trial which imprint themselves unforgettably: the Negro reporters, as they walked into court one day after lunch, being hailed by the Sheriff with 'Hello, Niggers.' Mrs Bradley, the mother of the victim, testifying that she told her son before he left for the South, 'to be very careful how he spoke and to say "yessir" and "no ma'am" and not to hesitate to humble yourself if you had to get down on your knees', Moses Wright – we salute his courage – testifying that when J. W. Milam came to get his fourteen-year-old nephew Emmett Till, he asked 'You from Chicago?' and when the boy answered 'Yes' Milam said 'Don't you say yes to me or I'll knock hell out of you.' Mrs Bryant's sexy whopper (which Judge Swango to his credit kept from the jury) that this fourteen-year-old boy with a speech defect had grabbed her round the waist, solicited her with an unprintable expression and boasted, 'I've been with white women before,' J. A. Shaw, Jr, the foreman of the jury, asked by the press what the jury thought of

Mrs Bradley's testimony replying 'If she tried a little harder she might have got out a tear.'

Emmett Till's broken body, with the bullet hole in the right temple and the gaping hole in the back of the head, as if broken in by a rock, testified to a maniacal murder. Those who killed him were sick men, sick with race hatred. The murder and the trial could only have happened in a sick countryside. Where else would a mother be treated with such elementary lack of respect or compassion? Where else would the defence dare put forward the idea that the murder was somehow 'framed' by the N.A.A.C.P.? Where else would newspapers somehow make it appear that those at fault were not the men who killed the boy but those who tried to bring the killers to justice? There is a sickness in the South. Unless cured, there may some day spring from it crimes as evil and immense as the crematoria of Hitlerism.

If Milam and Bryant did not kill Till, then who did? Nobody in the South asks the question, at least publicly. Who was the third man with them? Where are the two missing witnesses? Nobody cares. Mississippi went through the motions, and the motions were enough to muffle the weak conscience of the northern white press. The judge was honourable; the special prosecutor tried hard; who can quarrel with a jury verdict? But the jury was all white, in an area two-thirds Negro. And of what use was an upright judge and a special prosecutor when the case was rushed to trial without adequate preparation or investigation? This was only the final scene of a lynching, hastily covered with a thin veil of respectability by a shrewd Governor. The same Governor, Hugh White, as chairman of the Legal Education Advisory Committee, has just put forward a six-point programme to fight desegregation which calls for abolition of compulsory public schooling and legislation to 'prohibit interference with state law under cover of federal authority'. Hugh White is himself the leader of Mississippi's racists and nullificationists.

Before the war and the witch-hunt, where there were still organizations like the Southern Conference for Human Welfare, there would have been public meetings of protest under mixed auspices. It shames our country and it shames white Americans that the only meetings, in Harlem, Baltimore, Chicago and Detroit, have been Negro meetings. Those whites in the South and in the North who would normally have been moved to act have been hounded out of public life and into inactivity. To the outside world it must look as if the conscience of white America has been silenced, and the appearance is not too deceiving. Basically all of us whites, North and South, acquiesce in white supremacy, and benefit from the pool of cheap labour created by it.

Will the Negro take this latest outrage? Unless Negroes rouse themselves to make their indignation felt in some dramatic way, nothing will be done in Mississippi or in Congress. Philip Randolph last Sunday suggested a march on Washington like that which dramatized the E.E.P.C. fight before Pearl Harbor. Were thousands of Negroes to converge on the Department of Justice and demand action against the murderers of Till, and of the other Negroes whose recent murders have gone unpunished in the South, such a demonstration would have an impact. The American Negro needs a Gandhi to lead him, and we need the American Negro to lead us. If he does not provide leadership against the sickness in the South, the time will come when we will all pay a terrible price for allowing a psychopathic racist brutality to flourish unchecked.

3 October 1955, vol. 3, no. 36

The United States as Three Nations, Not One

The problem which confronts our country in the integration crisis may be illuminated if we regard the United States for a moment not as one nation but as three, the South as a land apart, the Negro as a people apart. The differences among the three may be seen in their sharply different responses to the President's action in calling out the troops in Little Rock. The white South was overwhelmingly hostile; the white North – which constitutes a majority of the whole people – was overwhelmingly approving. The white South was shocked at military 'occupation'; the white North relieved that we were not to give in before mob rule. The Negro's reaction was of a different kind. The Negro felt like Cinderella. When a station wagon guarded by army jeeps took little Negro children to and from school instead of leaving them to run the gauntlet of hate alone, the Negro felt that for the first time in American history he was being treated like a first-class citizen, that for a wonderful moment he was no longer on the outside, wistfully looking in.

'Satchmo' Armstrong's anguished cry, 'Sometimes it seems like the Negro doesn't have a country', must have echoed in every Negro's heart during the days in which it seemed as if Faubus and the mob would get away with it. Amid the hand-wringing over Little Rock by the so-called Southern moderates, and the (lily-white) conferences in the White House to negotiate withdrawal of troops, and to let Faubus save face, it is forgotten that for the Negro the law never looked more truly majestic than it does today in Little Rock where for once the bullies of the South have been put on notice that they cannot take out their venom on the Negro and his children.

Quite different is the scene through white Southern eyes. The white South feels like an oppressed minority because the white North has interfered to prevent it from oppressing its Negro minority. If one recalls the bitter feelings of the Irish to this day about Cromwell, it is less difficult to understand that for the white South the defeat of its armies only a century ago and its occupation by Northern troops are memories which the calling out of the army in Little Rock makes vivid again. The white South feels a victim of injustice, misunderstanding and brute force. That these are exactly what it visits on the helpless Negro who steps out of line merely illustrates the capacity of human beings to go on doing to others what they violently object to when done to themselves.

When three groups in one country see the same problem in such sharply different ways, it is difficult to find a common language. What the white South so proudly calls its way of life looks to the white Northern outsider as a dark and tangled complex created by slavery, reconstruction and sex. The mind of the white South seems sick with a strange hatred for the Negro people, though from this same hated people have come beloved playmates, nursemaids and mistresses. The outcry against 'mixing' is revealing in the century of Freud. 'Mixing' is what Southern white males have been doing with pleasure for generations. The recurrent outbursts of savagery in which Negroes are emasculated is a symbol no special training is required to decipher. A psychoanalyst would suspect that all this racialistic hysterics masks a longing to 'mix'. But what can the crude methods of politics do with tensions which would appal a psychiatrist?

When any effort is made to change this 'way of life', the reaction is nationalistic. White Southerners draw together, moderates and extremists, as a nation does when under attack from the outside. No voice is raised, in the white South itself to say that racialism is an illness, an anachronism. The moderates loyally insist that they, too, are for segregation. The best they can still argue today – it may be less tomorrow – is the need to uphold the law. But law has firm sanctions only in majority views of what is moral. The white Northern majority, which is also the majority of the U.S., feels that segregation is obsolete and wrong, though Northern whites practise segregation, too, in their own way. But the overwhelming majority of whites in the South believe segregation is right, as their forebears taught themselves to believe slavery was right. The problem of enforcing in the white South what the North considers 'law' but the South doesn't can easily become insoluble. Troops may be an answer in Little Rock but they will not prove an answer in Atlanta.

A time of troubles may be beginning, the most serious conflict of our generation, poisoning our politics for years to come, capable of fomenting volcanic eruptions of bloodshed. Integration cannot be stopped. If the country is not to be torn apart in the process, every American, white and black, Northern and Southern, who exercises any kind of leadership, must be willing for the sake of our common country to take an unpopular position against his own hotheads, and must resist the temptation of the easy popularity to be gained by pandering to the thoughtless emotions of his own 'nation'. If America, which has made so much progress in two centuries towards a fruitful and inspiring equality, could succeed at last in integrating the black man, too, America would again become a beacon for all mankind. The ideal is great enough, the dangers acute enough, to challenge and inspire a generation *if* the leadership can be found. None of us can yet comprehend fully how much depends on that if.

7 October 1957, vol. 5, no. 38

Yes, Virginia, There's Still a Red (*Red Men, That Is*) Menace

The *Weekly* has decided to establish an annual Bakunin award, commemorating one of the livelier traditions of the enlightened nineteenth century, and to confer it this year for distinguished public service on the Indians of Robeson County, North Carolina, who broke up a Klan segregation rally with buckshot and sent the Klan leader complaining to the police that he wanted the same protection – as he phrased it – 'given Negroes at Little Rock'. We regret only that the Indians, obviously corrupted by white civilization, took nightshirts but no scalps.

27 January 1958, vol. 6, no. 4

Hopeful Thought-of-the-Week

The President seems to have angered Negro leaders at their meeting here with his pleas for patience. Typical of the protests this aroused was Thurgood Marshall's remark, 'I'm the world's original gradualist. I just think ninety-odd years is gradual enough.' Negro anger, though understandable, may be too hasty. Mr Eisenhower, as the commander-in-chief, has access to much information which cannot be made public. He may have a reason for counselling patience. It may be that secret studies have shown that the next war will end discrimination based on colour. There is reason to believe all survivors will be the same shade of radioactive green.

19 May 1958, vol. 6, no. 19

The Lesson Faubus-Era America May Still Learn from Algeria

To look at our South after studying the Algerian situation is to see how lucky we still are. In Algeria, the 'coloured man' is fighting against integration. Here he is demanding it. In Algeria, the Europeans are trying desperately to stave off minority status in an independent Arab country by offering too late an integration which would have been welcomed twenty years ago. Twenty years ago the Arabs of Algeria were prepared for assimilation into French society on the basis of ever widening equality of status. Today they no longer want to be Frenchmen. We are fortunate that our Negroes still want to be Americans like the rest of us.

The situation may be different twenty years hence. Twenty years of disappointment in the face of Southern white intransigence and Northern white indifference can create a bitterness which might never be bridged. The Negro sees us ready to send troops halfway round the world to uphold law and order in Lebanon, but he wonders what we will do when court orders are violated as schools open next month again in Little Rock and across the Potomac in Virginia.

The overwhelming re-election of a Faubus is in Negro eyes evidence that he is really up against a race issue, that white men are overwhelmingly united in the South against his aspirations for equality and that white men in the North are basically indifferent.

In the years ahead, as Black Africa develops, there will also develop in conflict with the whites of South Africa, of our South, and of North Africa, a fierce Negro nationalism, a racism in reaction against ours, that may win our Negroes away from the ideal of assimilation.

There was warning foretaste of this in the Marcus Garvey Day celebration held in Harlem (2 August) by a group calling itself the United African Nationalist Movement, which is anti-Israel, pro-Nasser – and (most significantly of all) anti-N.A.A.C.P., i.e. against those Negroes fighting for equality and assimilation as Americans. Nationalism in Harlem and the memory of Garvey (a Negro nationalist, who launched a Back-to-Africa movement) were strong enough to bring Adam Clayton Powell, Councilman Earl Brown and Manhattan Borough President Jack to the meeting as speakers in honour of Garvey.

Liberian history, and native exploitation by American Negroes, are sour recommendation for Back-to-Africa solutions. The American Negro has little real bond with the African Negro; the former is racially mixed with the whites, often more white than Negro, culturally and spiritually an American like the rest of us. But rejection on the basis of colour, mistreatment at the hands of whites, have already created a sense of community between them which will grow as Africa develops and may some day have serious consequences for national unity.

11 August 1958, vol. 6, no. 31

To Understand the Integration Crisis Read Anne Braden's The Wall Between

Anne Braden grew up in the South on the right side of the tracks. She came, as they say in the South, of a good family. Very early she began to feel there was something wrong in the relations between the races. Her family was always kind to the Negro family who worked for them. 'But something happened to me,' Mrs Braden writes in her book, *The Wall Between* (Monthly Review Press, New York), 'each time I looked at the Negro girl who always inherited my clothes ... She would sit in a straight chair in our kitchen waiting for her mother. ... She would sit there looking uncomfortable, my old faded dress binding her at the waist and throat. And some way I knew that this was not what Jesus meant when he said to clothe the naked.'

Anne became a newspaperwoman and married a fellow reporter, Carl, who came most decidedly from the *other* side of the tracks. His family was Catholic, the father an agnostic and socialist who lost his job in the 1922 railway shopmen's strike.

The family had known poverty ever since. Carl, at the age of thirteen, went into a pro-seminary to prepare for the priesthood but at sixteen decided it was not for him. He became a newspaperman in Louisville, Kentucky. 'A police reporter,' he once told his wife, 'has to become one of three things, a drunk, a cynic or a reformer.' Carl chose the third course, and it led him in 1954 to agree when a Negro veteran, Andrew Wade, asked the Bradens to buy a house for him in a new white neighbourhood in Louisville, Kentucky. The house was dynamited and the state authorities, instead of prosecuting the dynamiters, indicted the Bradens and five other residents of Louisville for sedition. Braden, the first to be tried, was sent to jail for fifteen years, and saved only by the miracle of the Supreme Court's Steve Nelson decision.

Anne Braden has told the whole story in her book, *The Wall Between*, and told it with the depth and objectivity of a first-rate novel. All that is happening elsewhere in the integration crisis is lit up for us by this story of what that attack on housing segregation did in and to liberal Louisville. Mrs Braden writes with compassion for the prisons in which men seal themselves up. She sees the 'paralysed liberals' of Louisville, like its cross-burners, as 'trapped men'. She even tried, in one of the most memorable episodes of the book, to understand her fellow Southerner, the prosecutor, Scott Hamilton, who was trying his best to send her and her husband to prison on trumped up charges he himself had come to believe. 'If circumstances,' she asked herself, 'somewhere in the past of both our lives had been different, would I perhaps have been on his side of this battle or he on mine?' This was the same young woman who could firmly refuse to answer questions about the books she read and the organizations to which she belonged. 'I think we have enough McCarthys in this country,' she said defiantly when taken before a judge, 'without the Grand Jury turning into one.'

The Bradens walked through the valley of the shadow of the witch hunt. An F.B.I. informer perjured herself to call Braden a Communist; he denied it under oath. The House Un-American Committee sent down agents to frighten Andrew Wade, the Negro they had risked so much to help, and got him to say things only said about a man and a woman one does not trust. The transcript of what Wade said in a moment of weakness gave Anne Braden the most terrible moment of the whole experience, one in which she felt 'that the things we had been working for – a world without segregation, a world of understanding and brotherhood – had turned to dust in my hand'. But the moment passed. Both Wade and the Bradens recovered from it. Her book is a worthy record of a great experience, the warming story of a heroic couple's abiding faith.

15 September 1958, vol. 6, no. 36

The Ugly Questions Unanswered in That Lynching

In the 'Untold Story of Little Rock' (*Saturday Evening Post*, 23 May), Virgil T. Blossom, the former school superintendent, criticizes the failure of the Justice Department 'to indict or prosecute a single individual involved in mob action to thwart integration, although more than fifty were arrested by local police'. The untold story of the Poplarville lynching is proceeding along the same lines. The Federal government has withdrawn from the case and handed over the results of an F.B.I. investigation to Governor Coleman of Mississippi. Instead of summoning a special grand jury, Governor Coleman says he will await the regular grand jury next November. By November the ashes will be cold.

Those wise in the ways of official double-talk will note the peculiar wording of the Attorney General's announcement. It says the decision to withdraw was 'based upon a ruling that F.B.I. investigation had clearly established that the persons responsible for the death* of Parker had not violated the Federal Kidnapping Statute, and no other successful Federal prosecution could be maintained'. This is tantalizing. It is 'clearly established' that the anti-kidnapping law was not violated, i.e. the murdered man was not taken across state lines. But what of the Civil Rights statutes which make it a crime for a state official to

* 'Death' not 'lynching'. Note how delicately the words have been chosen, as if to spare Southern susceptibility.

conspire with a lynch mob, or even to fail in his duty to protect against it? Of this other possibility, we are told only that 'no other successful Federal prosecution could be maintained'. For lack of evidence? The atmosphere? Because witnesses might fear reprisals from state officials? And why the word 'successful'? Even an unsuccessful Federal prosecution may serve as a deterrent. Were this not the murder of one whom we white Americans consider, to borrow the German word with all its ugly implications, an *Untermensch*, the Attorney General would never be able to get away with such meagre explanation.

The doubts raised by the cryptic wording of the press release are sharpened by the letter New York radio station W.M.C.A. received from Poplarville, Miss., in answer to a $5,000 reward offer. The well-known Negro journalist Ted Poston was allowed to read the letter. In the *New York Post* of Friday, 22 May, he reported it 'named an elected official of Pearl River County as a close collaborator' of the lynch mob. This official arranged to have the Negro prisoner transferred back to Poplarville from a safe jail in Jackson, and served as 'lookout', telling the mobsters where the jail keys could be found. Station W.M.C.A. officials verified the accuracy of Mr Poston's report when we phoned them and added that they were trying to retrieve the letter from the F.B.I. before it could be handed over to Mississippi authorities, lest the writer of it be exposed to retaliation. Why *was* Parker moved back to Poplarville? And why was the jail unguarded when the lynch mob arrived? Was County Attorney William Stewart, the responsible official, questioned?

The morning this issue went to press, Governor Coleman was to testify before the Hennings Committee against civil rights legislation. We are waiting to see whether any senator asks him about these loose ends. Will anyone question him about the mysterious suicide attempts by Poplarville's jail janitor, Houston Amacker, and Helen Van Ness 'a woman prisoner who', according to an A.P. dispatch from Poplarville (*New York Post*, 12 May) 'witnessed the abduction'. Both are white. Shouldn't these witnesses be moved to a safer place?

We invite the attention of the Hennings Committee, too, to the House Appropriations testimony by J. Edgar Hoover. Why is he so venomous and suspicious about anyone who seeks to help the Negro? Why does he, so vocal on the dangers of Communism, never raise his voice on the dangers of racism, though a sense of rankling injustice on the part of a newer Negro generation may some day tear our great cities apart? Year after year his testimony chimes in with Southern racists' attempts to picture the Negro's struggle for justice and equality as a Red plot. How reliable are F.B.I. investigations of lynchings when its chief approaches the problem in the same lurid frame of reference as the more benighted elements of the South?

1 June 1959, vol. 7, no. 21

On a Certain Blindness to the Peril of Racism

Our hat is off to the Attorney General for acting with vigour and dispatch in Montgomery's outburst of white racist violence, and we hope the President will move into a position of active leadership if trouble spreads, as it is likely to do. For this is one of these strange situations in which law and order are no longer synonyms but suddenly almost opposites. If the young students now making history in the South persist in insisting that the government uphold the law's guarantee of equal treatment for white and black, there will be *dis*order. If they and the Negro community are persuaded to sink back into acquiescence, there will again be order.

But the South has too long been enabled to enjoy order at the expense of law, to persist in those peculiar customs which once meant slavery and now mean humiliation for the darker half of its citizens. The 'Freedom Riders' have achieved the first great success of Gandhi's non-violent tactics in America by striking at those crucial points in the system of white supremacy where direct action is possible. The South can drag its heels for years on school segregation, as it has for decades on voter rights, but the right to sit unsegregated in a bus or at a lunch counter is a right an individual can enforce for himself if he has the courage to face up to insult and injury, to persist, and to establish his moral superiority by turning the other cheek. It is not surprising that this sudden appearance of literal fidelity to the Gospel should so startle the supposedly pious South that the tactic is blamed on Marx rather than Jesus. The 'Freedom Riders' have again made Christianity a revolutionary creed.

Mr Kennedy has said in another connection that things will probably get worse before they get better. This is true in the South. A moment is rapidly approaching, perhaps in Mississippi, when Mr Kennedy will have to do what he criticized Mr Eisenhower for not doing – and that is to bring the full moral force of his high office to bear. The fact that only one Southern Senator, Ervin of North Carolina, has spoken up in support of the Federal government's action in Montgomery, that the whole Alabama delegation has asked for the withdrawal of the Federal marshals, that the governors of Mississippi and Arkansas have spoken up in support of the Governor of Alabama, that they all blame the 'agitators', indicates the dimensions of the challenge. The Southern mobster, like the Communist guerrilla in another context, is effective because he has tacit, popular sympathy; the Southern white may deplore violence, but he'd like to see the Negro kept down in an inferiority which is profitable and flattering to him.

Too many Southern men and women regard freedom to humiliate Negroes as their most precious constitutional right. The struggle for equality is in this sense as irreconcilable as was the struggle against slavery.

In this struggle public attention should be focused on the extent to which a curious lack of antipathy for extreme racist organizations like the Klan affects the forces, so-called, of law and order. On page three [of this issue of the *Weekly*] we print excerpts from a published report by Alabama citizens on the extent to which the police are actually infiltrated by the Klan. We also call attention to the recently released House Appropriations Committee hearings on the Justice Department budget. Here we find the head of the F.B.I. treating the sit-ins as a Communist plot in a way which can only encourage the racial paranoia endemic in the South. Though the Klan and allied organizations have been growing rapidly, Mr Hoover still clings to the senescent and dwindling Communist Party, U.S.A., as our no. 1 subversive menace. He claims to have 'some 200 known or suspected Communist front and Communist-infiltrated organizations' under investigation by the F.B.I., a number so inflated to anyone aware of the realities on the shrunken American Left that one assumes he must suspect Marxist–Leninists even in the patriotic bosom of the D.A.R. But there is not a word about keeping our rapidly expanding network of racist and Fascist groups under surveillance. Mr Hoover is fierce about Reds, pinks and – a favourite target of his scorn – 'do-gooders', but he never seems to warn against racism, just as Senator Eastland never subpoenas Klansmen as a menace to internal security nor Mr Walter preaches of race hatred as un-American.

29 May 1961, vol. 9, no. 20

The Negro, the F.B.I. and Police Brutality

We turn aside this week from more resounding events to devote this letter to the report on 'Justice' by the U.S. Commission on Civil Rights. The Berlin crisis will be with us for many months, Latin American convulsions for many years. But this newly released study of police brutality, particularly to Negroes, offers an opportunity that may not occur again for a long time. The report seeks to turn attention to a dark corner of our national life, where the poor and the defenceless suffer; many months of patient investigation went into it; it had the unanimous approval of six commissioners, two of them white Southerners and one a Negro; it offers some thoughtful recommendations and it dares even to imply some criticism of that sacred cow, the F.B.I. It is heart-breaking to see how meagrely it has been covered by most papers, how quickly it is being brushed under the rug. No phrase carries more opprobrium in the United States than 'police-state practices', none brings forth more firmly conditioned reflexes from editorial writers and commentators. But no burst of indignation has greeted this report on police-state practices in our own country, behind that other iron curtain which shuts off from view the realities under which the Negro lives in the rural South and in Northern slums.

Eleven 'typical cases of police brutality' are reported by the commission and there are many others in the extensive footnotes. Plutarch tells us how the Spartans terrorized and humiliated their helots, weeding out the spirited, to keep their slaves in line; the 'uppity' Negro is a target in the South for the same reasons. The police brutality is not 'senseless'. There is a cold racial logic behind it: to maintain the Negro in subservient status as a source of cheap labour. As Sheriff Z. T. Mathews of Terrell County, Georgia, told reporter Robert Baker of the *Washington Post*, after the fatal beating of James Brazier, a Negro, by two police officers in 1958, 'There's nothing like fear to keep niggers in line.' In the beating to death of Bobby Hall by Sheriff Claude M. Screws of Baker County, Georgia, an F.B.I. agent testified at the Sheriff's trial, 'Mr Screws . . . told me that he had had trouble with Bobby Hall, that he seemed to be a leader . . . when a Negro got in trouble with the law that he, Bobby Hall, would advise him.' So in the case of Brazier, fatally beaten before his wife and four children, it was said that he was 'uppity'. A year after the killing Sheriff Mathews told his widow, 'I oughta slap your damn brains out. A nigger like you I feel like slapping them out. You niggers set around here and look at television and go up North and come back and do to white folks here like the niggers up North do, but you ain't gonna do it. I'm going to carry the South's orders out like it oughta be done.'

Since the brutality serves the purposes of the dominant race, it is not surprising that the police are rarely punished and often promoted. One of the two officers who beat Brazier to death was promoted to Chief of Police in Dawson City, Georgia; no state or local action was ever taken against the killers and Federal Grand Jury refused to indict. In the Bobby Hall killing, white eye-witnesses made it possible to convict Sheriff Screws in a Federal prosecution in a landmark decision which must fill Negroes with despair. In it a badly split court held in effect that police officers who kill Negroes are guilty of violating the Federal Civil Rights Act only if there was 'specific intent' to deprive the Negro of his constitutional rights. If the killing was done in hate, meanness, spite, or just plain fun, it doesn't count, at least not in the Federal courts. In a new trial Sheriff Screws was then acquitted and in 1958 he was elected to the State Senate of Georgia.

The Department of Justice has not been too energetic in civil rights cases, for these bring it into conflict with the Southern oligarchy in Congress. Frank Murphy, who cared deeply about basic rights, established the first Civil Rights Section of the Department in 1939 and Congress elevated it to a Division in 1957. The new report says 'The Truman Committee wrote of the Civil Rights Section in 1947 that "the total picture . . . is that of a sincere, hard-working, but perhaps overcautious agency". This same statement would fairly characterize the Civil Rights Division today in its efforts against unlawful official violence.' This is putting it gently. Since its establishment, the report points out, the Division has obtained convictions or *nolo contendere* pleas in only six police-brutality cases, 'not' the report comments, 'an impressive statistical record for a period of over three years'. Inquiry by this writer disclosed that only one of these six successful cases was racial, involving the brutal beating of an Indian in Idaho. Though four of the six cases were in the South, none involved Negroes. As a matter of fact no police officer has been convicted of brutality to Negroes since two sheriffs, one from Texas and the other from Alabama, pleaded guilty after indictment in 1955. There has not been a conviction in a police brutality case, white or coloured, for more than two years, since 30 October 1959, though more than 1,300 complaints were received and fifty-two prosecutions authorized in the two and a half years from January 1958 to July 1960. This is not much of a record.

A major reason for the poor record lies in the attitude of the F.B.I. on which the Department depends for investigation of civil rights complaints. One of the virtues of this report is that it lifts the curtain, however queasily, on this untold aspect of the story. The first hint of this appeared in a footnote to the report of Truman's Committee on Civil Rights in 1947 which said there was 'evidence' that the F.B.I. considered civil rights investigations 'burdensome'. Footnotes* on pages 213–15 of this new report give excerpts from an exchange of letters between J. Edgar Hoover and Attorney General Tom Clark which Civil Rights Commission staff members dug up in the Harry S. Truman Library in Independence, Mo. In a letter dated 24 September 1946, Mr Hoover complained to the Attorney General that 'as a result of the aggressiveness of pressure groups or as a result of newspaper stories' the F.B.I. was being forced to expend 'a considerable amount of manpower investigating murders, lynchings and assaults, particularly in the Southern States' where it was improbable that violations of Federal laws had occurred. Mr Hoover felt this hurt the 'prestige' of his Bureau. Attorney General Clark replied the same day (the fusillade of formal letters seems to reflect frigid relations between them on the subject) that while many such investigations proved fruitless, 'If we do not investigate, we are placed in the position of having received the complaint of a violation and of having failed to satisfy ourselves that it is or is not such a violation.' The commission's investigators failed to notice that this exchange occurred just two months after four Negroes were lynched by a mob in Monroe, Georgia, and one month before Attorney General Clark announced that he was ordering a Federal Grand Jury investigation. Had Mr Hoover been opposing an F.B.I. inquiry into the Monroe, Ga, lynchings? The new report leaves the question unanswered. It says only (footnote 134, page 215), 'Such discussions between the incumbent Attorney General and the Director of the F.B.I. regarding Bureau investigation procedure in civil rights cases continued into subsequent years.'

This delicate subject is treated in the text of the new report with the tactful and apologetic circumspection accorded the lamentable weakness of a reigning monarch. 'It has been reported, from time to time,' the Civil Rights Commission says (at p. 61),

that the Bureau has little enthusiasm for its task of investigating complaints of police brutality. If the contention is accurate, the fact

* It is indicative of the F.B.I.'s untouchability and the timidity of its critics that such crucial matters are relegated to the obscurity of footnotes.

is, to some degree, understandable. The Director has used the strongest language to stress the need for cooperation between the Bureau and law enforcement officials at all levels. Apparently without this cooperation the F.B.I. could not maintain the excellent record it now enjoys in the enforcement of a long list of Federal criminal statutes. Although the Bureau states that it 'has not experienced any particular difficulty or embarrassment in connection with investigation of police brutality', there is evidence that investigations of such offenses may jeopardize that working relationship. The very purpose of these investigations is to ascertain whether or not state or local officials have committed a Federal offense. Even though the allegations may later prove groundless, the investigation of them may place the F.B.I. in a delicate position.

The plain meaning of this is that the civil rights statutes, like the Negro they were supposed to protect, are relegated to secondary status, expendable items in the chase for bank robbers and stolen cars.

A careful reading of the report and the footnotes shows that the F.B.I.'s procedure in handling civil rights complaints is hardly zealous. In most cases the F.B.I. field office forwards the complaint without preliminary investigation in so bare a form that it 'frequently lacks those minimal facts required to determine if a violation occurred or even if there is a need for a preliminary investigation'. The complaint goes to the Civil Rights Division and is assigned to an attorney. If he wants a preliminary investigation 'this must be cleared through his section chief, a higher Division Official, and Bureau headquarters in Washington'. This leads to 'time-consuming' delays; here another of these footnotes whispers, 'It has been claimed that delays have afforded guilty officials the opportunity to intimidate complainants and witnesses.' If a preliminary investigation is ordered, 'At the outset, the F.B.I. contacts the head of the agency and advises him of the complaint which has been received and that investigation is being ordered.' This advance notice, the Civil Rights Commission objects, 'can jeopardize a section 242 (Civil Rights) case. Police force superiors may adopt an unduly protective attitude towards their officers. They may share the racial prejudices of their subordinates and of their communities.'

So exquisite is the F.B.I.'s empathy for peculiar regional mores that 'In 1959 a case of an allegedly unjustified killing of a Negro by a State policeman was closed because of the [Civil Rights] Division's reluctance to have the Bureau [F.B.I.] notify the Arkansas Governor of a civil rights investigation during the tense school situation in Little Rock.' Apparently the F.B.I. would have refused to investigate the case without first notifying Governor Faubus. There are even, the report notes, 'some victims of violence who distrust F.B.I. agents, believing them to be in league with local officers'. But, the report goes on to say staunchly, 'the Bureau cannot, on their account, resign its heavy responsibilities in those fields of Federal law enforcement that require its close association with local officials'. This sounds as if it was revised by the F.B.I. before publication.

The report recommends three main reforms, a change in Section 242 of the Civil Rights Act to remove the stumbling block of the 'specific intent' requirement set up by the Screws case; another change to make it possible to sue cities and counties for damages in police brutality cases; and grants-in-aid to improve police training. But the man who could do most in this situation is J. Edgar Hoover. Three Federal inquiries in the past generation have shown that police brutality is wide-spread, and not confined to Negroes, Mexicans and Indians: the Wickersham Commission report in 1931, the Truman Committee in 1947 and now this Commission in 1961. In all these years Mr Hoover has been head of the F.B.I., in charge of police training programmes through the F.B.I.'s National Academy. The F.B.I., whatever its faults, has been trained to avoid rough stuff. Its example and Mr Hoover's admonitions, if they were forthcoming, could do a great deal to make the brutal cop a shunned exception. But though the magazines and newspapers are full of articles in which he holds forth on juvenile delinquency, smutty books, Communism, hitch-hikers and other of his favourite menaces, we do not ever remember his speaking out on the dangers of racism or the disgrace of police brutality. Commission attorneys reviewed the F.B.I. Law Enforcement Bulletin from January 1956 through August 1961 and found only one item dealing with civil rights, a piece by Roscoe Drummond flattering to the F.B.I.

The commission might have found it useful to study Mr Hoover's annual appearances before the House Appropriations Committee. The hearings during the last ten years show not a single occasion on which Mr Hoover has spoken against police brutality or for civil rights. On the contrary his presentation has been calculated to curry favour with the Southerners and reactionaries on the committee. On one occasion he warned against Communist exploitation of the sitdown movement; on another he assured the committee that civil rights cases are handled only 'by mature special agents' (1959 hearing on the 1960 budget). The figures he gave on three occasions showed how very few complaints against police officers result in prosecution. Mr Hoover had made it clear that the F.B.I. acts in civil rights cases only because ordered to. Finally it is a pity that the commission, in recommending prosecution by information, where Federal grand juries refuse to indict in Section 242 cases, fails to mention the biggest obstacle to this approach. It would require the F.B.I. to sign the supporting affidavit. This the F.B.I. does not want to do, for it would make it look like a crusader on civil rights. It prefers to crusade on safer subjects and against easier menaces.

27 November 1961, vol. 9, no. 44

Too Few Listen as Freedom Riders and Sit-In-ers Tell their Dramatic Story . . . Police Dogs, Savage Mobs, Sadistic Cops, Fail to Halt Liberation Movement

Norman Thomas, who back-stopped Mrs Roosevelt as chairman of the Committee of Inquiry, spoke of them as 'secular saints' – this handful of young Negroes in their teens and early twenties. They and a few white sympathizers as youthful and devoted as themselves have begun a social revolution in the South with their sit-ins and their Freedom Rides. In the sparsely filled small *Washington Post* Community Room last weekend they told their story and their needs to a 'Committee of Inquiry into the Administration of Justice in the Freedom Struggle'. To it Mrs Roosevelt, now bowed in body but tireless as ever in spirit, not only lent her name as chairman but flew to Washington and presided over the first day's session.

In the boxes on these two pages, in succinct summaries more moving than any eloquence, we provide glimpses in their own words of what they have encountered since that first sit-in at a Greensboro, N.C., lunch counter in February 1960. A report and a transcript of the two-day hearing will be published. They will provide the first comprehensive view of the movement which has sparked Negro resistance to white supremacy in the deep South for the first time since Reconstruction. Never has a tinier minority done more for the liberation of a whole people than these few youngsters of C.O.R.E. (Congress for Racial Equality) and S.N.C.C. (Student Non-Violent Coordinating Committee).

The sit-ins and the Freedom Rides have done something else, less sensational but more universally significant. As Mr Thomas said in his summation, 'They have fought entrenched discrimination and wrong without themselves indulging in violence and done this in one of the most violent periods of human history.' Everywhere else in recent years, terrorism has been accepted as a justifiable weapon in liberation struggles. From Palestine and Cyprus to Algeria and Indonesia, the knife, the bomb, the nocturnal attack, haphazard violence often at the expense of the very people being liberated, have been taken for granted.

Here in the United States the struggle against the imposed humiliation of the Negro has been carried out in Gandhi's spirit, with successful non-violence. History will record it to the honour of the Negro and of our country but too few are aware of it today. The hearings themselves attested in unintended fashion the degree to which this has been the work of a minority. Though Washington is the seat of Howard University and all through the South students have been aroused to act in this struggle, only a few local Negro students turned out. The N.A.A.C.P. did not even send an observer. A. Philip Randolph lent his name but not his presence. There was only one Negro on the panel either day. Dr Kenneth Clark, the New York City

College psychologist the first day; Rev. Gardner Taylor, a Brooklyn Baptist pastor, the second.*

The record, when published, will show the widespread use of dogs by the police to terrorize Negroes; the lawlessness and sadism of Southern police officials; the inability to get the F.B.I. to do anything about police brutality; the appointment of White Citizens Council members to the Federal bench; the use of heavy bail requirements as a means of crippling the sit-in movement, and undercover pressure from State agencies in Mississippi, to frighten bonding companies away from Freedom Ride cases.

James Farmer, C.O.R.E.'s impressive leader, testified that the Southern Regional Council estimates that there have been 5,181 arrests since the sit-ins began and that between two and three million dollars have had to be raised to bail them out. Louis Lusky, once a law clerk to Justice Cardozo, now a practising lawyer in Louisville, Ky, defence counsel in the famous Carl Braden sedition case, testified that in the mass arrests of Freedom Riders in Jackson, Miss., total bond requirements reached $373,000 and not a single bonding company was willing to put up bond.

Such tactics and the new use of criminal anarchy charges (on which we will report more fully in a later issue) are aimed to crush the movement. But it has succeeded in awakening Negroes even in Mississippi to the possibility of fighting for their rights and dignity. Most important of all, as Mr Lusky said in his deeply felt testimony, it has broken the comfortable white Southern stereotype of the Negro as a less-than-human creature ill disposed to fight for his emancipation.

4 June 1962, vol. 10, no. 22

---

* Others who lent their names but did not appear included Walter Reuther. Unlike Reuther, Wm Schnitzler, secretary-treasurer of the A.F.L.-C.I.O., at least sent a substitute, Boris Shishkin. The other name-lenders non-appearing were: Tallulah Bankhead, Harry Golden, Bishop James A. Pike, Justine Wise Polier, and James Wechsler. Those who sat in on the hearings part of the time were Telford Taylor and Joseph L. Rauh, Jr.

When's the President Going to Mention Racism?

Three questions stand out in the Mississippi crisis. The first is: was it befitting the dignity of the law and the presidency for Mr Kennedy to spend so many hours on the telephone dickering with a Southern governor who was acting in contempt of a final court order? The second is: how close to death did these dickerings and the Governor's false assurance bring James Meredith, the Federal marshals protecting him and assorted reporters and university officials in the besieged Lyceum building?

On two occasions the mob came within a hair's breadth of smashing the thin line of marshals, once when the mob tried to ram the marshals with a fire truck and the second time when mobsters tried to smash the line with a bulldozer which, fortunately, rammed into a tree. The marshals were almost out of tear gas when the first Federal troops arrived. Had they been delayed only a little longer, had the mob re-formed and rushed the marshals again in the interim, as it had several times before, then it might have overpowered the marshals and taken over the school grounds. The result would have been a massacre. This is what Mr Kennedy risked and so narrowly avoided.

The reason for taking the risk was, as Miriam Ottenberg, a reporter particularly friendly to the Department of Justice, wrote in the *Washington Star* (1 October) that 'Both the President and the Attorney General ... wanted to avoid sending in troops if at all possible' and were therefore 'particularly keen' to accept the assurances given them by Mississippi officials that State Police could handle the situation. In their eagerness to avoid using Federal troops, the President and the Attorney General let Governor Barnett trick them. As Stan Opotowsky, who wrote the best and most vivid account of the campus battle, reports in the *New York Post* (1 October), 'Barnett had his way. He insisted that Meredith be placed on the campus

---

Those who sat through the whole two days in addition to Norman Thomas were Roger Baldwin and John B. Culberton, a devoted white attorney from Greenville, S.C. Rowland Watts of the A.C.L.U. and Carl Rachlin of C.O.R.E. acted as counsel for the hearing board.

before the President went on radio and TV to address the nation.' The result was that 'the Federal men had to run the gauntlet of idle students, who on a day other than Sunday, might have been tied down by classes. Instead they eventually grew into a crazed and rioting mob'. This occurred, as Opotowsky reported, because 'the Justice Department wanted Meredith in the University before Tuesday so it could get Barnett and Lt Gov. Johnson off the hook at the deadline for their contempt of a Federal court order'. This desire to fix things up privately cost two lives, and risked more.

The third and most important question is: when is Mr Kennedy going to mention racism? All through his campaign for the presidency, Mr Kennedy criticized Mr Eisenhower for failing to use his high office for moral leadership in the integration struggle and promised to act quite differently himself. But in his radio-TV appeal to the Mississippi students and the nation last Sunday night, Mr Kennedy was as antiseptically neutral and uncommitted about civil rights as was Mr Eisenhower in the Little Rock crisis. Like his predecessor, Mr Kennedy spoke as if the President were a mere top Federal marshal, sworn to uphold the law, but not called upon to like it or discuss it. Once again at a critical moment, the weight of the presidency was not brought to bear in support of the court's integration rulings. Mr Kennedy and his brother, the Attorney General, in the latter's TV reply to Governor Barnett, both spoke of Meredith's battle as a 'private suit' with which the Federal government had no concern until called in a few weeks ago to enforce a court order. This is a position calculated to achieve the lowest common political denominator consistent with enforcement; it puts the President and the Attorney General shoulder-to-shoulder with the Southern moderates. That is not good enough.

It is not good enough because resistance to unjust law lies too deep in American tradition, as in that of every free society. We have too long been taught that resistance to tyranny is obedience to God, as indeed it is. Peaceful change in the South can only be brought about by moral leadership and ethical education, if we strengthen those silenced and besieged elements in the white South itself which realize that it is wrong to treat the

Negro as a second-class citizen, cruel to mark his children from their first days in school with the brand of apartness and inferiority, a sin to make another human being a 'nigger'. The fight cannot be won until the South is made to feel that integration is not just some ruling by a Supreme Court accidentally filled with Negro-lovers but a movement which springs from the deepest ideals of this nation and the most irrepressible aspirations of human beings, everywhere. Instead of a synthetic pep-talk, full of oratorical nonsense about Mississippi's great traditions, Lucius Lamar and Jake Lindsey, all lily-white, Mr Kennedy should have said a word about Meredith, about a Negro air force veteran who fought with honour in Korea and had a right to be treated as a first-class citizen on his return home. In all Mississippi's history, not one Mississippian has ever shown as much courage as this young Negro. Could the President not have appealed to young students to wipe away the ugly racial blunders of their elders, to see this as a challenge to their intelligence, their gallantry, at least their sportsmanship?

It is more disturbing than the mob scene that not one single student at Ole Miss. has had the desire or the courage to go over and shake Meredith's hand or to sit beside him in class. Those empty seats around him, those continued jeers, condemn Mississippi's younger white generation, even these its most privileged. But how expect them to behave differently when they see their elders egg on the mob or fall silent, when they see even the President and the Attorney General unwilling to go beyond the politically expedient, willing belatedly if necessary to call out the troops, but not to speak up for the justice and the morality of the principles they are enforcing?

Mr Kennedy's final appeal was to preserve the law and the peace so 'we can turn to the greater crises that are without and stand united as one people in our pledge to man's freedom'. This stale Cold War rhetoric was offensive on so serious an occasion. Devotion to freedom should begin at home. If we can't have it in Mississippi, we won't win it defending dictators in Vietnam. The crises without are nowhere near as real as the crisis within. A large secton of the white South is mentally sick on the subject of race, it draws support from paranoid minorities in the North who join it in seeing the Supreme Court as the seat of Communistic plotters, and integration as an artificial business stirred up by Jews from New York. Men like Eastland represent this psychopathic undercurrent which makes the mob feel righteous. This sickness could under certain conditions coalesce into a serious rightist threat to free institutions. The time to stop it is now, when it is still weak. This hard fight is Mr Kennedy's duty; easy flag-waving diversions about dangers abroad are no substitute for it. This sickness in a great nation like ours is a matter of world-wide concern. Only a quarter century ago another great and cultured nation, Germany, destroyed itself and half a continent from the virus of racism. When is the President going to mention it?

8 October 1962, vol. 10, no. 36

Suppose Not Negroes But Men of Property Were Being Beaten in Mississippi?

Of course we don't mean it seriously. We're merely putting it forward as a classroom exercise in jurisprudence. But let us suppose it was not the rights of Negroes but the rights of property which were menaced in Mississippi. Let us suppose that, thanks to a sudden disappearance of racism, poor whites and Negroes had suddenly united and elected their own men to the state government, replacing even the sheriffs and the police officers. And suppose that these new law-enforcement officers began to harass, to beat, to shoot and occasionally to kill men of property on one excuse or another – failure to pay minimum wages on the plantations, or failure to provide fair accounting in mills and stores. Suppose that when property owners tried to demonstrate police dogs were set upon them. Suppose that when they tried to appeal to the Civil Rights Commission in Washington, the Mississippi legislature passed special laws (like Sections 2155.4, 2155.5 and 2155.6 enacted in 1960) making it a crime punishable by five years in jail to make false statements to any Federal investigator, providing that in such prosecutions the two-witness rule for perjury would be suspended and one

witness would be enough for conviction, and applying this sanc-
tion even to immaterial statements (that is, any inconsequential
slip of the tongue). Suppose the Attorney General had timidly
refused to allow the Civil Rights Commission to hold public
hearings in Mississippi lest this disturb the atmosphere! Suppose
bombs had been thrown, not into some poor N.A.A.C.P. or
C.O.R.E. office, but into (forgive the expression) A BANK. Suppose the Civil Rights Commission in desperation had then
called on the President and the Congress to suspend all Federal
aid to Mississippi until it agreed to safeguard fundamental
rights guaranteed by the Federal Constitution. Q.: Would this
suggestion evoke a shush-shush of legalistic horror from the
liberal pundits of the great newspapers? Or would the U.S.
Army take over Mississippi tomorrow?

29 April 1963, vol. 11, no. 10

The Wasteland in the White Man's Heart

It's not so much the killings as the lack of contrition. The morning after the Birmingham bombing, the Senate in its expansive
fashion filled thirty-five pages of the *Congressional Record* with
remarks on diverse matters before resuming debate on the
nuclear test ban treaty. But the speeches on the bombing in
Birmingham filled barely a single page. Of 100 ordinarily
loquacious Senators, only four felt moved to speak. Javits of
New York and Kuchel of California expressed outrage. The
Majority Leader, Mansfield, also spoke up, but half his time
was devoted to defending J. Edgar Hoover from charges of
indifference to racial bombings. His speech was remarkable only
for its inane phrasing. 'There can be no excuse for an occur-
rence of that kind,' Mansfield said of the bombing, in which
four little girls at Sunday School were killed, 'under any possible circumstances.' Negroes might otherwise have supposed
that states' rights or the doctrine of interposition or the failure
of the Minister that morning to say 'Sir' to a passing white man
might be regarded as a mitigating circumstance. Even so
Mansfield's proposition was too radical for his Southern col-

leagues. Only Fulbright rose to associate himself with Mansfield's remarks and to express condemnation. There was more indignation in the Senate over Nhu's pagoda raids in Saigon.

If four children had been killed in the bombing of a Berlin church by Communists, the country would be on the verge of war. But when four Senators (Hart, Kuchel, Humphrey and Javits) framed a resolution asking that the Sunday after the Birmingham bombing be set aside as a national day of mourning, they knew their fellow Senators too well even to introduce it. They sent it on to the White House where it was lost in the shuffle. Despite the formal expressions of regret, the sermons, the editorials and the marches, neither white America nor its leadership was really moved. When Martin Luther King and six other Negro leaders finally saw the President four days after the bombing, it was to find that he had already appointed a two-man committee to represent him 'personally' in Birmingham, but that both men were white. This hardly set a precedent for bi-racial action. If Mr Kennedy could take a judge off the Supreme Court to settle a labour dispute, he could have taken one of the country's two Negro judges off the Court of Appeals to dignify a mission of mediation. He might have insisted, for once, after so terrible a crime, on seeing white and Negro leaders together, instead of giving a separate audience four days later to a white delegation from Birmingham. It is as if, even in the White House, there are equal but separate facilities.

The Negro leaders, facing the TV cameras outside the Executive Offices that Thursday afternoon, looked like men pursued by despair, afraid that at the slightest misstep they might be trampled under the hopeless fury in the ranks behind them. The white delegation, the following Monday, had underling written all over it. The President of the United States could take time out to hear white Birmingham, but the Mayor was too busy and sent his secretary. With him were neither the Big Mules nor their Northern capitalist overlords; it is as if they had assigned their office boys to see the President. If what they told the press afterwards was a sample of what they told the President, he too must have despaired of finding a solution. Even these supposed moderates could not shake loose from the mythology of white supremacy; if only outside agitators like Martin Luther King would stay away peace and quiet could be restored; many Negroes favoured segregation, but apparently were afraid to say so except privately to their white friends. Hire a Negro policeman? That was a 'profoundly difficult', 'almost impossible', problem. Just why was never explained; perhaps Negroes do not look good in blue, with brass buttons.

Four centuries of white supremacy have left their indelible mark in the double standard we whites instinctively apply to race relations. The Attorney General, rejecting a Negro appeal for Federal troops, said hearts could not be changed by bayonets. But few stop to think that the alternative is to leave the Negro community of Birmingham to the bayonets of the state troopers. Gene Grove in the *New York Post* (20 September) vividly pictured how the Negro community is ruled. When one reporter approached Colonel Al Lingo of the state police

with a question, the only reply was a shotgun in the belly. Wednesday night the troopers beat an aged man in the Negro district of East Thomas and a young boy in the Negro district of Parker Heights, both for failing to move off the street fast enough. Yesterday morning they rode down the street with carbines peeking from every window, shouting at Negroes sitting on their porches to 'get back in the house, niggers, get your ass the hell off the street'.

The Mayor's secretary looked surprised when a reporter asked him if he thought the manners of the state troops towards the Negroes were not provocative. He found no fault with it. Such ways and language, after all, are accepted institutions in the South, the way 'peace and quiet' have been preserved.

When I was in Germany, I felt the empty waste land of the German heart. I feel the same way about the hearts of my fellow white men in America, where the Negro is concerned. The good people there as here are in the minority and weak. Just as many Germans feel it was somehow the fault of the Jews that they got themselves cremated, so many whites here, North and South, feel that the bombing wouldn't have happened if the Negroes weren't so pushy. As a white housewife in a Birmingham supermarket told Robert Baker of the *Wash-*

ington Post (19 September), it was 'terrible' but 'that's what they get for trying to force their way where they're not wanted'. Worse than the bombing is this inhuman chill.

30 September 1963, vol. 11, no. 19

All Deliberate Speed – or How to Get Where You Don't Want to Go in 1,000 Years

Ten years after the Supreme Court's desegregation decision 98.8 per cent of the South's Negro children are still in segregated schools. Even this figure is deceptively low. The statistical charts at the end of the Civil Rights Commission's 1964 report on education reveal that one state, Texas, accounts for more than half of the integrated enrolment. It has an estimated 18,000 Negro pupils in desegregated schools. By contrast, in Alabama there are twenty-one and in South Carolina there are only nine Negroes going to school with whites. This is respectively .007 per cent and .003 per cent of the total pupils enrolled in desegregated schools. Mississippi had no school integration below the college level until this fall when a court order opened up three public-school districts. In one of these districts, in Clarksdale, no Negro pupil tried to register at a white school.

In other Southern States desegregation is concentrated in a few school districts. Louisiana had 1,814 Negro pupils in desegregated schools, but these are located in only 3 out of 67 bi-racial school districts. In Georgia only 10 out of 181 bi-racial districts are desegregated; in Arkansas 21 out of 228; in Texas 289 out of 899; in North Carolina 61 out of 171; in Florida 21 out of 67; and Tennessee 58 out of 142.

At this rate – little more than one per cent in a decade – it will take almost ten centuries to desegregate the South.

9 November 1964, vol. 12, no. 38

J. Edgar Hoover's Novel View of Racism

J. Edgar Hoover turned up at Gwen Cafritz's party here in Washington the other evening and found, according to the

Washington Star's society reporter (21 November) that he couldn't get past the entrance 'as he drew group after group of guests expressing admiration for his outspoken comments during an unusual three-hour press conference with women reporters earlier this week'. The spontaneous ovation showed that beneath the cynical surface of Washington society there beats a warm heart, ready to welcome the dissenter even in this age of conformity. Mr Hoover told the admirers thronging around him that he was surprised at the reaction from the country. He said he had received almost 400 telegrams, 'all favourable except for two or three who were critical or hostile' and these he said 'were probably from racist groups associated with Martin Luther King'.

We have often asked why Mr Hoover did not speak out on the subject of racism. We are encouraged to see that he has at last broached the subject, though from a novel angle. We had never thought of Rev. King or the organizations associated with him as racist, though we suppose that in a sense they are. Mr Hoover obviously considers as racist any organization which seeks to give the Negro equality with the white man, to set race against race by insisting that Southern registrars register Negro voters, too, and generally to stir up the Negro against white supremacy. This has, come to think of it, long been the South's point of view but no Southern spokesman has had the daring to express it in quite so original a way. It never occurred to Bull Connor to assert that he had set dogs on those demonstrators in Birmingham to protect the city from racism. Nor has Ross Barnett thought of defending the burning of Negro churches in Mississippi as a means of safeguarding the state from racist agitation. To call Martin Luther King 'the most notorious liar in the country' may have seemed a little extreme even to members of the White Citizens' Councils. But to come up with the idea that N.A.A.C.P., C.O.R.E., S.N.C.C. and Southern Christian Leadership Conference can be termed 'racist' organizations – that's close akin to genius.

This observation by Mr Hoover shows the wisdom of his attitude towards press conferences. Though Mr Hoover is constantly writing articles on various favourite menaces (usually red or pink) in the Sunday supplements, his usual practice on interviews is to answer prepared written questions submitted in advance. The lucky reporter gets the answers in written form and a handshake. In forty years as head of the F.B.I., Mr Hoover had never before held a general press conference, and even this first of its kind was restricted to women. According to *The Washington Post*'s society reporter, Marie McNair (21 November), Mr Hoover explained this at the Cafritz party. 'With men journalists,' he told his admirers, 'the questions are loaded and the reporters are trying to trip you up.' However, there are exceptions to this, he declared, naming half a dozen newspapers throughout the country in which he has confidence. It is reassuring to learn that Mr Hoover does not regard the entire American press with suspicion, and is prepared to grant clearance to six newspapers at least. It is easy to imagine what the run-of-the-mill subversive Washington correspondent (male) would have done at a press conference in which Mr Hoover implied that Martin Luther King was a racist. Some slippery fellow might even have asked Mr Hoover blandly whether he was perhaps thinking of arresting the Rev. King under the new Civil Rights Act.

30 November 1964, vol. 12, no. 40

If We Acted in Selma as We Act in Saigon

Senator Eastland of Mississippi made a speech in the Senate, 3 February. It was entitled 'Communist Forces Behind Negro Revolution in This Country'. It was the second major speech of its kind by Eastland. He made an earlier one last 22 July on 'Communist Infiltration into the So-called Civil Rights Movement', the latter remarkable because of its suggestion that the murder of the three civil rights workers last summer in Mississippi might be a hoax. It is instructive, and it may be therapeutic, to notice that Senator Eastland's theory of why there is trouble in our South is exactly the same as the theory propounded by Secretary of State Rusk as to why there is trouble in South Vietnam. The theory in both cases is that all would be well if only the North let its neighbours alone.

Like the State Department, Eastland sees not rebellion but an invasion, a 'mass invasion of Mississippi', as he said last July, 'by demonstrators, agitators, agents of provocation and inciters to mass violence, under the cover of the so-called civil rights movements'. Just as the Pentagon and State put out figures recently to show 'Troop Flow from Hanoi Up Sharply' so Eastland provided the names, the subversive records and the border-crossing dates of infiltration from the North. Eastland even cited the same alarmist journalistic sources. 'By April of this year,' Eastland told the Senate last July, 'so much evidence had piled up of Communist infiltration and Communist influence in racial agitations that Mr Joseph Alsop devoted one of his columns to what he called "the unhappy secret" of Communist success in infiltrating the civil rights movement.' To read the two speeches of Eastland and the supporting remarks of his Mississippi colleague, Stennis, is like reading the speech of Rusk and McNamara about South Vietnam before Diem was over-thrown – in both cases the picture is of a happy land and a contented people torn apart by outside agitators. One would never guess the misery, the beatings, the killings, the violations of elementary rights, the exploitation, which are the roots of the rebellions. No high-born mandarin from Hue could be more sorrowful than Stennis when he told the Senate (3 February) it was these Communist agitators 'who flouted all the customs and traditions of a social order to which people had been accustomed and had lived under for almost two centuries'. Eastland told the Senate the same day that ninety-five per cent of the Negroes in his area had 'spurned any association' with the invaders and Stennis said he found 'the same pattern' in his area. But somehow by esoteric means these infiltrators managed nevertheless here and there to disrupt 'the spiritual life of both races . . . the peace and harmony of the people'. This is how the South felt a century ago about the abolitionists: snakes in a patriarchal paradise.

The sickness of the South is the sickness of every ruling class in history. These always see conspiracy rather than suffering as the mainspring of every upsurge by the oppressed. Eastland buttressed his speech with quotations from J. Edgar Hoover and ideological police records from the files of the Un-American Activities Committee and his own Internal Security Committee just as the State Department's 'Blue Book' in 1961 justified our intervention in South Vietnam by citing evidence of Communist conspiracy against Diem. In one colloquy on the Senate floor (3 February) Eastland and Stennis agreed that South Vietnam and our own South were both confronted by the same universal conspiracy. They are as indignant about Washington's aid to the civil rights movement as Washington is indignant about Moscow's and Peking's encouragement to the guerrilla fighters in South Vietnam. One almost expects to hear Eastland and Stennis ask how Washington can claim to be for peaceful co-existence and yet insist on supporting 'wars of liberation' in the South, or accuse old Ho Chi Johnson of persisting in his dastardly ambition to reunify the country.

There are even the same contradictions in both areas. Just as our government in South Vietnam oscillates between treating the uprising as a rebellion and calling for social reforms to conciliate the people, so Stennis the day after Eastland's speech last week put into the Congressional Record the resolution passed by the Mississippi Economic Council, calling for law and order in the state. That resolution, the expression of Mississippi's better conscience, abandoned conspiracy theory and urged compliance with the civil rights laws. Stennis, to his credit, praised the council for taking a 'stand out front' for that 'obedience to law' which is the foundation of 'true liberty'. It is difficult to reconcile what Stennis said to the Senate on 3 February with what he said on 4 February.

Can we not learn something from the two situations? We see the idealism of the volunteers who go south here. Can we not see that in Vietnam we fight the same liberating zeal? In this double mirror, costly fallacies quickly show their face. If the Federal government handled Negro aspiration as it handles the revolt in South Vietnam, we would be sending 'counter-insurgency' teams from Fort Bragg into the South to kill civil rights agitators. We would be burning out with napalm the Negro neighbourhoods in which we suspected that C.O.R.E. or S.N.C.C. workers were hiding.

Conversely, if the South had an air force at its disposal, we would be hearing a clamour in Mississippi for escalation of the war by bombarding the source of all the trouble. Since Washington persists in giving aid and comfort to the civil rights rebels, why not bomb the supply lines and the source?

15 February 1965, vol. 13, no. 6

Why They Cry Black Power

There is a hopeful side to the riots and picketing in the slums. They indicate that the poor are no longer poor in spirit. This is the spark that hope has kindled, the real achievement of the poverty programme, the beginning of rehabilitation. The negative side is the spread of race war. The Negro, the Puerto Rican and the Mexican-American will no longer wait humbly at the back door of our society. For them its shiny affirmation of equality is a taunt. Either we make it real or see our country torn apart. A race is on between the constructive capacity of our society and an ugly white backlash with Fascist overtones. The crossroads of America's future is not far off.

Our country is the last hope of multi-racialism. The French, for all their civilizing gift, were unable to create that multi-racial community Ho Chi Minh was once willing to enter. The British Commonwealth is splitting up over British unwillingness to act against the dictatorship of white minorities in Rhodesia and South Africa. Racialism and tribalism are the curse of mankind, anachronistic contemporaries of the astronaut. Where white supremacy is gone forever, Arab and Negro slaughter each other in the Sudan; Malay and Chinese riot in Singapore; tribalism is breaking up Black Africa's most promising nation in Nigeria.

Racism here is only another example of a universal human disease. The cry of 'black power' is less a programme than an incantation to deal with the crippling effects of white supremacy. The 'black' affirms a lost racial pride and the 'power' the virility of which the Negro has been robbed by generations of humiliation. Its swift spread testifies to the deep feelings it satisfies. It is not practical politics; it is psychological therapy. Stokeley Carmichael's burning explanation of it in the 22 September issue of the *New York Review* is to be read as the poetry of despair. The United States is not Mr Carmichael's cherished model, Lowndes County; there are few other counties which have its overwhelming black majority. And it is typical New Left *narodnik* mysticism, albeit in Negro form, to call for 'the coming together of black people' to pick their own representatives and at the same time to reject 'most of the black politicians we see around the country today'. Who picked Adam Clayton Powell, Harlem's absentee political landlord?

But rational argument will not meet the appeal of 'black power'. It affirms separation because it has met rejection. When Senators go out on the golf links to forestall a quorum rather than vote on 'open occupancy', when hateful faces in the North greet Negro demonstrators with cries of 'kill the jungle bunnies', when whites flee the cities as if the Negro were some kind of rodent, how else salvage pride except by counter-rejection? It is the taking of white supremacy for granted that is the danger, not the cry of 'black power', which is as pathetic as a locked-out child's agony. Nothing could be more disastrous than to divert attention from the real problems of our society by setting off on a witch-hunt against S.N.C.C. In Atlanta, as in Watts, trouble began not because of S.N.C.C. but because the cops are trigger-happy when dealing with black men.

Without extremists to prod us into action, we will not take the giant steps required to rehabilitate the coloured and the poor. The Negro still wants in; he cannot go back to Africa; his only future is here. Not black power or white but a sense of belonging to one human family can alone save this planet. But the time is short before hate shuts the doors. The time is coming when we will regret the billions wasted in Vietnam. The time is coming when we may regret the number of Negroes we have trained there in guerrilla war. There is hardly a city where the Negroes do not already dominate the strategic areas through which the affluent commuter passes on his way to the inner core. S.N.C.C.'s hostility to the war is not disloyalty but wisdom. We cannot rebuild that sense of community so essential to our beloved country's future by engaging in a white man's war in Asia while a black man's revolt rises at home.

19 September 1966, vol. 14, no. 28

The Fire Has Only Just Begun

The assassination of Dr Martin Luther King, Jr, was the occasion for one of those massive outpourings of hypocrisy characteristic of the human race. He stood in that line of saints which goes back from Gandhi to Jesus; his violent end, like theirs, reflects the hostility of mankind to those who annoy it by trying hard to pull it one more painful step farther up the ladder from ape to angel.

The President and the Washington establishment had been working desperately up until the very moment of Dr King's killing to keep him and his Poor People's March out of the capital; his death, at first, promised to let them rest in peace. The masses they sang were not so much of requiem as of thanksgiving, that the nation's no. 1 agitator had been laid to rest at last. Then a minority of his own people, and not all of them the ignorant and the hungry, celebrated his memory with an orgy of looting while black radicals and New Leftists hailed the mindless carnival as a popular uprising. Since the liquor stores were the no. 1 target, it might sourly be termed the debut of Marxism-Liquorism in revolutionary annals. Those among his own people who sneered at his non-violent teaching as obsolete now seized upon his death as a new excuse for the violence he hated. Thus all sides firmly united in paying him homage.

Dr King was a victim of white racism. Its record encourages such murders. Dr King was only the most eminent in a long series of civil-rights victims. The killers are rarely caught, even more rarely convicted; the penalties are light. The complicity, in this case, may go further. It is strange that the killer was so easily able to escape when the motel in which he was killed was ringed with police; some came within a few moments from the very direction of the fatal shot. Violent anti-Negro organ-

T–F

izations like the Klan have their cells in many police forces. The Memphis police had shown their hatred in the indiscriminate violence with which they broke up Dr King's march a week earlier. The Attorney General should be pressed to include the Memphis police in his investigation of the slaying.

Though Dr King was the greatest Southerner of our time, few Southern political leaders expressed any sorrow over his passing. Most, like Stennis of Mississippi, ventured no more than antiseptic and ambivalent condemnation of all violence. In the House on 8 April the few Southerners who spoke deplored the riots more than the killing. The one exception was Representative Bob Eckhardt of Texas who dared call Dr King 'My black brother'. Privately many white Southerners rejoiced, and their influence was reflected in the scandalous failure to declare a holiday in the district the day Dr King was buried. Though stores closed, government offices were open and Negro mailmen delivered the mail as usual. This is still, despite its black majority, a Southern-ruled town; it shuts down on Washington's birthday, but not Lincoln's.

The most powerful of the district's absentee rulers, Senator Robert C. Byrd (D., W. Va) went so far as to imply in a Senate speech (5 April) that Dr King was to blame for his own death. Byrd said those who organize mass demonstrations may 'in the end . . . become themselves the victims of the forces they set in motion'. While Dr King 'usually spoke of non-violence,' Byrd went on smugly, 'violence all too often attended his action and, at the last, he himself met a violent end.' This should make Byrd the South's favourite criminologist.

Byrd is the Senator to whom the blacks of Washington must come for school and welfare money. As chairman of the Senate Appropriations subcommittee on the District of Columbia budget, Byrd wields far more power than the city's figurehead Negro 'Mayor'. He has used this key position to block liberalization of welfare rules not only in the district but in the country, since the Federal government can hardly apply elsewhere rules more liberal than those he will allow in the district. Byrd has become the national pillar of the 'man in the house' rule. This, as the report of the Commission on Civil Disorders protested, makes it necessary for the unemployed father to 'abandon his family or see them go hungry'. In this sense not a few of the child looters in our gutted ghettoes can trace their delinquency straight back to Robert C. Byrd.

For whites who live like myself in almost lily-white north-west Washington on the very edge of suburbia, the ghetto disorders might have taken place in a distant country, viewed on TV like Vietnam (which it begins to resemble), or as a tourist attraction on a visit in the bright spring sunshine before curfew to the sullen and ruined ghetto business districts. It was not until five days after the trouble started that two young soldiers turned up for the first time to guard our own neighbouring shopping centre – 'as a precautionary measure', they explained – and tape appeared on its liquor store windows. Even sympathetic and radical whites found themselves insulated from what was going on not just by the military cordons but even more by an indiscriminate black hostility. Even some liberal and leftist families with children moved out of integrated neighbourhoods on the edge of the ghetto in apprehension. These were our first refugees from black power.

Nothing could be more deceptive than the nationwide mourning. Beneath the surface nothing has changed, except perhaps for the worst. The President has called off his address to a joint session indefinitely. His Senate majority leader, Mansfield, warns the Congress not to be 'impetuous' in reacting to the disorders. How fortunate we should be if all our dangers were as remote as this one! The new civil rights bill, if it passes, is more likely to bring new evils in its anti-riot provisions than reform in housing.

In Washington, as in most cities hit by black violence, the police and the troops have been on their best behaviour to the point where business spokesmen are complaining that there has been too much leniency in dealing with looters. For once, to the Administration's credit, lives have been put ahead of property. Had police and soldiers begun to shoot, the killings would have become a massacre and the riots a black revolution. As it is, in Washington at least, the black community has been grateful for the protection afforded it. But this leniency is unlikely to survive when and if white rather than black areas begin to go up in smoke. There is little time left for the big multi-billion dollar programme which can alone rehabilitate the hopeless and bitter generation of blacks that racial discrimination and the slums have bred. Whites still think they can escape the problem by moving to the suburbs, and as long as they think so, nothing will be done. There are already 55,000 troops in our 110 scarred cities – more than we had in Vietnam three years ago. Already the police talk of guerrilla war. If it comes, a half million troops will not be enough to contain it. A looting suspect told one reporter at a police station here, 'We're going to burn this whole place. It might take years but we'll do it.' This is the agony of a lost race speaking. If we cannot respond with swift compassion, this is the beginning of our decline and fall.

15 April 1968, vol. 16, no. 8

When Will Nixon's Top Black Officials Walk Out in Protest . . . ?

If we were black, we would be filled with a bottomless despair. The events of the past two weeks show the essential indifference if not downright hostility of the white majority in this country. The killing of six blacks, all shot in the back, in Augusta, and the murderous fusillade against a black women's dormitory in Jackson, Miss., where two girls were killed, have elicited little protest in the white community and very little reaction even among blacks, accustomed to such brutality. The President's skimpy message of protest was amazingly frigid and extraordinarily non-committal. The Attorney General went South but to a lily-white upper-class Delta Council meeting where he discussed the stock market! 'Since he became Attorney General,' Aaron Henry said bitterly in a story on that appearance which the *Washington Star* yanked after its early edition, 20 May, 'he has done more than any one man to create the climate that makes white policemen feel they can shoot our people down, like they did at Jackson State.'

A Chicago grand jury reports police perjury and wilful

murder in the Black Panther raid which killed Fred Hampton and Mark Clark but could find no evidence on which to indict! 'Few things would contribute more to bring us together,' Samuel C. Jackson, black assistant secretary of housing and urban development said in a speech to whites here, 22 May, 'than the growth of law and order among the forces of law and order.' Agnew and Mitchell were his obvious targets and he had sharp words to say of the Administration's D.C. crime bill with its 'no-knock' and pre-trial detention provisions. But he stays in the Nixon Administration. The last straw for Nixon's black officials should be his decision to support tax exemption for segregated white schools in the South. If James Farmer, Assistant H.E.W. Secretary, and the other top blacks in Nixon's entourage had any guts they would stage a mass-resignation in protest.

1 June 1970, vol. 18, no. 11

2: Poverty

The Rich March on Washington All the Time

To see the Poor People's March on Washington in perspective, remember that the rich have been marching on Washington ever since the beginning of the Republic. They came in carriages and they come on jets. They don't have to put up in shanties. Their object is the same but few respectable people are untactful enough to call it handouts. Washington owes its very existence as the capital to a deal for the benefit of wealthy speculators. They had bought up the defaulted bonds issued to finance the Revolution, paying as little as fifteen cents on the dollar to the needy original investors. The speculators wanted repayment at full face value. It was only by promising to move the capital from Philadelphia to a new city to be built on the Potomac that Alexander Hamilton could get enough Southern votes to swing the deal.

The fiscal and banking system of the new Republic was thus solidly established on the basis of a $20 million handout to the rich and on the Hamiltonian theory that if the new government would channel enough of the national wealth to the top some of it would eventually trickle down. In the meantime the farmer and the consumer would pay the taxes and the tariffs to keep the investor fat and happy. Ever since then the public treasury and the public lands have been a major source of the great American fortunes down to our own day of never-ending oil depletion allowances. The tax structure and the laws bear the imprint of countless marches on Washington; these have produced billions in hidden grants for those who least need them. Across the façade of the U.S. Treasury should be engraved, 'To him who hath shall be given.'

One easy and equitable way to finance an end to abject poverty in this country would be to end the many tax privileges the wealthy have acquired. A twelve-man committee of industrialists and financiers has just recommended to Governor Rockefeller of New York a form of that guaranteed income the marching poor will demand. The committee proposes a negative income tax to raise 30 million of our neediest above the poverty level. Instead of paying income taxes they would receive enough from the Treasury to bring their incomes up to a minimum of $3,300 a year for a family of four. The additional cost would be about $11 billion a year. That is what the more obvious tax loopholes for the rich now drain from the U.S. Treasury.

Few people realize that our present tax and welfare structure is such as to encourage the wealthy to speculate and the poor to vegetate. If a rich man wants to speculate, he is encouraged by preferential capital gains and loss provisions which give him a twenty-five per cent cushion against losses and take less than half as much on his speculative gains as on his normal earnings. But if a poor man on relief took a part-time job he had until very recently to pay a 100 per cent tax on his earnings in the shape of a dollar-for-dollar reduction in his relief allowance. Even now after a belated reform in the welfare system, a poor man on relief after his first $30 a month in extra earnings must turn back to the Treasury seventy cents on the dollar while the rich man need pay the Treasury only twenty-five cents of every dollar he wins on the market even when his normal income tax rate is more than fifty per cent. Such is the topsy-turvy morality of the Internal Revenue laws.

A heart-breaking report on hunger by a Citizens Board of Inquiry has just lifted the curtain on why the poor are marching. In the richest country in the world people eat clay to still the pains of an empty belly, children come to school too hungry to learn, and the infants of the poor suffer irreversible brain damage from protein deprivation. Much of the crime in the streets springs from hunger in the home. Much of this hunger is also linked to handouts for those who do not need them. Some of its roots may be found in subsidy programmes designed to encourage farmers to make more money by producing less food. The effect has been to push the poor off the land and into the ghettoes. A programme designed thirty years ago ostensibly to help the desperate family farmer has become a source of huge handouts to big farmers and farm corporations.

In 1967 the 42.7 per cent of our farmers with incomes of less than $2,500 a year received only 4.5 per cent of total farm subsidies paid by the government while the top 10 per cent, many of them farm corporations or vertical trusts in food processing, received 64.5 per cent of these subsidies. The contrast between these handouts for rich farming interests and the stingy surplus food allotments for the poor is dramatically displayed in the statistical appendices of the Citizen's Report on Hunger. In the calendar year 1966 a quarter of a billion dollars in farm subsidies were paid to a lucky landowning two one-hundredths of one per cent of the population of Texas while the 28.8 per cent of its population below the poverty line received less than $8 million in all forms of food assistance. Such grotesque maldistribution of Federal aid is not limited to the South. That same year the U.S. Treasury paid almost $36 million in farm subsidies to one-third of one per cent of the population of Nebraska while only $957,000 in surplus food allotments went to the 26.1 per cent of its population which is in poverty. One farm company in California, J. G. Boswell, was given $2,807,633 in handouts by the Treasury that year and the Hawaiian Commercial and Sugar Company got $1,236,355 in Federal sweetening.

Such are the huge hogs that crowd the public trough. Other even bigger corporations live on the gravy that drips from the military and space programmes. We may never reach the moon – or know what to do with it when we get there – but the race for it has already created a new generation of Texas millionaires. The arms race and the space race guarantee the annual incomes of many in the country-club set.

Even before the marchers began arriving, the President at his latest press conference was already inviting them to leave. Their demands would be 'seriously' considered, he said, 'and then we expect to get on with running the government as it should be'. For years, 'running the government as it should be' has meant financing and planning these programmes which are the welfare systems of the American upper classes. Three quarters of the poor get no help. Two thirds of our hungry schoolchildren are not reached by the school-lunch programme. But finding the money to help them is not part of 'running the government as it should be', i.e. with a budget allocated 80 per cent to the Pentagon and 10 per cent to health, education and welfare.

Ours is a warfare, not a welfare state. And unless the better conscience of the country can be mobilized, it will wage war upon the poor, too. Only twice before in our history have the poor marched on Washington – Coxey's Army of the jobless in 1894 and the bonus marchers in 1932. Both times they were easily dispersed by force. The last heartless chapter of the flinty Hoover Administration was the attack of General MacArthur's troops upon the encampment of the bonus marchers on the Anacostia flats. This time the shanties will not be burned down nor the poor scattered so easily. A clash could set off the hottest summer yet of our nascent civil war. The poor may prove an irresistible force. The Congress is certainly an immovable object.

At this dangerous juncture we need a crusade of the progressive well-to-do to supplement the efforts of the poor people's march. We are glad to see that S.A.N.E. and a group of other organizations are calling for demonstrations of support throughout the country for Saturday, 25 May. We need volunteers to stand on street corners and collect money to feed the encampment of the poor in Washington. And we need an army of young white idealists to ring doorbells in the suburbs and awaken the middle class to the crisis the poor may precipitate. What lies ahead may be far more important than the election.

We wish the unaware millions of the suburbs could have heard the extraordinary collection of spokesmen for the poor whom the Rev. Ralph David Abernathy brought to Wesley A.M.E. Church for a preliminary rally here last week. The volcanic despair of our Negroes, Puerto Ricans, Indians, Spanish Americans and poor whites has thrown up new and unknown leaders able to present their case with an untaught and unmatchable eloquence. The descendants of the enslaved, the conquered and the dispossessed have found voices which makes one realize what human resources lie untapped among them. It was also thrilling in a time of rising separation to join hands again with blacks in singing 'We Shall Overcome' and to feel how truly this movement stems from Martin Luther King's teaching. If this fails, multi-racialism and non-violence will fail with it. Yet fail it must unless the middle class and the suburb can be aroused to pressure Congress for the steps required to wipe out poverty. 'There is nothing,' Martin Luther King said, 'except a tragic death wish, to prevent us from reordering our priorities, so that the pursuit of peace will take precedence over the pursuit of war.' Now is the time for the white and the fortunate to organize themselves for this work of solidarity. This – it cannot be said too often – may be our last chance.

13 May 1968, vol. 16, no. 10

How They Fix the Poverty Line

The government now estimates that there are 25.4 million Americans living below the poverty line. The McGovern hunger report shows that this line has been placed unrealistically low. The poverty line is based on the Department of Agriculture's 'economy' food plan for a family of four. This is then multiplied – again unrealistically – by three (instead of four) to allow for all other expenses. The latest estimate by the Census Bureau places this at $3,700 a year. But the Department of Agriculture itself warned last year that this 'economy' good budget was only suggested for 'emergency' use. 'The cost of this plan,' it said, 'is not a reasonable measure of basic money needs for a good diet.' It suggested that welfare agencies use the U.S.D.A. Low-Cost Food Plan 'which costs about 25 per cent more'. This would now be about $1,541 a year and bring the poverty line for a family of four up to $4,600 a year. The McGovern report says Social Security estimates that about 38 million Americans are below that line. The 25.4 million of the Census Bureau estimate are very poor indeed. Yet almost half of the country's blacks live below this $3,700 poverty line ($3,886 is their median family income). The Census Bureau also discloses that half the 'gainfully' employed in three occupations earn far less: service workers ($3,660), farm labourers ($854 – yes, per year) and other labourers, except in the mines ($2,652). These lower-income regions are the kingdom of hunger.

9 September 1969, vol. 17, no. 16

3: Democracy

An Appalling Choice to Head the C.I.A.

The C.I.A. is an intelligence organization run from the rather stuffy conventional wealthy businessman's point of view. It is staffed, from the top down, by Wall Streeters, Ivy League dilettantes, superannuated colonels from the armed forces and scholars, whose loyalty can be kept certified only by a fanatical anti-Communism. The main lesson of the Cuban fiasco is that an organization of this kind cannot be relied upon to know what ordinary people are thinking. But President Kennedy does not seem to have learned that lesson at all. In replacing Allen W. Dulles by John A. McCone, he picked a man who is if anything considerably less literate and less knowledgeable than Dulles, and fully as incapable of understanding the resentments and the aspirations that are the dynamic factors in today's world.

Mr McCone's rising fortunes, financial and political, have been associated with the war and the arms race. In 1937 he helped to form the Bechtel-McCone-Parsons Corporation, a construction and engineering firm. In January 1941 he organized and became the president of the California Shipbuilding Company; the Bechtel concern was then given a management contract to run the shipbuilding company. After the war the General Accounting Office told a House Merchant Marine Committee investigation that the company had made $44,000,000 on an investment of $100,000. The same committee a few months later complained that Mr McCone's company was paid $2,500,000 by the government to take over a shipyard costing $25,000,000 and containing surplus material costing $14,000,000.

Mr McCone did not confine his interests to shipbuilding. Bechtel-McCone-Parsons also built a huge installation at Birmingham, Alabama, during the war for the air force and became a leading construction firm for the A.E.C. Mr McCone also organized a private shipping company which did a big transport business for some of the largest A.E.C. contractors, firms like Union Carbide and Dow Chemical. These diverse enterprises had a common stake in armament expenditure, and Mr McCone made his debut in public service as a member of Truman's Air Policy Commission which in 1948 advocated a stepped-up indefinitely prolonged arms race. The report became the bible of the aviation lobby. His views recommended him to the alarmist Secretary of Defence Forrestal who made Mr McCone his deputy. In 1950–51 he was Under-Secretary of the Air Force.

With the Democrats out, Mr McCone returned to California and Republican politics. There his principal associations, political and religious, were of the right. He became a major money raiser for former Senator Knowland, often referred to as the Senator from Formosa, and he was close to Cardinal McIntyre of Los Angeles, not one of the more liberal members of the American hierarchy. In 1958, Admiral Strauss picked Mr McCone to succeed him as Chairman of the Atomic Energy Commission; they shared the same hostility to public power and to cessation of nuclear testing. At his nomination hearing, one of the exhibits was an angry letter Mr McCone had sent in 1956, as a Caltech trustee, to ten Caltech faculty members (including Harrison Brown and a Nobel laureate in physics) for releasing a statement supporting Adlai Stevenson's proposal for a ban on H-bomb testing. Mr McCone, a friend and admirer of Edward Teller, accused the ten professors of echoing Soviet propaganda in what he called an attempt 'to create fear in the minds of the uninformed that radioactive fallout from H-bomb tests endangers life'.

To control the nation's intelligence is to be in a position to shape decisions of war and peace. The C.I.A. is an enormous bureaucracy, with millions at its disposal to corrupt men abroad and perhaps at home; a rival, shadow State Department with a foreign policy even less enlightened. Its network of cloak-and-dagger operatives abroad move in a murky realm where provocations can make peace untenable. The U-2 was one sample. The Joint Intelligence Board over which Mr McCone will also preside coordinates all the multifarious snooper organizations of our government – there must be half a dozen beside the C.I.A. and the F.B.I. – and also our growing para-military agencies which can engage secretly in war. Mr Kennedy could not have made a more appalling choice for so crucial a post.

9 October 1961, vol. 9, no. 37

When a Two-Party System Becomes a One-Party Rubber Stamp

When a country is denied a choice on the most burning issue of the time, the war in Vietnam, then the two-party system has become a one-party rubber stamp. This is the first and essential point to be made in the wake of the Democratic and Republican conventions. The Establishment and the military have locked the ballot boxes. If the results are an intensified alienation among the youth who must fight this war, an increase in resistance to the draft, a rise in street demonstrations and violence, this is the cause and not some occult conspiracy. The real conspiracy was the one which wove together Eisenhower's last inflammatory message to the Republican convention with the iron control Johnson and Daley exercised over the Democrats. Both parties, both candidates, have been drafted. The Pentagon has won the election even before the votes are cast.

The second thing which needs to be said is that the country owes a debt of gratitude to the tatterdemalion army of yippies, hippies and peaceniks – and to their leaders David Dellinger, Tom Hayden and Jerry Rubin – who frightened the Establishment into such elaborate security precautions in Chicago. They made opposition to the war visible. The special barbed-wire fences around the amphitheatre which turned 'Stalag '68' into the favourite joke of the convention, the system of electronically checked passes so intricate that it led to a whole series of angry clashes with the delegates themselves, the vast concentration of police, National Guardsmen and troops, as if in preparation for a revolution, dramatized for the whole world to see that there was something indelibly undemocratic about this Democratic convention.

Of course security precautions were justified. The Secret Service, the F.B.I. and the Chicago police had a right to be fearful of what might happen, especially if Johnson himself had turned up and this was the grim eventuality I believe they had in mind. But the question not to be lost sight of is why for the first time in American history a convention and a President required so much protection. This was the scandal it proved impossible to hide and this is why the police were so brutal in dealing with the cameramen and the reporters. They were the main enemy of the proceedings, the eyes and ears of the country. The unwelcome witnesses of the rigging within the convention and the repression without. Johnson and Daley, alike in so many ways, are alike in their obsessive animosity to the press. Daley's big and beefy police seemed to crack the skulls of the TV and press reporters with a special gusto and as if given free rein by their masters. Their conduct was in its own way a resounding tribute to the First Amendment. It also gave middle-class whites a taste of the police brutality which is an old story to blacks.

The convention was a triumph of what the Russian Communists would call 'democratic centralism', that submission of 'the lower organs of the party to the higher' which they are reimposing in Prague. The delegates chosen were less representative of the party rank-and-file than of the party machines, and the committees were even less representative than the delegates. A Citizens' Committee, to include respected retired jurists, ought to be formed to take testimony from delegates, demonstrators and the police on the whole question of how this convention and the protests against it were handled. It would show I believe that security was used as a way to control the convention. If assassination plots were as thick as Daley and the police now claim – and Humphrey idiotically echoes them – then it is strange that no attempts were made, no shots fired, no bombs thrown. For in the crowded hallways of the main hotels, including the Hilton, it would have been easy for an assassin to take a potshot at any one of the candidates. There security was poor.

On the other hand, at the amphitheatre, guards were used to harass McCarthy and McGovern delegates. The opposition on the floor was hamstrung by lack of phone communications and by the arbitrary and arrogant rulings that Carl Albert as chairman applied to any attempt to protest. The Johnson steamroller stopped the effort of the Humphrey forces to put a slightly milder face on the pro-war Vietnam plank. Not the slightest deviation was allowed. Johnson and Daley are masters of meticulous detail, accustomed to rule their kingdoms with an iron hand. So it was that a convention strikingly cool despite its unrepresentative majority to any mention of Johnson's name was forced to wear his brand in the platform plank on Vietnam and the choice of Vice-President. A candidate who might have placated blacks and anti-war delegates was Fred Harris of Oklahoma. But he was the vice-chairman of the Kerner commission whose report Johnson disliked. Johnson and Daley preferred a safe and bridle-broken liberal like Muskie of Maine (Johnson put a saddle on him long ago), with an appeal to Chicago's Polish Americans and an 'ethnic' offset to Agnew.

To wander in Lincoln Park among the hippies and yippies, to drop in on the headquarters of the New Left demonstrators, to talk at random with the youths in Grant Park and the streets, was to feel that in revulsion against the war the best of a generation was being lost – some among the hippies to drugs, some among the radicals to an almost hysterical frenzy of alienation. There were a few among them I am sure who sought deliberately by taunts and obscenities to provoke a confrontation with the police, but far more were driven to angry resistance by Daley's unwillingness to let them sleep in Lincoln Park and to grant permits for peaceful demonstrations and parades. These would have let off steam and been far easier to police than crowds which felt their elementary rights were being trampled. Even Joseph J. Lefevour, president of the Chicago lodge of the Fraternal Order of Police, in the middle of a press conference called to defend police tactics, admitted (*Chicago Tribune*, 30 August), 'Most of the kids in the parks,' i.e. Lincoln and Grant parks, 'have been orderly. They've obeyed our orders and joked with us. But then their leaders work them up to fever pitch and disappear, leaving the kids to take the consequences.' But could they have been worked up 'to fever pitch' without the brutal nightly sweeps at curfew time in Lincoln Park, and the indiscriminate and sadistic way the police beat and tear-gassed not only peaceful demonstrators in Grant Park but onlookers behind the police's own barricades in front of the Hilton?

Daley has long run a one-party state in Chicago, with just that combination of brutality, social welfare handouts and co-operation with big business which is also the essence of Johnson's own conception of personal government. The way Humphrey has stepped out as Daley's apologist, even after the climactic raid on the McCarthy headquarters in the Hilton, is an index of what we can expect from a Humphrey Administration, of what he means by law and order, and of what lies behind his platitudinous evangelism. Another index – to be forgotten at our peril – was his appearance before the Catholic War Veterans on the eve of the convention when he threw away a moderate prepared script and delivered a warmongering address. These two events have finally decided for me that Humphrey is no lesser evil than Nixon. A vote for Humphrey is a vote for Johnson's war and Daley's police-state tactics.

I confess that I do not know what to do politically at this juncture. The three main ways open are Allard Lowenstein's effort eventually to take over the Democrats, Marcus Raskin's attempt to form a New Party, and the New Left's call to go into the streets. To meet the crises of race and war which confront the country, time and patience, faith in persuasion, are required. But how preach these virtues to a youth who may be called up any day for the army? The war is destroying our country as we are destroying Vietnam. Hate and frenzy are poor substitutes for political thinking, yet the *enragés* among the youth, with their romanticism about guerrilla war, may set the tune for the whole country. A handful may provoke the government to such over-reaction as to polarize the country between extremes.

The New Left and even its moderate allies are still operating in a fog of misconceptions. The main one is that 'the people' are against the war. The people on the contrary are confused and divided. To say that the streets 'belong to the people' as Tom Hayden has done is to overlook those people who feel the streets belong to them, too, for the ordinary business of their lives. 'Let that party,' Raskin said of the Democrats the other day in calling for a New Party, 'be the party of the cops, the military, the big city bosses and the non-people'. There are an awful lot of 'non-people'. The need is for dialogue, not mono-logue, to win them over. If law and order really break down, if democratic processes are abandoned, it is we of the left, the anti-war forces and the intellectuals who will be the first to suffer. To play with revolutionary talk and tactics as the New Left is doing, when there is no revolutionary situation, is to act as the provocateurs for an American Fascism.

The deeper tragedy lies in the increasing abandonment of non-violent tactics by black and white dissenters alike. To howl down those with whom we differ, to use obscenities instead of arguments, to abandon persuasion for direct action, to de-humanize the other side with cries of 'pigs' and worse is to embark on a game the rightists are better equipped to play, and to set examples which American Storm Troopers may some day apply to us. Hate is still the main enemy of the human race, the fuel that heats the furnaces of genocide. How build a better world by relapsing into primitive and sanguinary habits?

9 September 1968, vol. 16, no. 18

The Price We Pay for Empire

The revelations of the Symington subcommittee report on 'Security Agreements and Commitments Abroad' would fall into better focus if it began by saying plainly that the U.S. since World War II has become the biggest empire the world has ever known. The huge military and intelligence establishments required to maintain that empire become increasingly difficult to control. Their size and secrecy make ours a partially closed society. The truth is that no one, not the President or the Sec-retary of Defence, or even the heads of secret-service agencies like C.I.A., D.I.A. or N.S.A. much less the Congress can fully control these monstrous bureaucracies. In their murky depths moves are made which may turn out later to have set the course for disastrous military interventions. We are all trapped by the sheer inertial mass of the machinery required to run the empire. In dozens of ways it frustrates free decision by freely elected government, and there is always the danger that it may, if challenged or given the chance, apply at home the methods it employs abroad. Widespread Army spying on anti-war civilians may be seen as the application at home of the 'pacification' techniques the military intelligence apparatus has developed in Vietnam. As in ancient Rome, the price of empire may be the downfall of the Republic.

'Under the Constitution, the Congress, particularly the Senate,' the report begins, 'has a responsibility to keep itself fully informed about matters of foreign policy.' The twenty-eight pages are packed with examples of how poorly informed – and often deliberately misinformed – the Congress has become. Senate leaders did not learn until the Symington hearings that our bombing operations in Laos began, not with interdiction of the Ho Chi Minh trail, but in support of Royal Lao forces in Northern Laos. The Nixon Administration talks of improving relations with China but raids on the mainland continue from Taiwan, unmanned U.S. reconnaissance planes still fly over China, air bases on Taiwan have been enlarged to handle B-52 bombers and the Nationalist Army, 'despite U.S. efforts to make it appear otherwise', still trains (with U.S. supplied equipment) for return to the mainland. Until the Symington hearings, no one knew that the U.S. had conducted joint military exercises with Franco's army to combat a hypothetical uprising. 'Creeping commitments' spark new wars in fighting old ones: 'After Thai approval of U.S. use of Thai bases for bombing in Laos and Vietnam, insurgent elements surfaced in Thailand. In turn, the U.S. increased its counter-insurgency forces.' In Ethiopia, to obtain the use of Kagnew Station (obviously for U-2 flights over the Soviet Union), the U.S. secretly agreed in the fifties to finance a 40,000-man army for Ethiopia. U-2 flights have been replaced by satellites but Kagnew station is still in operation. It is now threatened by Arab-supported Eritrean guerrillas, and the Soviets have reacted by supplying arms to Ethiopia's traditional enemy, Somalia. So Cold War engulfs another part of the globe.

Every businessman knows the problem of keeping tabs on what goes on in his own business. Imagine trying to ride herd on the biggest business in the world: U.S. military and intelligence operations. Nobody knows the full cost but it probably comes close to $100 billion a year. 'As but one illustration of the incredible duplication and waste,' the report says, 'at one time the three military services, along with A.I.D., U.S.I.A. and C.I.A. were each operating independent counter-insurgency programmes' in Thailand. The report discloses that no mechanism exists in the executive branch to eliminate duplication between civilian and military snoopers and that even in the Pentagon there is no overall review of competing military intelligence programmes – this despite the establishment by McNamara years ago of a D.I.A. (Defense Intelligence Agency) supposed to coordinate all Pentagon gumshoe work. The total cost of military intelligence in 1970, the report reveals, was $2.9 billion, no bagatelle even in the Pentagon.

The secret services are big enough to run their own secret wars. 'Everyone recognizes,' the report says, 'that national security imposes limits on the disclosure of information. But the multimillion dollar support of a 30,000-man army can in no way be considered an intelligence operation.' The reference is to the C.I.A. in Laos. There may be some benefits in secrecy. Considering the monumental misjudgements of U.S. intelligence in the past two decades in Korea, in Cuba, and in Vietnam, it's just as well that intelligence reports are confined to a select circle. The Symington report has a lovely quotation from Walter Lippmann. He once wrote of the information funnelled into our policy makers that the men reporting to them realize 'that it is safer to be wrong before it has become fashionable to be right'. Every bureaucracy likes its intelligence apparatus to confirm its preconceptions. But couldn't this reassuring yesmanship be done more cheaply?

The passion for secrecy, and its use to hide misjudgements

from those who must ultimately foot the bill in lives and money, was the main obstacle in this two-year investigation. If ever there was a David-and-Goliath operation, this was it. A newspaperman, Walter Pincus, and a lawyer, Roland A. Paul, were the two-man staff of this special subcommittee of Senate Foreign Relations under Senator Symington. Their job was to survey commitments to more than forty-three nations represented 375 major, and 3,000 minor, U.S. bases abroad. They visited twenty-three countries and held thirty-seven days of hearings. The published record fills over 2,500 heavily censored but nevertheless revealing pages. The hearings were made possible by Symington's conversion in recent years from a pillar of the military establishment to one of its severest critics. The report deserves wider reading and closer study than it is likely to get.

The subcommittee's greatest difficulty was in dealing with the subject of nuclear weapons. We seem to have scattered these all around the globe. Some day rebels against governments we support may 'kidnap' and use some of them for a kind of blackmail. A leak during the hearings disclosed that our military feared something like this in Greece. The danger to these sacred monsters we have planted around the globe may yet serve as additional rationale for helping a Chiang, a Papadopoulos or a Franco to put down a rebellion against the lack of freedom in so many corners of our 'free world'. At one point 'the Executive Branch claimed that this subject is of such high classification that it could not be discussed before this Foreign Relations subcommittee under any circumstances'. Subsequently it relented and agreed to a single-day world-wide briefing of the full Senate Foreign Relations committee but only on condition that there be but one transcript, and this to be held by the State Department! This is a long way from the Constitution, which begins to seem a quaint relic.

The bureaucracy, with its gift for reassuring euphemism, sold the country long ago on 'containment'. It sounded neat and sanitary. No one ever put the question, 'Shall we sow instant death around the borders of the Soviet Bloc and China by ringing them with nuclear devices and delivery systems?' This is what has been going on since the fifties. The report reminds us that the U.S. went to the brink of nuclear war in 1962 'when faced with the possibility that the Soviet Union was putting missiles in a country ninety miles from the U.S.' We must assume that 'the Soviets, as they view our placement of tactical nuclear weapons in countries far closer to their borders than Cuba is to ours, will seek to break out of the nuclear ring that has been drawn around them'. New missile crises may not be resolved as peacefully as in 1962. How can Congress and the country take preventive measures when censorship blacks out so much of what we need to know? The full price of empire has yet to fall due.

11 January 1971, vol. 19, no. 1

4: The Presidents

At Least There is the Promise of Bigness in Kennedy

The strongest testimony to the collective intelligence of the delegates at the Democratic convention was their indifference to the proceedings. We do not remember ever seeing before so inattentive a convention, and we regard the inattention as a sign of growing national maturity. The convention showed itself too sophisticated for the elocutionist nullities of Idaho's Senator Church, who started on the road to fame by winning an American Legion oratorical contest and demonstrated at the convention how richly he deserved that prize. Governor Collins of Florida turned out to be commonplace; Chester Bowles, without lift and unimpressive. Only Governor Pat Brown of California, with his plea that we stop pretending that Communist China does not exist, dared touch on any real issue.

It was not until the demonstrations for Adlai Stevenson that the convention came to life, though this was in part an illusion created by the galleries. Two speakers only, Mrs Roosevelt and former Governor Lehman, in their hopeless appeals for Stevenson, achieved a passionate and memorable sincerity. Mrs Roosevelt drew deep down within herself for strong powers of utterance quite extraordinary for her years, and by her power overshadowed every other participant in the proceeding including Stevenson himself, who emanates an air of preciosity. By far the biggest man available – what a pleasure it would have been to see in the White House a man of stature and education suited to the dimensions of our country and its power – yet it must be admitted the man lacks something in the way of virility and fire. This unfavourable view consoles one in his defeat, as does the hope that he may become Secretary of State if Kennedy wins.

With Humphrey (if only Stevenson had his fighting energy!)

defeated, Kennedy seems clearly the best of those available. Amid such empty figures as the moronic Symington and sophomoric Jackson, and even beside so able a man as Lyndon Johnson, Kennedy shines. His grace, his tact and his intelligence are unmistakable. His press conference replying to Mr Truman's rather wild charges was a demonstration of high skill in the management of men and events. His encounter with Johnson before the Texas delegation left Johnson looking small and petty. Though his nomination is the product of money and a Madison Avenue machine, Kennedy added ingredients of personal appeal and power without which he could not have succeeded. He has attracted to his banner men and women we trust – Mrs Edith Green of Oregon, to name one. In the gamble that is the inescapable nature of every presidential choice, Kennedy is promising. He might turn out to be a big man. This cannot be said of his close rivals in the last lap at the convention, nor can it be said of Nixon. Never did our country and the world need a big man in the White House more.

The platform on which Kennedy will run is outstanding in its civil rights programme, which includes a cheer for the wave of sit-ins by which Negro youth and its allies have done more for the Negro in a few breath-taking months than three generations of normal political activity. Otherwise its liberalism is of the A.D.A. and George Meany variety, i.e. it combines social welfare measures with a stepped-up arms race. We hope the Russians noticed the undercurrent of belligerence and alarm over Mr K.'s latest on the Monroe Doctrine. The Democrats will be tougher to deal with than the Republicans. We hope the Russians have the good sense not to engulf our election campaign in reckless talk. The Congo affair on top of everything else as we go to press gives the world the atmosphere of a bar-room on the verge of a brawl.

18 July 1960, vol. 8, no. 28

As If the Prophet Jeremiah were Caught Cheering

At the risk of alarming steady customers, inured to a weekly diet of apocalyptic pessimism, I must confess that I am becoming optimistic. This may seem in its way perverse. Just when a new President sends Congress a first message filled with perilous tidings at home and abroad, your Washington reporter suddenly begins to see hope ahead. I even feel a little embarrassed, like the prophet Jeremiah caught giving three lusty cheers. But ever since John F. Kennedy's first press conference, I haven't felt the same.

The swift movement of events here is bewildering; one would have to print morning, evening, noon and night to keep up with it. The appointments, the policy positions, have something in them for everybody. Mr Kennedy's heroes are Churchill and the two Roosevelts, but his dazzling sleight of hand most resembles de Gaulle's – and de Gaulle, remember, for all the misgivings of the French left is pulling off the miracle of getting France and the French army slowly to accept the idea of an independent Algeria. I believe Mr Kennedy, by a similar dexterity, may succeed in bringing about a settlement, first with the Soviet Union and then with Peking, in ways and on terms some of us may find surprising and even unpalatable, but the result can pull us away from the brink.

Some readers may remember that back in the spring of 1953, we shocked some of them with a piece called, 'Challenge to the Left: Back Ike for Peace', which proposed that we circumvent the pall of McCarthyism and make Mr Eisenhower's moves towards a Korean truce the rallying point for public support of a broader settlement; we asked the left to get rid of its stereotypes and see that the new Republican soldier President was a potential force for peace. So he would have been but for Chancellor Adenauer's skilful torpedoing of one constructive possibility after another on the way to the abortive summit last year, and the tragic accident of the U-2. The latter was due to Mr Eisenhower's lazy slovenliness about his job; the former, to the pro-Bonn orientation which John Foster Dulles so long gave U.S. policy. The days of the Bonn–Washington axis are I believe over; Adenauer's sudden moves towards a settlement with Poland reflect his fear of being left high and dry by bilateral talks between Washington and Moscow; 'not a word on Berlin'

Die Welt of Hamburg complains of Mr Kennedy's State of the Union message.

As for a new incident or provocation similar to the U-2, its possibility is not to be excluded. There are mountainous bureaucratic and corporate forces against a settlement, with huge funds and resources at their disposal. But they will no longer find a slack hand and an absent mind at the White House. I cannot tell you with what pleasure I watched the new President at his first press conference; his performance washed away a long-held and indeed cherished anti-Kennedy bias. Necessity may make his course tortuous but the direction is clearly towards peace. I feel that for the first time since Roosevelt we have a first-rater in the presidency, a young man of energy, zest and ability. It is a post in which any man of any quality must grow, but when a man starts out with the gifts Mr Kennedy so clearly has, we have the right to hope he will grow to greatness, and perform valiantly in the cause of mankind.

Many difficulties and disappointments lie ahead. The narrow victory in the House Rules fight will invigorate the coalition of Republicans and Southern Democrats, who see that Mr Kennedy will have to pay dearly in concessions to get the precarious margins required for his domestic programme, but it will also invigorate Mr Kennedy, and I predict that his personal appeal over TV will give him a better margin in the next House elections two years hence. It is obvious that he loves nothing better than a hard fight; indeed he seems to have a weakness for seeing an Armageddon everywhere. In this respect, the State of the Union message would have benefited by a little understatement. This is neither Britain in September 1939 nor America in 1933, nor has Fort Sumter just been fired upon.

In one sense, of course, the crisis is greater and global, but the hangover of fervent Cold War clichés still impedes Mr Kennedy's efforts to express it with a just sobriety. Much of what the President will do in this connection, the peace movement will find incomprehensible and distasteful, and we intend to criticize watchfully but no longer in a tone of despair. In moving towards peace, Mr Kennedy must carry with him somehow a party and a labour movement strongly attached to the arms race, and a country which would be startled if it too soon heard an entirely different tune on Soviet-American relations. In this, Mr Kennedy's problem is much like Mr Krushchev's; both must conciliate rigid fanatics in their ranks; both must make coexistence appear as only another form of struggle to liberate the other's sphere of influence; neither can afford to appear 'soft', the one on capitalism, the other on Communism. But both are master politicians, and both are well aware of the crossroads to which history has brought them.

The immediate issue, the crucial main point, is the successful negotiation of a nuclear test ban treaty and its ratification by the Senate, which requires a two-thirds vote. This is a formidable hurdle. To achieve this arduous goal, the necessary first step towards wider settlement and relaxation of tension, all the contradictions and compromises plainly visible in the Kennedy programme and official family – and there will be more of them – are justified. The President can be freed from these political necessities only by a more aroused and better informed public opinion. Never was there greater need for a broader peace movement than now; never was there a President more open to fresh ideas and more ready for flexible tactics. But the success of such a movement in affecting the course of events will depend on its unconventionality; its freedom from pacifist and party line stereotypes and a demonstrated independence of Moscow. What we need is not an organization to sell any particular panacea but to draw more and more people into discussing the problems of foreign policy and of peace. What we ourselves need most to lose are the chains of our old clichés.

Any President's power to act is limited by the people's power to understand. A whole series of unstable situations abroad may easily upset negotiations on critical wider issues. It would be good if public opinion understood that many of Mr Kennedy's problems abroad are less the result of Soviet machinations than of the C.I.A.'s, the heritage of poor State Department policy and melodramatic thinking at home. It is silly to talk of Laos, the Congo and Cuba as tests of Soviet sincerity. Mr Krushchev cannot chase the Pathet Lao out of the jungle for us nor turn Mr Lumumba into a willing tool of Belgian-American big business and he certainly cannot control Fidel Castro. If Dr Castro were really a Communist, he could be turned on or off like a party line spigot, but he is a real revolutionary and a handful. In Cuba, more than anywhere else, there is need for private negotiation; the alternative is bloody intervention direct or covert, which would enflame the hemisphere; it is by our attitude towards Cuba not by new promises of new aid, mañana, that the Latin American masses will judge us. It is in this Lilliputian quarrel that I see the greatest danger.

6 February 1961, vol. 9, no. 5

We All Had a Finger on that Trigger

There was a fairytale quality about the inaugural and there was a fairytale quality about the funeral rites. One half expected that when the lovely princess knelt to kiss the casket for the last time, some winged godmother would wave her wand and restore the hero whole again in a final triumph over the dark forces which had slain him. There never was such a shining pageant of a presidency before. We watched it as children do, raptly determined to believe but knowing all the time that it wasn't really true.

Of all the Presidents, this was the first to be a Prince Charming. To watch the President at press conference or at a private press briefing was to be delighted by his wit, his intelligence, his capacity and his youth. These made the terrible flash from Dallas incredible and painful. But perhaps the truth is that in some ways John Fitzgerald Kennedy died just in time. He died in time to be remembered as he would like to be remembered, as ever-young, still victorious, struck down undefeated, with almost all the potentates and rulers of mankind, friend and foe, come to mourn at his bier.

For somehow one has the feeling that in the tangled dramaturgy of events, this sudden assassination was for the author the only satisfactory way out. The Kennedy Administration was approaching an impasse, certainly at home, quite possibly abroad, from which there seemed no escape. In Congress the

President was faced with something worse than a filibuster. He was confronted with a shrewdly conceived and quietly staged sitdown strike by Southern committee chairmen determined to block civil rights even if it meant stopping the wheels of government altogether. The measure of their success is that we entered this final month of 1963 with nine of the thirteen basic appropriation bills as yet unpassed, though the fiscal year for which they were written began last 1 July and most of the government has been forced to live hand-to-mouth since. Never before in our history has the Senate so dragged its heels as this year; never before has the Southern oligarchy dared go so far in demonstrating its power in Washington. The President was caught between these old men, their faces set stubbornly towards their white supremacist past, and the advancing Negro masses, explosively demanding 'freedom now'. Mr Kennedy's death, like those of the Birmingham children and of Medgar Evers, may some day seem the first drops portending a new storm which it was beyond his power to stay.

In foreign policy, the outlook was as unpromising. It was proving difficult to move towards coexistence a country so long conditioned to Cold War. Even when Moscow offered gold for surplus wheat, it was hard to make a deal. The revolt in Congress against foreign aid illustrated how hard it was to carry on policy once tense fears of Communism slackened even slightly. The President recognized the dangers of an unlimited arms race and the need for a *modus vivendi* if humanity was to survive but was afraid, even when the Sino-Soviet break offered the opportunity, to move at more than snail's pace towards agreement with Moscow. The word was that there could be no follow-up to a nuclear test ban pact at least until after the next election; even so minor a step as a commercial airline agreement with the Soviets was in abeyance. The quarrel with Argentina over oil concessions lit up the dilemma of the Alliance for Progress; however much the President might speak of encouraging diversity, when it came to a showdown, Congress and the moneyed powers of our society insisted on 'free enterprise'. The anti-Castro movement our C.I.A. covertly supports was still a spluttering fuse, and in Vietnam the stepping up of the war by the rebels was deflating all the romantic Kennedy notions about counter-guerrillas, while in Europe the Germans still blocked every constructive move towards a settlement in Berlin.

Abroad, as at home, the problems were becoming too great for conventional leadership, and Kennedy, when the tinsel was stripped away, was a conventional leader, no more than an enlightened conservative, cautious as an old man for all his youth, with a basic distrust of the people and an astringent view of the evangelical as a tool of leadership. It is as well not to lose sight of these realities in the excitement of the funeral; funerals are always occasions for pious lying. A deep vein of superstition and a sudden touch of kindness always lead people to give the departed credit for more virtues than he possessed. This is particularly true when the dead man was the head of the richest and most powerful country in the world, its friendship courted, its enmity feared. Everybody is anxious to celebrate the dead leader and to court his successor. In the clouds of incense thus generated, it is easy to lose one's way, just when it becomes more important than ever to see where we really are.

The first problem that has to be faced is the murder itself. Whether it was done by a crackpot leftist on his own, or as the tool of some rightist plot, Van Der Lubbe style, the fact is that there are hundreds of thousands in the South who had murder in their hearts for the Kennedys, the President and his brother the Attorney General, because they sought in some degree to help the Negro. This potential for murder, which the Negro community has felt for a long time, has become a national problem. But there are deeper realities to be faced.

Let us ask ourselves honest questions. How many Americans have not assumed – with approval – that the C.I.A. was probably trying to find a way to assassinate Castro? How many would not applaud if the C.I.A. succeeded? How many applauded when Lumumba was killed in the Congo, because they assumed that he was dangerously neutralist or perhaps pro-Communist? Have we not become conditioned to the notion that we should have a secret agency of government – the C.I.A. – with secret funds, to wield the dagger beneath the cloak against leaders we dislike? Even some of our best young liberal intellectuals can see nothing wrong in this picture except that the 'operational' functions of the C.I.A. should be kept separate from its intelligence evaluations! How many of us – on the left now – did not welcome the assassination of Diem and his brother Nhu in South Vietnam? We all reach for the dagger, or the gun, in our thinking when it suits our political view to do so. We all believe the end justifies the means. We all favour murder, when it reaches our own hated opponents. In this sense we share the guilt with Oswald and Ruby and the rightist crackpots. Where the right to kill is so universally accepted, we should not be surprised if our young President was slain. It is not just the ease in obtaining guns, it is the ease in obtaining excuses, that fosters assassination. This is more urgently in need of examination than who pulled the trigger. In this sense, as in that multi-lateral nuclear monstrosity we are trying to sell Europe, we all had a finger on the trigger.

But if we are to dig out the evil, we must dig deeper yet, into the way we have grown to accept the idea of murder on the widest scale as the arbiter of controversy between nations. In this connection, it would be wise to take a clear-sighted view of the Kennedy Administration because it was the first U.S. government in the nuclear age which acted on the belief that it was possible to see war, or the threat of war, as an instrument of politics despite the possibility of annihilation. It was in some ways a warlike Administration. It seems to have been ready, soon after taking office, to send troops into Vietnam to crush the rebellion against Diem; fortunately both Diem and our nearest Asian allies, notably the Filipinos, were against our sending combat troops into the area. The Kennedy Administration, in violation of our own laws and international law, permitted that invasion from our shores which ended so ingloriously in the Bay of Pigs. It was the Kennedy Administration which met Khrushchev's demands for negotiations on Berlin by a partial mobilization and an alarming invitation to the country to dig backyard shelters against cataclysm.

Finally we come to the October crisis of a year ago. This set a bad precedent for his successors, who may not be as skilful as he was in finding a way out. What if the Russians had refused to back down and remove their missiles from Cuba? What if they had called our bluff and war had begun, and escalated? How would the historians of mankind, if a fragment survived, have regarded the events of October? Would they have thought us justified in blowing most of mankind to smithereens, rather than negotiate, or appeal to the U.N., or even to leave in Cuba the medium-range missiles which were no different after all from those we had long aimed at the Russians from Turkey and England? When a whole people is in a state of mind where it is ready to risk extinction – its own and everybody else's – as a means of having its own way in an international dispute, the readiness for murder has become a way of life and a world menace. Since this is the kind of bluff that can easily be played once too often, and that his successors may feel urged to imitate, it would be well to think it over carefully before canonizing Kennedy as an apostle of peace.

9 December 1963, vol. 11, no. 24

Johnson Far Below J.F.K. in Sophistication, Breadth and Taste

The scramble for positions of influence with the new Johnson Administration makes it almost impossible to get an objective view of the man; everybody from the politicians to the Washington correspondents are, with few exceptions, outdoing themselves in flattering of the new monarch. His vanity, his thin skin and his vindictiveness make even the mildest criticism, or approach to objectivity, dangerous.

The negative aspects of Johnson are these. In sophistication, education and taste, he is a sharp drop from Kennedy. He has hardly read a book in years; never reads when he can help it; prefers to get information by ear, but rarely listens. He is one of the most long-winded men in Washington; a Babbit, with a remarkably small stock of basic ideas; these consist of a few clichés about freedom, which he translates largely into the freedom of the entrepreneur to make a buck. Money and power

have been the motivating passions of his life. He was a New
Dealer when that was the road to power, he became a conservative when that was the way to stay in. He is the perfect
extrovert, with no convictions and a passion for 'getting things
done', a nothing. He rose as rapidly as he did in the House and
later the Senate by endless sitting at the feet, after hours, of
Sam Rayburn and later Senator Russell. *Then* he listened, the
respectful and flattering young man; he had a genius for in-
gratiating himself with the old men of the Southern oligarchy.
But he kept his lines open to the liberals, in order to deal with
them, too, and he likes to picture himself as a Westerner rather
than a Southerner.

Johnson's skill as a legislative manipulator may be over-
estimated. In the Eisenhower period, he was an effective middle
man between the Republican and Democratic conservatives. In
the special session of 1960, after the election, however, he and
Kennedy together found it impossible to put through a mod-
erately liberal programme. Johnson is not a racist or a reac-
tionary; he once told a visiting civil-rights group that he had
learned all he knew on the subject from Aubrey Williams (of
the Southern Conference Educational Fund, once Johnson's
boss in the New Deal's National Youth Administration) and
Mary McLeod Bethune. As a shrewd politician, he knows he
must move slightly leftward and make civil rights his no. 1 issue
if he is to change the view of him as a Southern politician, with
a basically standpat philosophy. In Texas the liberals distrust
him deeply for running out on them and his New Deal past; the
conservatives hate him for having been a more than loyal
Kennedy lieutenant on Civil rights.

The Republicans suddenly feel a chance to win the next election and he will have a very short honeymoon. The Kennedy
assassination has not softened the hearts of the Southern oli-
garchs and their coalition with the Republicans may easily and
quickly be resumed. The vulnerable point of the new President
is his old protégé, Bobby Baker, a mercenary corkscrew of a
character whose extraordinary influence in the Senate throws a
horrifying light on the decayed underside of that august institution, and on Johnson's own aesthetic standards. The Repub-

licans may have trouble in exploiting the Baker case, however, because it probably links up with as many ugly deals on their side of the aisle as on the Democratic side. It will take all Johnson's skill and energy to hush up this scandal and get action out of Congress. Men like Fulbright and Benjamin V. Cohen will be good influences in this Administration, but on the whole Johnson like Truman will bring a lot of rather unseemly cronies to town and its level of literacy and civilization will fall again, as it did after F.D.R.

The hope is that men change and grow. A man's past is not necessarily a guide to his future, especially when he reaches the highest posts of a society. The sense of role, the maturing effect of responsibility, the consciousness of duty and love of country, the sense of humanity and history, all have their effect. Tom Clark, a one-time Texas lobbyist, not much of a lawyer, but a decent human being and never a racist, has made an honourable record and grown in stature on the U.S. Supreme Court. There may be surprises in Johnson, and we wish the new President luck. The manner and energy of his debut stir hope.

9 December 1963, vol. 9, no. 24

The Fatal Lure of World Domination

The Department of Commerce publishes a daily bulletin in which the government advertises various wants for bidding. There in the issue of 29 April, as our Marines were landing in Santo Domingo, appeared an ad which deserves to be preserved for the historian. Amid requests for bids on tyres, spare aircraft parts and survival kits, was this item:

Service and materials to perform a RESEARCH STUDY ENTITLED 'PAX-AMERICANA' [capitals in original] consisting of a phased study of the following: (a) elements of National Power; (b) ability of selected nations to apply the elements of National Power; (c) a variety of world power configurations to be used as a basis for the U.S. to maintain world hegemony in the future. Quotations and applicable specifications will be available upon request, at the Army Research Office, 3845 Columbia Pike, Arlington, Va., until 1 May 1965.

What better time to study the problems of maintaining American world hegemony than the moment when our combat troops were going ashore in Vietnam on the South China sea in one hemisphere and in the Caribbean in the other? Coupled with this ad were three others from the army. One was a study of the foreign aid programmes of the West European nations. The second was 'U.S. Involvement in the Emerging Nations', a study 'to determine the quality and quantity of total U.S. presence and influence in Latin America, Africa and Asia, to identify salient trends and to project the latter into the 1975–80 time frame'. The third was the most disturbing, 'Investigation of the feasibility and desirability in the 1970 time frame, of providing selected U.S. allies a significant nuclear defense capability *without necessity for maintaining U.S. controls or custody over weapons systems or their employment*'. (Our italics.) These contracts provide an insight into what is going on within our military bureaucracy, the extent to which it is invading the State Department's province in making foreign policy, and the kind of foreign policy the armed forces project for the future – one in which they play policemen to the world, even handing out nuclear weapons to favoured allies in the task! This is a formula which can only end by spilling the blood of our best youth in an endless attempt to dominate the planet. This is in the background of Johnson's increasingly militaristic policy in Asia and Latin America. Like Bismarck, we are resorting to blood and iron.

Two of Kennedy's utterances come to mind as one watches the steady degeneration of policy under Johnson. One was in Kennedy's American University Speech in June 1963: 'What kind of peace do I mean and what kind of peace do we seek? Not a Pax Americana enforced on the world by American weapons of war.' The other was at the University of California that year when Kennedy warned, 'We must reject oversimplified theories of international life – the theory that American power is unlimited, or that the American mission is to remake the world in the American image.' Such views are now out of fashion. They are stigmatized as neo-isolationist while ultra-nationalist ambition parades as internationalist idealism.

All kinds of excuses could be made for Johnson's Vietnam policy. He inherited the war from Kennedy. He needed a position of strength from which to negotiate. But the Dominican affair and the 'Johnson Doctrine' put Vietnam in a different light. For what Johnson is saying is that despite the Charters of the United Nations and of the Organization of American States we arrogate to ourselves the right to intervene whenever and wherever we believe a Communist regime may take over. This doctrine has two deplorable consequences. Like the Vietnamese war it must tend to solidify the Communist bloc just when centrifugal forces had made an appearance within it; American policy in Europe under Eisenhower and Kennedy had begun to encourage independence within the bloc by treating each European (though not Asian) Communist regime differently. Now that different types of Communism have begun to appear, and with them liberalizing trends, we enunciate a doctrine that no longer distinguishes among them. The effect may be to risk a new Stalinist Ice Age in the bloc as its members draw together again in fear of the U.S.

The implications are also serious for the non-Communist world. Social reform movements and anti-military uprisings in Latin America and elsewhere will be at the mercy of American definitions of what constitutes Communism. The Johnson Doctrine is McCarthyism in foreign policy. Like McCarthyism at home, it faces the same basic dilemma and that is to determine who is a Communist. Foreign policy generally tends to be to the right of domestic policy; the familiar accusation of Communism was unable to block the New Deal and the Fair Deal at home when popular feeling and democratic institutions overrode rightist propaganda in the press and communications generally. But in foreign policy, where popular feeling rarely registers, we often tend to regard with suspicion in Latin America regimes which are no more leftist than was F.D.R.'s. This is why countries like Chile, Uruguay, Costa Rica, Venezuela and Mexico – all non-Communist regimes – look with suspicion on our Dominican intervention. The sources on which the government depends in foreign policy decisions are all heavily weighted against the non-Communist reformer. Big business, the military, the intelligence apparatus and the Foreign Service tend to share the views of their opposite numbers in the countries with which we deal, and in Latin America these sectors of society are even farther right than in our own. To this influence must be added that of the Catholic Church. Cardinal Spellman – himself a major factor in U.S. foreign policy – was long a pillar of both the Diem regime in South Vietnam and the Trujillo dictatorship in the Dominican Republic. If such forces decide who is Communist, then social reform in the hemisphere and elsewhere is indeed in trouble.

Here we come to a sharp difference between the Kennedy and Johnson administrations. The former was friendly to Bosch but Standard Oil of New Jersey was hostile to him, as was (to its shame) the A.F.L.–C.I.O. While our Ambassador, John Bartlow Martin, warned the Dominican military against a coup to unseat Bosch, his warnings were undercut by our Military Mission in the island, some of whose members agreed that Bosch was a Communist. The Catholic Church, which had opposed Bosch's election, was angered by the adoption of a secular Constitution. So, after seven months, the first freely elected Dominican regime in a generation was overthrown. Bosch was all we claimed we wanted: a truly democratic social reformer absolutely free from any taint of Communism, as his friends Betancourt of Venezuela and Figueres of Costa Rica and our own Norman Thomas were prepared to attest. I was in the Dominican Republic when Bosch was in power, and I was impressed by his inspiring eloquence, his devotion and his uncompromising civil libertarian principles. But for the military and big business and the C.I.A. to be a genuine liberal was by definition to be 'soft on Communism'. Kennedy, to his credit, shut off all aid to the new military regime after Bosch was overthrown and refused to recognize it. Only the military dictatorships of Spain, Portugal, Formosa and Honduras extended recognition in the month after the coup, while the U.S. held off. But Johnson, soon after Kennedy's assassination, reversed that policy. Johnson, with Tom Mann, swung away from the social reform emphasis of the Alliance for Progress and towards military dictatorships submissive to American business interests –

like Brazil's which Rusk hailed as a victory for democracy and constitutional government!

There is no country for which U.S. intervention has a grimmer meaning than the Dominican Republic. The long and bloody night of the Trujillo dictatorship was ushered in by a similar U.S. Marine occupation. That Caribbean Nero was himself trained by the Marines, later armed by U.S. military aid, and praised by our Eastlands and Ellenders and McCormacks during the terrible years he imposed upon his people. The cry of Communism is familiar to them; for thirty years every opponent of the Benefactor was labelled a Communist. 'I beg President Johnson and the American people,' Mrs Juan Bosch, herself a Cuban aristocrat, said at an anguished press conference here, 'to understand that we are your friends. We are not "rebels". We are democrats fighting to *regain* the liberties which were stolen from us by General Wessin. We need your help and understanding, not your paratroopers ... not your bullets.' Never was the Red Menace more fraudulently trotted out than against Bosch and his supporters. Every American who knows what such interventions have cost the Latins in the past must blush with shame over Johnson's revival of gunboat diplomacy.

10 May 1965, vol. 8, no. 18

A Man the Whole World Has Begun to Distrust

After a year and a half with Lyndon Johnson as President, one thing can be said about him with certainty. It is dangerous to trust anything he says. His favourite stance on the platform is that of a country preacher, brimful of Gospel. Events have shown that beneath his corny brand of idealism is a hard-boiled operator who believes in force. The difference between him and Goldwater is that the latter candidly espoused what the former covertly practises. The Arizonian lost because he was more honest and less clever. But there is a limit to cleverness, and Johnson has about reached the limit.

The good will built up by Kennedy for our country in every

section of the world except East Asia has been dissipated by his successor. It is no exaggeration to say that Johnson is today distrusted everywhere: in Latin America, where he has destroyed the hopes aroused by the Alliance for Progress; in Western Europe, where he is regarded as impulsive and high-handed; in India, where he affronted Shastri by cancelling his visit rather than risk hearing an Asian dissent on our Vietnamese war; and in Eastern Europe, where the Russians had expected a continuation of the *detente* begun under Kennedy and the satellites had hoped for a continued thaw in the Cold War as their one sure means of liberation. Rarely has one man blasted so many hopes so quickly.

In Mr Johnson's recent V.E. day address to Europe, he touched on 'the dramatic contrast between this twenty years and the twenty years which followed World War I' and said that on 11 November 1938 'Munich was just six weeks old and war less than a year away.' Perhaps he spoke too quickly. Many of his listeners must have wondered whether a general war might not again be only another year away. Others must have recalled that it was behind the Pied Piper banner of anti-Communism that the Japanese began their incursions into China in the thirties and the Germans their mobilization for their second attempt in a generation to rule the world. The League of Nations was destroyed in the process as the United Nations is being destroyed by our own policy of unilateral military intervention. Humanity has long feared that some day a reckless man would have his finger on the H-bomb. Johnson has himself to blame if people are beginning to fear that maybe he is that man.

In a flurry of recent speeches and press conferences, Mr Johnson has shown himself on the defensive. He is finding his critics much less ready than they were in the campaign to be taken in by sweet talk. He has tried first of all to counteract the widespread resentment in the press corps and in the colleges over his inability to take criticism and his effort to stifle independent reporting and foreign policy debate. He is trying to sound like Jefferson in public while he sounds more like McCarthy in private. He told an entourage of reporters at the

White House recently that he knew that Communists were behind the teach-ins. He said he had instructed J. Edgar Hoover to root them out. 'How rare is the land and extraordinary the people,' he said at the National Cathedral school, 31 May, 'who freely allow, and encourage as I have on many occasions, citizens to debate their nation's policies in time of danger.' But after so warmly patting himself on the back, he refused to answer at press conference next day when asked whether this meant that he approved 'university teach-in techniques'. Even a pretended magnanimity is beyond him. The real Lyndon Johnson is reflected in *U.S. News and World Report* (7 June) which says. 'The White House is known to be concerned about the number of extreme "left-wingers" getting across their views in newspapers and on television and adding to U.S. troubles.' This will be news even to moderate 'left-wingers' accustomed to being sealed off from access to major communication media. Apparently any criticism is regarded in the White House as 'extreme' left-wing.

The teach-in on the campuses has been paralleled by something which might be described as a stall-in in the Organization of American States. Here again Mr Johnson is on the defensive, and trying to hide the truth about our isolation in the hemisphere. A long-winded filibuster style reply at press conference was an attempt to hide the political bankruptcy of his Dominican policy. Even as he was talking he was encountering great difficulty in getting the O.A.S. to send an *ad hoc* advisory committee to Santo Domingo. The revealing blow was when Gonzalo Facio, the Costa Rican Ambassador to the O.A.S. and the only democratic representative suggested for this three-man body, declined to serve on it. He said he could not serve because of his country's policies against military dictatorship and military participation in politics. The O.A.S. meetings, characteristically, are held behind closed doors but Facio made a public statement (*Washington Star,* 1 June). When the three-man mission was finally approved after a debate which lasted into the morning hours, the Ambassador of the rightist military dictatorship in El Salvador had to be substituted for Costa Rica. The other two members will be the U.S. and the Brazilian military dictatorship. The biggest and most democratic regimes in the hemisphere either voted 'no' (Uruguay and Mexico) or abstained (Argentina, Venezuela and Chile).

Mr Johnson said at press conference that the other countries in the hemisphere had long ago declared Communism incompatible with the Inter-American system. This does not mean they agreed that the U.S. Marines could march in whenever and wherever we thought a government leaned too far left. Just how far offbase we are in Santo Domingo is indicated by the fact that two well-known anti-Communist Latin American experts, both violently anti-Castro, have attacked Johnson's Red scare excuse for intervening in the Dominican Republic: Theodore Draper in the 24 May issue of the *New Leader* and Robert J. Alexander in the 20 May issue of *New America*, organ of the Socialist Party. The Administration's Dominican intervention was not made to look less silly by Secretary Rusk's defence of it at press conference, 26 May. 'There was a time,' Mr Rusk said, to demonstrate the power of a handful, 'when Hitler sat in a beer hall in Munich with seven people.' The Washington correspondent of *The* (London) *Times* (27 May) commented tartly, 'Apparently, however, tens of thousands of American troops are not to be deployed whenever eight suspicious men gather together over glasses of beer.'

What we found most repulsive in the press conference was Mr Johnson's unctuous call for plastic surgeons to go to Vietnam. An easier way to meet that need would be to stop dropping napalm on its people.

7 June 1965, vol. 13, no. 22

So What's a Little Isaiah between Friends?

The Nixon inaugural must have set a record for the number of invocations. We counted four before Nixon took the oath and one afterwards. Indeed it might be said there were six, for Nixon's own inaugural address was in the same genre, so much so that at one moment when our attention wandered we thought Billy Graham had been elected President. From Nixon's first reference to 'the majesty of this moment' to that peroration in which he urged us to build a 'cathedral of the spirit' we realized we were hearing a Golden Treasury of the pulpit's most venerable purple phrases. The ministry lost what the country has gained.

Isaiah is our favourite prophet. Ordinarily we would have been pleased when Nixon let it be known that he would take the oath of office on a Bible with its pages open to Isaiah. But we could not forget that Johnson – who could also sound like Billy Graham – started out by leaning heavily on Isaiah, too. His favourite quotation, particularly in his campaign against Goldwater, was Isaiah's 'come let us reason together' but it fell into disuse after he began bombing North Vietnam.

Nixon chose that page of Isaiah in which the prophet spoke of beating swords into ploughshares. This would be heartening if Nixon's speeches on the need for bigger arms spending during the campaign, and his choice for Secretary of Defence, did not seem to suggest that we might have to beat ploughshares into swords. Melvin Laird hasn't been spending his years on the House Appropriations defence subcommittee trying to sell the armed services on Isaiah. Laird has written about a Strategy Gap. Nixon has spoken about a Security Gap, a Submarine Gap and an Armament Research Gap. Perhaps it would be safest to put this Isaiah incident down to a Rhetoric Gap, like the Gospel Gap which enables Billy Graham to denounce materialism – as he did at the inaugural – while remaining a favourite spiritual back-scratcher of the pious rich.

We would be more impressed with the peaceful sentiments expressed in the Nixon inaugural if they had not become standard fare. Kennedy and Johnson, too, spoke evangelically in their inaugurals of the terrible power of the new weaponry, the need for peace and for diversion of resources to human need. Then they added a 'but' about remaining strong, and this – if strength can be measured in more arms – was serious. 'Let us cooperate,' Nixon said, 'to reduce the burden of arms ... But to all those who would be tempted by weakness, let us leave no doubt that we will be as strong as we need to be ...' Kennedy, too, made the same pledge and then in almost the same words added, 'We dare not tempt them with weakness.' Kennedy proceeded to step up the arms race and Nixon is pledged to do the same. Nixon announces an era of negotiation as Johnson promised 'we will be unceasing in the search for peace.' In less than two months he was bombing North Vietnam. Henry Cabot Lodge was then his special adviser and soon to be Ambassador in Saigon as he will now be Nixon's at the Paris talks. Though the objective circumstances have changed, the parallels are not reassuring.

Our Presidents at their inaugurals have all come to sound like card-carrying members of the Fellowship for Reconciliation. It's easier to make war when you talk peace. They make us the dupes of our hopes, as the newspaper headlines the morning after inaugural about Nixon's 'sacred commitment' attest. Johnson, too, snowed the country with a similar performance when he went up on Capitol Hill for a last boast-in and sob-in among his old cronies, those aged pygmies in aspic, preserved from reality by the gelatinous mutual flatteries which fill the Congressional Record. They are all *g-r-e-a-t* statesmen, like Lyndon and Sam and Gerry and what's-his-name. The surprise was not the last performance of Johnson-playing-Lionel-Barrymore-playing-Lyndon but the fact that he got away with it; the press by and large acted like sob-sisters in the 1890s covering a society ball to help the poor. Amid the sniffles no one was so uncouth as to peep into Johnson's fantastic exaggerations, like his claim to be spending $68 billion 'for such things as health and education' the next fiscal year. More than $35 billion of this is normal expenditure from social security, where the government takes in more from the lower brackets than it pays out and the munificence is attested by Johnson's proposal to raise the minimum from $55 to $80 *a month*, just enough to keep a beneficiary from dying too visibly.

Johnson, too, talked of peace but it will be years before we stop paying all the costs – fiscal and social – of his Vietnam war. He said it was 'imperative . . . to resist inflation'. But it wasn't imperative enough for him to impose taxes on the profits his war inflation created in the upper brackets. The poor and the black will now pay with unemployment to fight that inflation, as they paid disproportionately with their lives to fight this war. He, too, talked of the need 'to scale down the level of arms among the superpowers' so that 'mankind' could 'view the future without fear and great apprehension'. But he may have set off a new spiral when he approved the 'thin' anti-ballistic missile. And new arms for a fantastically overarmed nation take first priority in his final budget.

In the masterly flim-flam of budgetary accounting, the new estimates gloss over the fact that the war this year will cost $3 billion more than we were told before. A $3.4 billion decline is promised next year (largely due to the saving on planes and explosives if we continue to stop bombing the North). *But* the savings are already whisked away in a $4 billion increase in arms expenditures in the year beginning 1 July. Total military spending will be $81.5 billion, nosing past the peak of the Second World War – how's that for Isaiah!

The poverty programme remains just short of $2 billion but arms research and development will go up $850 million to a total of $5.6 billion, including work on such new goodies as missiles which can be hidden on the ocean floor. There's not a gap Nixon mentioned that the Johnson military budget does not fill – a 'new generation' of missiles (how beautifully they breed!) with multiple warheads, five squadrons of new FB 111 bombers (to keep Fort Worth and General Dynamics prosperous), $2.4 billion to give the navy three fast new nuclear attack submarines, the quiet variety which won't disturb sleep in the ghettoes. There is more money for the air force's advanced bomber. Just to make sure we don't run out of new Vietnams there's three-quarters of a billion this year and a billion next for those overpriced C 5A carrier planes which can get troops fast to any new trouble spot and millions more for three of those Fast Deployment Logistics ships which will take the place of foreign bases and have heavy equipment ready for the troops when the C 5As get them there. Even a submissive and somnolent Congress several years running has turned down the D.P.L.s as an engraved invitation to more trouble but Johnson's budget asks Congress to come and reason together with him again about the item.

No wonder this is a smooth transition. It's practically one continuous performance, and better than ever for the Pentagon. So what's a little Isaiah between friends?

Part Four:
Beyond the
Western World

1: China and
South-East Asia

Was the War No Surprise to Chiang Kai-shek?

The Senate report on McCarthy makes it possible to throw new light on one of the most tantalizing episodes in the Korean War. This concerns the burst of speculation in soybeans on the eve of the war. In touching on McCarthy's own successful flier in soybeans later that same year, the report asks whether he had confidential information 'with respect to the trend of the soybean futures market' and adds an intriguing parenthesis. It says 'Just prior to the transaction in question, the Commodity Exchange Authority of the Department of Agriculture conducted an investigation of alleged soybean market manipulation involving, among others, a number of Chinese traders.'

The report on McCarthy is not too intrepid a document. It was not surprising, on inquiry at the Department of Agriculture, to discover that the Senate Subcommittee on Privileges and Elections had omitted from the report its own biggest news 'scoop' in the soybean story. Inquiry at the Department turned up (1) the full text of a report on its investigation into soybean speculation and (2) a list of the Chinese who took part in this trading. The original report, issued on 10 August 1950, passed almost unnoticed at the time outside grain publications. It withheld the names of the Chinese speculators. But in the file of the Agriculture Department's later press releases on the subject there turned up a statement of last 26 November saying that the Senate Subcommittee on Privileges and Elections had asked for the names and addresses of the Chinese traders 'referred to, but not identified' in the original report. Attached was a list of names, with their holdings in soybean futures when the Korean war began.

The Department declined to identify the names further, but

one of the largest speculators on the list turned out to be T. V. Soong's younger brother, T. L. Soong. 'T.V.' is, of course, Chiang Kai-shek's brother-in-law. One of the smaller speculators was Nationalist China's executive director on the board of the International Bank for Reconstruction and Development. These directors are appointees of the governments they represent. Though such names confirm what had hitherto only been suspected – that 'insiders' close to Chiang and his government played a prominent part in the speculation – the Senate committee did not even mention its discovery.

If the Korean war was a surprise attack, how is it that Chinese close to Chiang began to speculate in soybeans in the weeks before the fighting broke out? The question was first raised by the *Monthly Review* in its issue of October 1951. A 'Footnote to Korea' by the editors, Leo Huberman and Paul Sweezy, called attention to the unsuccessful effort of the late Senator McMahon during the MacArthur hearings to elicit information from Secretary of State Acheson on reports that certain Chinese had cornered the American soybean market at the time the Korean war began. The 'Footnote' put that obscure colloquy into new and startling light by coupling it with an item published two months later, on 16 August 1951, on the financial page of the *New York Herald Tribune*. This item said that some fifty Chinese living in the United States and abroad had cleaned up $30,000,000 in speculative operations in soybeans 'just before' the war.

Just how extensive these operations were was not clear until now. The original Department of Agriculture study to which the McCarthy report calls attention shows that Secretary Acheson was perhaps less than candid in his answers to Senator McMahon. The Senator wanted to know whether Acheson had ever discussed with Secretary of Agriculture Brannan 'a corner that's supposed to have existed in the soybean market a year ago last June in the hands of certain Chinese in this country'. A 'year ago last June' was when the Korean war began. The casual listener would assume from the Acheson replies that the matter was of little importance and that little was known about it (p. 287, vol. 3, MacArthur hearings):

SECRETARY ACHESON: Yes, I have discussed it with him.
SENATOR MCMAHON: Is there anything that you can say at this time concerning the personalities who were engaged in that operation?
SECRETARY ACHESON: I don't know that I ever knew who the personalities involved were.

In the light of the information now turned up, this 'I don't know that I ever knew' seems superbly evasive. If the Secretary of State discussed the matter with Secretary of Agriculture Brannan, they must have considered it of more than routine importance. Brannan could hardly have failed to tell Acheson that a full investigation had been made by the Agriculture Department's Commodity Exchange Authority and that the names of all the participants were known, as the report of 10 August 1950 shows.

This neglected report begins to indicate the full dimensions of the skeleton the Secretary of State wished to keep securely closeted. The story the Department of Agriculture report unfolds begins several months before the Korean war. The war broke out on 25 June 1950. Four months earlier, the Commodity Exchange Authority of the U.S. Department of Agriculture began to receive 'a large number of complaints' from processors of soybeans in this country that the soybeans futures market had fallen 'so completely under the control of speculators' that it could no longer serve for legitimate hedging operations. One complainant pointed out that more soybeans were being traced on the Chicago market than all the other principal grain futures combined; another, that the sudden sharp rise in soybean prices 'is helping only the speculators as a large majority of the farmers have already disposed of their farm holdings'. The Commodity of Exchange Authority began to investigate and found 'very sizeable trading by persons with Chinese names, and in some cases with Hong Kong addresses'. Speculation in futures by Chinese is not unusual but 'no previous instance had been found', it said, 'in which Chinese held as large a proportion of the total open contracts in any commodity.'

The Commodity Exchange Authority wondered why the

Chicago Board of Trade reduced speculative margins on soybeans on 13 March 'from the already low level of 8.3 per cent to 6.1 per cent ... in the face of an active market'. In the four weeks which followed, the daily average volume of trading rose to 15 million bushels a day, as compared with 10 million daily in the preceding four weeks. Since few suspected that war was coming in the Far East, it was thought that Chinese Nationalist interests were trying to corner the market. On 7 August 1950, the *Chicago Journal of Commerce* carried a front-page item stating that the President of the Chicago Board of Trade had refuted previously published reports that a virtual corner of soybeans by 'Chinese Nationalist' interests had been instrumental in causing prices to soar from $2.20 to $2.45 a bushel. The refutation was made to look somewhat sickly when three days later the Commodity Exchange Authority issued its report on 'Speculation in Soybeans', the report from which the quotations here were taken. This showed that by 30 June 1950, fifty-six Chinese accounts held almost half of all open contracts for July futures on the long side of the market, i.e., of those playing for rise in price.

The inference is irresistible though not necessarily correct that inner Chinese Nationalist circles knew war was coming and cashed in on their knowledge. If this ugly inference is false, the Nationalists should be anxious for a Congressional investigation which would clear them of suspicion that a group of them made themselves a nice little profit of $30,000,000 on a war which had cost the American people and its allies heavily in lives and money. It may be, of course, that they had informers in Red China who tipped them off to a coming attack from North Korea. It may also be, as I indicated in my book, *The Hidden History of the Korean War*, that Chiang and Syngman Rhee provoked the attack from the North. It should not be forgotten that in this, as in any other unsolved crime, it is useful to begin by determining who benefited. The biggest beneficiary of the Korean war was Chiang Kai-shek. The war diverted the Chinese Reds from their plans to attack Formosa. It gave him a virtual American protectorate over Formosa, and an increased flow of American aid. The $30,000,000 in that perspective is small change, but an investigation into that small change might throw a flood of new light on the origin of a conflict which threatens to engulf the globe in the Third World War.

Now the U.N. Must Liberate the U.S.A.

With the signing of a truce in Korea, the main political task of the U.N. in a sense must be the liberation of the U.S.A. There can be no independent Korea until the United States has regained its own independence of all those forces symbolized and mobilized by the China lobby. It will be difficult to unify Korea until some progress has been made in unifying the United States. More serious than the 38th Parallel across Korea is the wall of paranoid suspicion crypto-Fascist forces here have been erecting around and across the United States, dividing Americans from each other and the rest of the world.

The Korean war would have been avoided if the U.N. had resisted pressure from Syngman Rhee and John Foster Dulles for the creation of a separate state in South Korea. The war with China might have been avoided if the U.N. in the winter of 1949–50 had rescued Acheson and Truman from imprisonment by the China lobby and insisted on the admission of Communist China to the U.N. The task now is harder, the danger greater. The problem now is to avoid the Third World War. The principal beneficiaries of the Korean war, Syngman Rhee and Chiang Kai-shek, are determined to see it resumed on a larger scale than ever, for if the truce becomes a peace neither can survive as a political force. In a peaceful world, recognition of Communist China is inevitable. It took martial law to ensure Rhee's re-election as President last year; he cannot hope to survive in a unified Korea, unless indeed it is unified for him by American arms and his government is given the means to fasten the same kind of police state on North Korea that Rhee rules in the South.

The key to a settlement in the East is unification of Korea, as the key to settlement in Europe is the unification of Germany but in both areas neither of the two contending great powers has been willing to let go of its own satellite share for fear the other's bloc might get the whole of it. Both have been agreed on unification in principle but both in practice had appended conditions unacceptable to the other. One way out for the U.S. would be to offer to withdraw from Korea altogether and hand over the problem of unification to the neutral Asian powers, if the Russians and Chinese would do the same. Such a move would create much good will for the U.S. and wipe out entirely the ugly effect of the 'let Asians fight Asians' slogan, which translated itself too easily into using colonial coloured peoples as cannon fodder against those who had won their independence. An offer of the kind suggested here would imply a sort of Monroe Doctrine for Asia and create the cement necessary to hold the area together as an independent bloc between the powers. But such bold and creative diplomacy seems to be made impossible by the obsessions of containment, and the political comfort of a mulishly inert diplomacy.

Now if ever is the time for the smaller powers to use their U.N. leverage creatively. They have much to learn from the Korean war. Korea was a terrible object lesson for all countries and areas which allow themselves to be divided between the American and the Russian power. The war showed that the American people, though instinctively kind and generous in dealing with distress, may easily be doped and duped by military leadership into permitting the kind of unnecessary havoc our air force wreaked in many parts of Korea. The war also showed that the American Air Force is infested with publicity men who are among the world's biggest liars; their inflated figures and inflammatory reporting are a menace. The war demonstrated again the delusion of victory by airpower and firepower, the ability of colonial coloured peoples to handle jet planes and anti-aircraft radar effectively, the tremendous military power of the new China, and the willingness of the Chinese and the Russians to swallow one provocation after another in their desire for peace.

In this picture, the American people seem a passive mass. The military have been able to drag out the truce talks by one phoney issue after another for many months without popular protest in this country. The desire for peace is there, but the thought-control drive has succeeded in stifling the forces and organizations which would have given it expression. The fear that peace might mean loss of jobs and business has been a potent factor, too, affecting workers as much as their employers. Militant rightist minorities easily sway this sheep-like mass, and cut down sharply the political and diplomatic manoeuvrability of the Eisenhower Administration. The new President promised peace in Korea and has fulfilled his promise, but the achievement of a precarious truce seems to have just about exhausted the political potency of the new Administration. Eisenhower's own desire for peace is a positive factor, but as against this the promise to walk out of a political conference after ninety days gives tremendous power for evil to Rhee and the American military men behind him.

Were there a peace move left in this country, two of its main objectives in the crucial six months ahead would be clear. One would be to restore greater political freedom in South Korea so that peace forces there could provide some check on Syngman Rhee. The other would be to focus the spotlight on the coming Rhee–Dulles talks. These two Catos were among the chief architects of the war. The key points to watch are the conditions to which Rhee will try to commit the United States for unification of Korea. His own conditions require unconditional surrender, and that way lies resumption of the war.

1 August 1953, vol. 1, no. 28

On Indo-China

'A severe winter, with destitute men, women and children frozen to death in Paris, has crystallized public opinion into a great outcry to end the colonial war in Indo-China. The press and everyone I have spoken to are indignant that the French government has spent seven billion dollars in fighting this war but has failed to build housing for the growing population of Paris.' So wrote Henry Wales from Paris last Wednesday in that well-known Midwestern organ of pacifism and radicalism, the *Chicago Tribune*.

Here in Washington, when three senior Southern Democrats with the committee positions and prestige of Senators Stennis (Miss.), Byrd (Va) and George (Georgia) attack the Administration for sending air force mechanics to Indo-China, a major political battle is impending.

During the debate in the Senate last Tuesday, the two most important points made by the Democratic opposition went generally unreported. Stennis said there were Filipino, Korean and Japanese mechanics qualified to service these planes, that their use 'was considered, but . . . for one reason or another, the idea was rejected and the plan to use U.S. Air Force mechanics was adopted'. Stennis also said he had seen French mechanics repairing jet engines and jet planes at our bases in France and asked why they could not have been sent instead.

What the Democrats scent is a deliberate effort to involve the U.S., first through 'token' forces of mechanics and then with troops. As to this, Mansfield (D., Mont.) who knows the Far Eastern situation intimately told the Senate the French and the Associated States already had 400,000 men as against Ho Chi-Minh's 300,000. 'What good would it do,' Mansfield asked, 'to send any more men from outside . . . when there is a superiority not only in manpower but in equipment as well?'

Eisenhower at press conference on Wednesday and Wilson the day before expressed the views of top Administration officials fighting a rearguard action against pressure from the military for intervention. The China lobby sees Indo-China as its opportunity and Admiral Radford, chairman of the Joint Chiefs of Staff, is ready with some of his favourite recipes including a blockade of the China coast, use of Chinese Nationalist forces in Indo-China and even active intervention by U.S. air and naval units. (Remember how it was said that air and naval support would be enough to end the Korean war?)

One little-noticed remark by Wilson at his press conference may reflect an argument being used by the military to belittle the risk of Chinese intervention. The Secretary of Defence said the terrain and logistic situation was such that large-scale Chinese intervention was impossible. (This also recalls some other expert advice on Korea.)

15 February 1954, vol. 2, no. 4

Why the Chinese 7th Fleet is in Long Island Sound

China's first line of defence is on Long Island. We are honour bound to support on that island the only legitimate American government, that of Herbert Hoover, who was forced from the mainland by Democratic subversion in 1932.

Staten Island admittedly is in a different category. Our Congress, in authorizing war at any time in defence of Long Island, wisely left it to the discretion of the President to determine at the time of any attack whether it was also in our interest to defend Staten Island and Martha's Vineyard.

Since that declaration by Congress both offshore islands have become more important to the defence of Long Island and to Mr Hoover's hope of reconquering the mainland where his picture is said to be displayed openly at the Banker's Club, the Union League and other popular rallying places.

Mr Hoover's Republicans have deployed about a third of their strength on Staten Island and Martha's Vineyard. From the former they have cut off almost all shipping into the Port of New York while the forces on Martha's Vineyard harass the Port of Boston.

The unfriendly nature of the Democratic regime has been demonstrated by its response to these developments. The Voice of America has been threatening Long Island. Staten Island has been bombarded from the mainland.

Wars have often occurred in the past because great powers failed to make clear the point at which they would fight. We have put the regime in Washington on notice that any attack on Long Island would be an attack on China.

At the same time we have no intention of making Washington's military planning easier by letting it know in advance what we will do if the Americans try to seize the offshore Islands. We are also going to keep them guessing as to whether

American aggression against Staten Island will bring massive atomic retaliation against New York. Some nervousness in other countries is we suppose natural but the free world may rest assured that all these questions will be answered in good time by our great leader, who is keeping in close touch with the situation from the Peking golf links.

In the process of determining its policy towards the United* States, China has taken into account the various statements and arguments advanced by proponents of extending diplomatic recognition to Washington. One of the most commonly advanced reasons for recognition is that reality must be 'recognized' and 170,000,000 people cannot be 'ignored'.

While superficially appealing, both statements themselves overlook the realities of the situation. Chinese policy is, of course, based on full appreciation of the fact that the American Democratic regime is currently in control of the mainland.

Our attitude towards the people of the United States remains what it historically has been, one of sympathetic understanding; our Confucian missionaries long laboured among them and are ready to return any time they overturn their present Godless and materialistic regime. It is an earnest of our enduring friendship that Long Island sits on the Security Council of the United Nations, wielding a veto as one of the five great powers of the earth.

Moreover, the People's Republic of China is convinced that the American Democratic regime does not represent the true will of the American people but the fruits of a conspiracy by Franklin D. Roosevelt and his successors; our intelligence agents, who watch events in the interior closely, tell us that guerrilla forces of the N.A.A.C.P. led by a Negro named Faubus have already seized control of Arkansas.

Thus our policy of withholding recognition is in actuality in the ultimate interests of the American people. China holds the view that democracy's rule in the United States is not permanent and that it one day will pass.

* Any resemblance between what follows and the wording of the U.S. policy statement on non-recognition of Communist China (9 August) is not purely coincidental.

By withholding recognition from Washington, and keeping our Embassy in Mr Hoover's splendid capital in Rockville Center, we hope to hasten that passing.

8 September 1958, vol. 6, no. 35

Putting the Spotlight on the Trouble Brewing over Cambodia

Cambodia is another of those far countries in which our military and intelligence agents do pretty much as they please. It is in such areas that wars can be hatched. We invite attention to it because trouble is brewing there now, and because to see Cambodia as it must appear from Peking is a useful mote-in-our-own-eye exercise.

Cambodia is one of the three independent countries created by the Geneva accords of 1954 which ended the war in French Indo-China. Cambodia has an ancient history and a curious present; its dominant political figure is Prince Norodom Sihanouk who gave up the throne to head a Popular Socialist Party and become Prime Minister. He is a shrewd man who has made neutralism pay by getting aid from China and Russia on the one hand and the U.S. and France on the other. The result of this competition, incidentally, is that our aid programme in Cambodia is said to be one of the best in Asia.

The U.S. under the direction of John Foster Dulles disliked the Geneva accords on Indo-China, declined to take part in the conference which ended that war, but pledged itself reluctantly not to upset the settlement. This pledge has not been honoured. For a long time we seem to have been giving covert encouragement to forces from neighbouring South Vietnam and Thailand which have been trying to overthrow Sihanouk's neutralist regime.

Early this year an attempt to overthrow Sihanouk was thwarted when Communist and Western embassies in the capital tipped the plot. But when *Realités Cambodgiennes* (a Cambodian French-language weekly available at the Library of Congress) asked the Prince (issue of 24 January) whether the

U.S. Embassy was among those which helped him, he replied 'Although our American friends have a very active and richly endowed intelligence service, with assured facilities in our neighbours of the West and East [i.e. Thailand and South Vietnam] they did not think it their duty to inform us, thus allowing many of our compatriots to doubt their impartiality.'

On 26 February Prince Sihanouk called in all the ambassadors in his capital and laid before them the evidence that this plot was financed and armed from South Vietnam, a U.S. satellite. On 2 March the Ambassador of South Vietnam was recalled on the request of the Cambodian government. Then last 31 August there was an attempt to assassinate the King and Queen of Cambodia with a bomb which killed Prince Norodom Vakrivan, assistant director of the royal household. The government charged that this, too, was 'plotted from abroad'.

In Cambodia, as in Laos and Vietnam, the Geneva accord set up an International Commission for Observation and Control made up of a Polish, a Canadian and an Indian member, the latter being the neutral chairman. The existence of this commission in Cambodia is of some protection to its neutral government. Now the Soviet government in a note to the British government (these two provided the co-chairmen who still preside over the Geneva settlement) accuses the latter of trying to liquidate the commission in Cambodia. Moscow based its note on a British proposal passed on to it by the Cambodian government. The lame British reply of 4 October was to deny that it proposed the dissolution of the commission but admit that it suggested the commission adjourn, subject to recall. This is what happened to the commission in Laos last year, and it has proved impossible to recall it.

As seen from Peking, these manoeuvres must appear a series of attempts to upset a peaceful settlement in neighbouring Indo-China and to end a successful experiment in peaceful coexistence. Under the circumstances it could not have been easy for Khrushchev to make Mao Tse-tung believe that, nevertheless, our President wants peace.

12 October 1959, vol. 7, no. 38

Never Were So Many Warnings Ignored as in Laos

At a gay reception given the new Congress by the Women's National Press Club here last night, Chairman Fulbright of the Senate Foreign Relations Committee seems to have been alone in taking a gloomy view of the Laotian crisis.* 'There may be a war over Laos,' he told an impromptu interviewer. 'Once again they may call us the War Party. Nobody will remember that we Democrats inherited this situation in Asia.' Few also will remember that the Democrats and the country had ample warning that something was rotten in the state of Laos. In 1958 the waste and corruption which marked our aid programme in Laos were disclosed by the General Accounting Office, publicized in the *Wall Street Journal*, *Reader's Digest* and the *Reporter*. The Porter Hardy subcommittee of House Government Operations took 984 pages of testimony on the Laotian situation in the spring of 1959 and published a scathing report on the role played by our Ambassador J. Graham Parsons in presiding complacently from 1955 to 1957 over what was probably the most corrupt of all U.S. aid operations and in railroading out of the country for 'nervous disorder' a General Accounting Office auditor who came 'close to discovering the truth' about the net of bribery and perjury which shielded the waste of millions there. Yet Fulbright's Senate committee remained as unaware of these revelations in the press and on the other side of the Capitol as if they were occurring on the moon. His Foreign Relations committee unanimously endorsed Parsons, 26 May 1959 for promotion to Assistant Secretary of State for Far Eastern Affairs, a post in which he was confirmed by the Senate without discussion, and from which he has been helping in the current crisis to shape the policies pushing us towards direct military intervention in Laos.

* Other somewhat less than clairvoyant comments collected by Dorothy McCardle for the *Washington Post*: Adlai Stevenson's 'Laos is serious because the loss of any territory to the Communists is serious' and Hubert Humphrey's 'Laos is no more important than any other place in the world. Latin America has top priority. As a matter of fact we have to deal with totalitarianism all across the board.'

The Laotian crisis illustrates how ineffectively democratic controls operate in overseeing our vast American empire and in checking on the activities of the obscure satraps who determine its destinies. It is one episode in a story of costly misjudgement. We spent $2,300,000,000 helping France carry on the eight years of futile jungle war by which she tried to keep control of Indo-China. When the French early in 1954 began to talk wearily of peace, Dulles, Nixon and Radford tried unsuccessfully to drum up support for U.S. military involvement. When peace was made in Geneva in July of that year, Dulles refused to attend the conference and set himself to undercut the settlement. We used our influence to prevent the agreed-upon elections which were supposed to unite Vietnam in July 1956 and we have done all in our power – and spent another $300,000,000 – to block fulfilment of the Geneva agreement in Laos. This called for reunification of the country by free elections under the supervision of a tripartite international commission (Canada, India and Poland) and the establishment of a coalition government with the Pathet Lao who controlled two north-eastern provinces adjoining Communist China and North Vietnam. The neutralist Prince Souvanna Phouma succeeded over our objections in holding these elections in 1958 but within a few days after the International Commission left Laos, there was a rightist coup, the leaders of the Pathet Lao were thrown in jail, an army dictatorship was brought into power and the civil war resumed. In 1959 the Laotian rightists did their best to bring about U.S. military involvement with stories about invasions from China and North Vietnam which proved untrue. In August of last year a paratroop battalion under Captain Kong Le overthrew the rightists, restored Souvanna Phouma to power and promised investigation of the military and civilian leaders 'who have been making huge profits' out of the instability in Laos.

Mr Parsons was soon back in Laos last fall trying to upset the new government. According to disclosures made by Prime Minister Nehru at a press conference in October, Parsons was sent to Vientiane by the State Department to threaten Prince Souvanna Phouma with loss of American aid if he did not 'cease his attempts to negotiate with the Communist Pathet Lao movement and end all contact with Captain Kong Le', which he refused to do, threatening in turn to ask the Soviet Union for aid if U.S. aid were withdrawn. The London *Economist* (29 October) in reporting these revelations by Nehru commented that 'the policy of grading economic aid according to the anti-Communist credentials of recipient governments' went back to 'Mr Dulles's dictum that "neutralism is immoral" ' and pointed out that this policy had been shown to be not only obsolete but 'counter-productive'. 'Domestic Communism,' it said, 'has been far weaker in neighbouring Cambodia, which has been determinedly neutralist since independence and which draws aid from all sides, than in Laos, where a succession of anti-Communist governments have paid their soldiers and civil servants out of the American taxpayer's pocket.'

It is American policy which has strengthened the Leftists in Laos. The Porter Hardy report in June 1959 showed that the State Department in deciding to support a huge Laotian army 'despite contrary recommendations by the Joint Chiefs of Staff' had so flooded the country with money as to set off a disastrous inflation which doubled the cost of living from 1953 to 1958 and by enriching a handful of Vientiane merchants and officials 'tended to lend credence to the Communist allegation that the Royal Lao government was "corrupt" and "indifferent" to the needs of the people'. Our policies by cynically supporting anti-parliamentary military coups when it served our purposes has also discredited democracy in the eyes of Laotian intellectuals. More recently we pushed Prince Souvanna Phouma into dependence on Moscow by supplying the rightist military forces against him directly and through Thailand with tanks and artillery. This, and the Thailand economic blockade against Vientiane, led Phouma before his recent fall to ask the Soviets for gasoline and military supplies. These supply flights through Hanoi in North Vietnam to what was then clearly the legitimate government of Laos now figure in the proof unveiled at the State Department of outside aid. Prince Phouma fled from the U.S.-supported rebels on 9 December. The worsening situation since amply confirms the *Economist*'s comment (24 December) that it would have been better if Prince Phouma had 'been allowed to pursue his patient task of conciliation, unhampered by an American-aided right-wing rebellion'.

Nothing illustrates more vividly the bankruptcy of our policy in Laos than the repeatedly demonstrated weakness of the army we have so generously supported there. It is the highest paid army in Asia and variously estimated (the canny Laotians have never let us know the exact numbers, perhaps lest we check on how much the military payroll is diverted into the pockets of a few leaders) at from 23,000 to 30,000. Yet it has never been able to stand up against handfuls of guerrillas and even a few determined battalions like those mustered by Captain Kong Le. We can only hope that British, French, Indian and Japanese objections will now keep us from plunging into war in a trackless mountainous jungle land where our superior weapons will count for little, but where we may easily become involved in a broader conflict with neighbouring North Vietnam and then China. The path to peace lies in reconvening the international supervisory commission and in return to the principles of the 1954 Geneva accords.

9 January 1961, vol. 9, no. 1

Hardly Setting an Example of Adherence to World Law

The Kennedy Administration is not being at all candid about the dispatch of troops to Thailand. It has sought to create the impression that the troops were sent in response to an appeal from Thailand for protection from a threat of aggression, and that action was taken in accord with the South-East Asia Treaty Organization (S.E.A.T.O.) and the Charter of the United Nations. Our official letter of notification to the United Nations dated 15 May said U.S. military forces were being sent to Thailand 'in response to a request by the government of Thailand ... which now faces a threat of Communist aggression'. This communication was signed not by Adlai Stevenson but by his deputy, Charles W. Yost. It may be that after the Cuban affair Mr Stevenson has grown reluctant to put his signature to these little white prevarications. There has been no sign of any Pathet Lao advance towards the Thai border since the Royal Lao troops fled from Nam Tha. There is no appeal on the record from Thailand for U.S. troops.

When Mr Kennedy at press conference 18 May was asked to explain his 'rather swift action to move American troops into Thailand', he replied that 'in our desire to stabilize the situation we got in touch with the Government [of Thailand] which was already in touch with us, and worked out the proposed course of action.' This wording is curiously circuitous. If Thailand had appealed for U.S. troops, it would have been easy to say so. The official troop announcement from the White House two days earlier also failed to say there had been an appeal from Bangkok for aid. It said the action was taken following 'joint consideration' by the two governments. Again the phrasing was odd. There is reason to suspect that our government, rather than the Thai, initiated this 'consideration', that our government rather than Thailand's has been pressing other members of S.E.A.T.O. to send token forces. This, I believe, explains the evasive replies given by the State Department all last week when asked to clear up these matters. The key to Thai reluctance may be found in a dispatch to the London *Daily Telegraph*, 6 May, from its correspondent in Saigon who reported that the Thais had asked the U.S. to deploy its troops 'well outside the capital, Bangkok' in order 'to avoid giving the impression that the country, which has never been under white colonial rule, has come under alien occupation'.

The return of white combat troops to the mainland of Asia is not a popular move. The struggle against colonialism is too recent. This is true not only of neutralist but of independent anti-Communist states. S.E.A.T.O. has itself been suspect from the beginning, as primarily an alliance of white imperial powers. Most of the peoples it purported to protect declined to join. India, Burma, Ceylon and Indonesia turned down John Foster Dulles's invitation to the organizing meeting in Manila in September 1954; Malaya, which became independent since, refused to become a signatory. Nehru saw the Dulles plan as 'likely to change the whole trend towards peace that the Geneva conference has created by its decisions on Indo-China'. Pakistan, the Philippines and Thailand were the only Asian countries to join the U.S., Britain, France, Australia and New Zealand in forming the pact. The same queasy feelings have made themselves apparent in Asia in the wake of U.S. action. Japan objected to the sending of troops from her territory as a violation of her defence agreement with the U.S. The Prime Minister of Malaya, 20 May, announced that his government would not agree to permit British Commonwealth troops stationed in Singapore to be sent to Thailand. Neither Pakistan nor the Philippines have responded to our request for token contingents. Lyndon Johnson was warned by the Filipinos during last year's uproar over Laos not to send U.S. combat troops.

In the cynical atmosphere of Washington, where the troop movements are dismissed light-heartedly as a means of containing the Republicans before the next Congressional elections, little attention is paid to such wider considerations. It is a dangerous myopia that overlooks the instinctive reactions of Asia's vast millions. The action is not even in accordance with the pact we fathered. When Mr Kennedy was asked at his 18 May press conference what was 'the legal basis for our sending troops into Thailand' he replied 'the actual legal basis was to put us in position to fulfil our obligations under the S.E.A.T.O. treaty'. This was disingenuous. The treaty requires unanimous agreement for armed resistance to aggression, consultation in the event of any other threat to 'the inviolability or integrity' of any state covered by its guarantees. We acted first and consulted afterwards. We sent in troops and then having created a fait-accompli put pressure on the other members to make it look legal by adding token troops of their own. The pact was supposed to be a joint venture to protect the stability of South-East Asia. Suppose some other member thought the sending of U.S. combat troops to Thailand threatened to upset that stability by provoking similar movements by China? Our unilateral action was hardly in accordance with the treaty, as it was hardly in accordance with the U.N. Charter. If there was a threat to the peace, the charter should have been invoked. Our obligations to the U.N. were not fulfilled by sending it a little chit after the event saying (as did our note of 15 May), 'Consistent with the policy of the United States to keep the United Nations fully informed as to events affecting the maintenance of international peace and security in South-East Asia, I am informing you of the President's action.' What does the Secretary General reply to that! 'Thanks a million, and please let us know if you drop any A-bombs . . .'? This wilful disregard of charter and treaty hardly accords with all those fine speeches we make about world law.

What if China were to send combat troops into Mexico as a warning to the U.S. to keep hands off Cuba, would we accept this as a purely defensive move intended to maintain peace in accordance with the U.N. Charter? Or would we suspect China was using Cuba as an excuse to establish a base in North America?

28 May 1962, vol. 10, no. 21

Another Fact-Evading Mission

Five months after his inaugural, President Kennedy sent Vice-President Johnson to Vietnam on a fact-finding mission, where the latter hailed Diem as 'the Churchill of today'! Five months later Mr Kennedy sent General Taylor and Walt W. Rostow. Every few months, the White House sends another fact-finding team to Vietnam. Now it is sending Secretary McNamara and General Taylor. To the future historian, these missions will appear not as efforts to find the facts but to evade them. One fact is that a clique of rich Catholic mandarins can't go on ruling a Buddhist country. Another fact is that you can't go on pouring napalm on villages and poisons on crops, uprooting people and putting them in prison-like compounds, and expect to be liked. A third fact is that you can't stabilize South-East Asia without coming to terms with its biggest neighbour, China. Talk with Sihanouk in Cambodia, or de Gaulle in Paris, with a view to mediation – this is what the occasion calls for, not another frantic mission to Saigon.

30 September 1963, vol. 11, no. 19

A Crisis and a Turning Point Approaches in Vietnam

The war in Vietnam is being lost. Only a few weeks ago, Secretary McNamara and General Taylor reported on their return from Saigon that 'the major part' of our military role there could be 'completed by the end of 1965'. Now Hanson W. Baldwin, our most respected military expert, writes (*New York Times*, 7 December) that 'unless public support in the U.S. and among its allies can be maintained *during years of frustration*, there is no possibility of victory'. The italics are ours. President Johnson at his first meeting with the press that same day announced that Secretary McNamara is going back to Vietnam on another tour of inspection. It begins to look as if the Secretary of Defense has become a commuter between Washington and Saigon.

It is clear that we are heading for a new crisis in South Vietnam; rebel attacks are mounting in size and frequency; the loss of arms to them is growing. At the same time Cambodia has formally asked Britain and the Soviet Union as co-chairmen of the 1954 Geneva Conference on Indo-China to reconvene it. In August of last year, when Cambodia asked the Geneva conferees to reassemble and guarantee its neutrality, President Kennedy shied away from the idea. But this time the attitude of the American government seems to have changed. When the Foreign Minister of Cambodia was here to attend the President's funeral, he spoke with Under-Secretary of State Harriman and was assured that we would not place obstacles in the way of reconvening the conference for this purpose. The first Geneva Conference met, it will be recalled, to end the Korean war, and then went on to end the first Indo-Chinese war as well. The new session could become a vehicle for the peaceful ending of the war in South Vietnam too. We are approaching a turning point, either to risk widening the conflict by intervening with our own combat troops, or settling the war at the conference table.

Prince Sihanouk of Cambodia indicated these wider possibilities when he called for an independent South Vietnam linked in a neutral confederation with Cambodia. 'The reunification of Vietnam is the end to be attained but it is for the moment premature if not impossible, as responsible leaders of North Vietnam have admitted to me,' said Prince Sihanouk (Agence France-Presse, *Le Monde*, 4 December), adding that he thought 'the Communist camp would content itself with a South Vietnam completely neutral, as is Cambodia.' An article in the *Peking Review* (22 November) confirms this view. China would like new trade ties with the West to replace the broken trade ties with the Soviet Union. Peace in South Vietnam would remove a major obstacle to such relations. In South Vietnam itself the National Liberation Front has made clear in a clandestine interview (*Le Monde*, 24 August) that it did not wish to 'exchange one dictatorship for another'. A democratic South Vietnam, an honourable and face-saving peace are possible. Unfortunately the U.S. public have been conditioned to such oversimplified and fallacious views on Asian foreign policy as to make negotiation difficult. The Cambodian Foreign Minister had a friendly talk with the new President, but if Mr Johnson were a combination of Machiavelli and King Solomon we would still have trouble with this one. Three ideas widely held in this country are obstacles to a sensible settlement. One is that problems arising in the areas bordering China can be settled without taking its views into account. We had to negotiate with China to end the Korean war and we will have to sit down at Geneva with China again to end the Vietnamese war. The second is that neutralism is a menace second only to Communism, though the only one of three Indo-Chinese states which is stable today, free from guerrilla war and any internal Communist threat is neutralist Cambodia.

The third obstacle to peace is public acceptance of the C.I.A. as a proper agency of government. The first thing to be said of the C.I.A. is that in South-East Asia, at least, it has proven itself politically incompetent. Its favourite Indo-Chinese protégés, Diem in South Vietnam and Phoumi Nosavan in Laos, have been utterly discredited; the latter only opened the door to Communism, the former had to be 'removed' when his failure and instability became too notorious. The one Indo-Chinese ruler the C.I.A. has always regarded with disfavour is the only one who has succeeded. Cambodia under Sihanouk's leadership, Majority Leader Mansfield told the Senate the other day (20 November), 'has developed within its borders a remarkable degree of progress and political cohesion and stability and a level of human freedom and political participation in the life of the nation which exceeds most if not all of the other nations of South-East Asia'. Yet as the *Washington Post* said in a recent editorial (14 November), the C.I.A. 'has for a long time tended to consider the non-aligned Sihanouk as a pernicious fellow'.

The second thing to be said of the C.I.A. is that the very existence of a secret agency which boasts of 'cloak-and-dagger' activities in countries with which we are at peace creates suspicions which poison our foreign relations. Both President Johnson and Secretary Harriman denied to the Cambodian Foreign Minister that the C.I.A. had been engaged in plots against its government. But no one can be sure that the right hand of our government really knows what this left hand is doing.

Cambodia's first charges of a C.I.A. plot were made in 1959 when it expelled Victor Matsui, an official of the U.S. Embassy, for activities incompatible with diplomacy; Cambodia claimed that rebel groups had been given radio transmitters with which they kept in touch with the U.S. Embassy. The next incident was the capture of an anti-Sihanouk emissary with 270 kilograms of pure gold for the rebels; he confessed that he had been in contact with C.I.A. agents not only in Cambodia but in Washington. Later an elaborate 'gift' was presented at the Royal Palace and turned out to be an ingenious bomb intended to kill the King and Queen; three members of the court lost their lives when it exploded. It had come by ship from Vietnam and its intricacy led the Cambodians to suspect skilled C.I.A. hands at work. Then they learned that the secret radio was operating from a house in Saigon under the very nose of U.S. and Vietnamese authorities, and felt this could not happen without their connivance. Another assassination attempt came last spring, when the President of Communist China visited Cambodia. Conspirators were caught in an attempt to mine the road over which he would pass with Prince Sihanouk on his way from the airport. The latest incident was the confession of a rebel infiltrator from South Vietnam that anti-Sihanouk forces worked out of strategic hamlets near the Cambodian border in close liaison with both Vietnamese and U.S. military authorities. These are the incidents which led Prince Sihanouk to break off American aid, fearing that aid agencies were a means by which hostile American agents penetrated his country.

Again I ask – in the wake of our own President's assassination – how long are we going to maintain what other nations consider an assassination agency of our own?

23 December 1963, vol. 11, no. 25

Withholding the Truth on Weapon Losses

In our reply to the State Department's White Paper last March 8, we pointed out that the government's own figures indicated only about $2\frac{1}{2}$ per cent of the Vietcong's weapons were of Soviet bloc origin. Now in checking at the Pentagon on the year-end tally of weapon losses in 1965, we learn that information on the origin of captured weapons has been classified. A press officer implied that most of the guns were Chinese imitations of Russian models. If this were true it would support the case for stronger action against China. We assume the Vietcong have been getting more outside aid but we suspect the figures have been classified because they would show that the number of Chinese and other Soviet bloc weapons are still smaller than those the guerrillas get from our side. The weapon loss figures for last year (see U.P.I. tally, *Washington Post*, 2, January) also omit weapon losses by U.S. troops; this, too, has been classified. The figures given for South Vietnamese army weapon losses are hard to believe. The Pentagon tally for 1964 showed 4,900 weapons captured from the guerrillas and 13,700 lost to them; a surplus in their favour of 8,800. This year's tally shows 14,690 captured from them and 15,972 lost to them, or a surplus in their favour of only 1,282. Considering the increase in fighting, the sharp rise in weapons captured from the guerrillas is credible, but the slight rise in weapons lost to them is not. A footnote to the table says cryptically, 'U.S.

authorities refused to list the exact number of weapons lost.' We have no trouble at all in believing that the figures are not exact.

10 January 1966, vol. 14, no. 1

Where Johnson's New Bombings Lead

Easy, wrote Virgil, in a passage every schoolboy once knew, is the descent to hell. And to the moral standards of the damned. This is the path on which Lyndon Baines Johnson is leading our country. His is a Satanic cleverness John Foster Dulles would have envied. Everything becomes transmuted in Johnson's hands until we lose the capacity to distinguish good from evil. So in his TV-cast press conference last night from his opulent ranch in Texas he somehow managed to appear the aggrieved victim, the unjust target, in the bombing of the oil depots in Hanoi and Haiphong.

Over and over again the President identified criticism with Communism. Some of the Communist countries, he said, 'were rather vicious in their statements ... that we were bombing civilian targets'. Perhaps they were only premature. 'Most of the Communist countries expressed disapproval,' he said. (So, for that matter, did most of the non-Communist.) 'We expected the regular Communist response,' he said in another passage, 'namely, that this would harden the opposition, that it would not lead to negotiations ...' The unwary listener would never guess that this is overwhelmingly world opinion, that it is the view of the Vatican, of the Japanese, Canadian and Indian governments, of the Secretary General of the United Nations, of every West European government, except perhaps West Germany's; that almost every small country in Latin America, Africa and Asia looks on in horror as the world's largest military power is allowed to burn and bomb at will a country too small and weak to retaliate in kind. Johnson could point for support only to those countries 'who', as he elegantly put it, 'have bodies there', i.e. South Vietnam, bodies we pay for in the case of the only large supplier, which is South Korea.

If enemy planes suddenly appeared in the skies over New York or Washington and began to bomb the oil depots on their outskirts, if they returned three days in a row and we had no way of knowing whether this time or next they would hit the centre of the city, if it became dangerous to venture out into the streets as the skies rained hot and deadly fragments of shrapnel from the anti-aircraft guns with which we tried vainly to ward off the invaders, we too might be just a little 'vicious', as Johnson complained, in our comments. Johnson explained self-approvingly that we 'were very careful to select military targets that were not in the centre of the area, and to spare all civilians ...' But even God, with whom our leaders sometimes seem to confuse themselves, could not be that precise if he hurled down the lightning of his judgement. Maps published by the London *Sunday Times* (3 July) show clusters of houses within a few hundred yards of the oil depots in Hanoi and Haiphong and built-up suburban areas within a mile. No doubt the Air Force tried for precision and largely succeeded, but how were the poor people on the ground to know this, and who were we to decide in our omnipotence how far we were to go in punishing and frightening them, like some giant tormenting an ant-hill with huge and clumsy foot?

The fear which seized Hanoi was vividly described by Jean Raffaelli, the Agence France-Presse man in the North Vietnam capital. 'The noise of the bombers,' he reported in a cable to that same issue of the London *Sunday Times,* 'the explosions and anti-aircraft fire reached such an intensity that suddenly it brought an element of fear. People took refuge in the shelters, or jumped into the trenches, which zigzag across private gardens. Shrapnel rained down upon the pavements, injuring dozens of people. ... Accounts which were forthcoming in the evening suggest that the raids were precision jobs, with the bombs well grouped. It was not possible to assess the casualties, but the coming and going of ambulances, and the bustle at the principal hospital ... suggested that they had been relatively heavy.' Washington officials quickly hailed the bombings as 'superb' but assured us that they had killed only 'one or two civilians, if any', though admitting heavy smoke hampered reconnaissance (*New York Times*, 3 July). This smug arithmetic of the bodycount is always being adjusted upward or downward, as if with omniscient exactness, to prove our prowess or our rectitude.

Hanoi is taking no chances on our highly advertised mercy. Strict evacuation orders have been issued and the capital is being emptied as rapidly as possible of all those not engaged in essential tasks; the population is expected to be reduced from 1,200,000 to 300,000. It is rapidly becoming a ghost town. The authorities fear not only the bombardment of the city and the demoralization of its inhabitants, M. Raffaelli reported from Hanoi on the Agence France-Presse ticker, 2 July, but also the possibility that the American fliers may hit the dikes which protect the populous Red River Valley and its rice-fields from inundation. Heavy rains in Yunnan have already swollen the river beyond normal. Parts of Hanoi are below the level of the waters held back by the dikes. These are constantly patrolled and improved by special teams. Destruction of the dikes, especially now as the waters rise, could drown and starve out a substantial portion of the North's most heavily populated area. Hanoi fears that we may duplicate in North Vietnam the war crime the Germans committed by bombing the dikes in Holland. This is the fear aroused as we tighten the screws on North Vietnam's people and intensify the terror in what Johnson blandly calls 'a policy of measured response'.

Plain words are disappearing from circulation as the government floods us with counterfeit phrases of this kind. The real word for the policy we are following is that *schrecklichkeit*, that frightfulness, the Germans proclaimed as their strategy in the First World War, also as a means of shortening the war by frightening their enemies the more quickly into submission. I can remember as a boy the contempt the Germans aroused as a people who could so openly proclaim so devilish a tactic. We are more clever than they, and portray a massive rain of fire from the skies as somehow the token of our benevolence.

It is only as terror and economic warfare designed to bring all Vietnam to its knees on our terms at the bargaining table that the escalation can be rationalized. Pentagon sources eager for new and more deadly targets are already leaking the truth about the oil depot raids. Richard Fryklund, a military affairs reporter with good sources in the Air Force, reported in the *Washington Star* (30 June) that despite the raids the infiltration of North Vietnamese regiments was expected to increase, as it has since the bombings of the North began in February of last year. He reported that the enemy had been stockpiling more supplies than they had been using and that 'the enemy would require delivery of about 150 tons of material a day if they went on the offensive' and 'at the present modest tempo of the war' need only about ninety tons. That is nine ten-ton truck-loads a day, not much for a little country McNamara's computers credit with 10,000 trucks. Oil can be found for that trickle no matter how much we bomb. As recently as 21 January, as Senator Fulbright recalled at the Senate Foreign Relations Committee hearing 30 June, McNamara said the amount of fuel necessary for their supply trucks could be found even though we were to shut off the supply by mining Haiphong. He added, 'Even if they got no fuel for trucks, they have demonstrated many, many times in the Orient that they can move the quantities of supplies now being moved into the south by animal and manpower.' The secret of these raids, which McNamara repeatedly opposed in private talks with reporters at Honolulu and since, lies in domestic political considerations. Johnson hopes to make up for the falling confidence in him within the ranks of the Democratic and the peace-minded by winning the 'hawks' and the Republicans. He is shaping up as their ideal candidate for 1968, since he has succeeded in doing what Nixon unsuccessfully advocated in 1954 and Goldwater in 1964. When Johnson speaks of keeping one's word, as he did at Omaha, one remembers all those words he has brushed under the rug since he won the last election by promising so fervently to do what he is doing.

Slowly and gradually Johnson has set us on a course whose end neither he nor anyone else can foresee. He is reported to be in a Messianic mood, seeing himself as the misunderstood leader of a holy crusade. He is surrounded by hawks and hardliners, and by comparison with them can still believe himself moderate. Always super-sensitive to criticism, he now begins to see it as treasonable. If the enemy can only win in our home front, as he now proclaims, like the French rightists before him in similar circumstances, then criticism of the war is aid and comfort to the enemy. A disturbing note was sounded in his speech at Omaha, with its insistence that he and he alone had been chosen to decide the issues of war and peace. 'If everyone in this country,' he said in Texas last night, 'was working as hard to support the principles of democracy as the men in Vietnam are, I think we should have little to worry about.' Does it foster democracy to talk the language of one-man rule?

If the cost of aggression, as the President says, is to be increased at its source, why stop short at the bombing of North Vietnam? The source of the oil we are trying to shut off is in the Soviet Union. So is that of the anti-aircraft which ring Hanoi and Haiphong. Arms, and other supplies, come from China, and across it from Russia and the rest of the Soviet bloc. If we bomb North Vietnamese oil storage tanks, why not Soviet oil refineries? If we bomb the railroads and roads which carry supplies in North Vietnam, why not those which carry supplies in China? If we attack North Vietnam without a declaration of war, picking and choosing our targets, why not those of China and the Soviet Union? The answer is that we hesitate to do to such formidable big countries what we feel free to do to a helpless small one, with only a negligible Navy or Air Force. But how long before our frustrated hawks call for ultimatums threatening to widen the war to these privileged sanctuaries unless all aid is shut off? 'We shall see this thing through to the end,' President Johnson says. What does he mean by 'the end'? The Third World War?

11 July 1966, vol. 14, no. 24

Why China Builds Bombs at the Expense of Bread

Those whom the gods would destroy they first render complacent. China's giant strides to nuclear power represent the most important political and military development of our time. But both the great capitals challenged are doing their best to pretend nothing has happened. *Pravda*, in the prize journalistic underplay of the century, gave sixteen words at the bottom of page 5 to the news that China had successfully tested a guided missile with a nuclear warhead. In Washington the *Daily News* hit the streets with a banner headline which should be preserved for the wry amusement of posterity. It said, 'Red China's Missile Test Doesn't Scare Pentagon'. If we had been editing that paper we would have put a second line under it, 'But Pentagon's Smugness Scares Us'.

Secretary Rusk, seven days after the first Chinese nuclear explosion in 1964, assured the country that it would be 'a very considerable number of years before there is anything there', i.e. in China, 'that would impose any serious problem'. This remark should rank with his assertion in 1950 that Communist China was only a 'Slavonic Manchukuo', i.e. a Russian puppet state. In their fourth nuclear test in two years, the Chinese have shown that they could (1) perform the difficult feat of miniaturizing a nuclear warhead for it, (2) build an operational intermediate ballistic missile and (3) perfect the safety factor to the point where they could detonate it over their own territory. These were no small achievements. They were enough to make *Le Figaro* (28 October) say that China had overtaken both England and France in the field of nuclear missiles (neither has yet tested a missile with live nuclear warhead) and must now be regarded as the no. 3 nuclear power.

Chinese nuclear capacity has been even more underestimated than was the Soviet Union's. In a Senate speech, 18 October, just before the last Chinese blast. Senator Jackson (D., Wash.) expressed surprise at 'the weapons sophistication displayed' in the first three Chinese tests. The surprise in the first was the use of enriched uranium-235 instead of plutonium, which meant that the Chinese could build up a stockpile faster than expected. The surprise in the third, last May, was the use of 'thermonuclear materials', which indicated that they could build H-bombs of an advanced type. The new feat, requiring a high degree of engineering competence, was accomplished faster than Secretary McNamara expected in the predictions he made last December to the N.A.T.O. Council. His forecast of a

Chinese I.C.B.M. by 1975 may be an underestimate. 'Considering the progress made in developing a nuclear missile system with an operational warhead,' the famous nuclear physicist Ralph Lapp told the *Weekly*, 'it would not be surprising if the Chinese could test an I.C.B.M. in two years.' Senator Jackson, who is chairman of an atomic military applications subcommittee, believes China might put nuclear missiles on those of its submarines which are outfitted with tubes for surface launching of missiles. This would be enough to threaten our coastal ports. The Chinese may be able to deter us from an atomic attack on them earlier than we expected. The mere prospect will change the politics of Asia and the world.

The Chinese announcement of their nuclear missile test is too quickly being dismissed as propaganda. Much can be learned by a thoughtful reading. When they say that 'at no time and in no circumstances will China be the first to use nuclear weapons', this is no more than a recognition of our nuclear superiority. All they can hope to do for many years to come is to have enough missiles to be able to inflict unacceptable damage on us if we make a nuclear attack on them. If they can hold two major cities like San Francisco or New York hostage in this way, that may be enough. This is also the logic of the French *force de frappe*. The idea was born when Moscow, in the Suez crisis, threatened London and Paris with nuclear missiles. The French would never dare attack Russia with their inferior nuclear force but they believe the threat that they might be able to 'take out' Moscow and Kiev would be enough to deter Russia from making a nuclear attack on France. The Chinese are talking sober nuclear strategy when they say their weapons are 'entirely for defence'. If they can build enough nuclear strength to neutralize ours, we could only wage conventional war against them. There they have the advantage of their huge manpower and their readiness to fall back on a guerrilla 'people's war'. These are assets which can be used on the defensive only, but the combination would make China impregnable to successful attack. This is the strategic meaning of the Chinese missile and this is what makes it irrelevant for President Johnson to warn the Chinese as he did in Malaysia, 30 October, that any nuclear potential they may acquire will be counter-balanced by our superior power. The Chinese do not need to match us to deter us.

The lesson of the Chinese missile is that to stop the pro-liferation of nuclear weapons is a political, not a technological problem. When a nation as poor as China can develop the nu-clear missile so quickly, it should be clear that they are no longer available only to large rich nations. To stop the spread of nuclear weapons requires some means of guaranteeing the smaller powers security without them. Now is the time to recall those occasions in the late fifties and sixties when China appealed to us in vain for a nuclear-free Pacific, and for a pledge that nuclear weapons would not be used against non-nuclear powers. That was the time to stop the Chinese nuclear missile.

The Chinese demand then is the same demand being made now by some forty non-nuclear powers in the current debate over non-proliferation at the U.N. General Assembly. They are unwilling to renounce nuclear weapons unless the nuclear powers, in the words of the resolution, 'give an assurance that they will not use, or threaten to use, nuclear weapons against non-nuclear weapon states'. Neither the Warsaw Pact powers nor the N.A.T.O. powers are supporting this resolution. This is why the Ambassador of India was so bitter in his speech at the U.N., 31 October. India is not disposed to sign a non-pro-liferation treaty unless the big powers agree to stop expanding the vast nuclear arsenals at their disposal. India wants nuclear arms and their delivery vehicles reduced and then eliminated. It wants nuclear renunciation to be mutual, and not for smaller powers only. Even if nuclear 'umbrellas' are offered the smaller powers, it would be at the price of lost independence and the risk of deals made over their heads. It must seem hypocritical to the smaller powers for Johnson to say, as he did in Malaysia, that they would be making bombs at the expense of bread. To them this may seem the price of survival in the nuclear jungle. Our bombing of North Vietnam gives them a taste of what the defenceless may expect.

7 November 1966, vol. 14, no. 35

Saigon Afire Now – Will it be Washington in April?

It is no longer necessary to argue the mendacity of our leaders and the incompetence of our military. Mr Johnson has assured us that the successful surprise attack on 100 South Vietnamese cities and towns was really a Vietcong defeat; if they suffer a few more such defeats, we'll be lucky to settle for a coalition government in Hawaii. No nation ever had the misfortune to be led by a bigger team of clowns than those Johnson and Rusk, Westmoreland and Bunker, put through their daily capers in Washington and Saigon; their body-counts alone are enough to make Bob Hope jealous: these seem to be based on an extension to warfare of instalment credit principles – count now, kill later.

We still don't know what hit us. The debris is not all in Saigon and Hue. The world's biggest intelligence apparatus was caught by surprise. Our no. 1 whiz kid, the retiring Secretary of Defense McNamara, capped his record of mis-judgements on Vietnam by preparing a final defence 'posture' statement in which he reported 'a drop in [Vietcong] combat efficiency and morale'! The day he read this report to the Senate Armed Services Committee the Vietcong made their nationwide raids. Neither under Japanese nor French occupation were the rebels ever able to stage such widespread and coordinated attack. Yet we have 500,000 troops in the country as compared with the 60,000 of the French; our army is incomparably better supplied with firepower and airpower; and for three years we have been bombing the North so heavily that every town and city except Hanoi and Haiphong is in ruins.

When the bodies are really counted, it will be seen that one of the major casualties was our delusion about victory by airpower: all that boom-boom did not keep the enemy from showing up at Langvei with tanks. Three years of interdiction by airpower and the rebels are steadily better equipped; the days when they depended on weapons captured from our side are long over. Another casualty is the reputation of Westmoreland and our Joint Chiefs of Staff. On TV Westmoreland and Wheeler began to look more and more pathetic as they clung to those inflated body-count box scores which only they still take seriously. It is as if they mistake the art of warfare for the demolition and extermination business. Giap is proving that superior military and political skill can win over vastly superior firepower, i.e. brainpower over bulk. This is what did in the dinosaur.

Two events during the uprising were deadly. They will never be forgotten as symbols the world over of what the Pax Americana really means for the people we claim to be protecting. One occurred at Bentre after it was shelled 'regardless of civilian casualties', as the ordinarily unemotional A.P. reported 7 February, 'to rout the Vietcong'. A U.S. major explained, 'It became necessary to destroy the town to save it.' This will go down in the history books as typical of our whole Vietnamese campaign. The whole country is slowly being burnt down to 'save it'. To apply scorched-earth tactics to one's own country is heroic; to apply it to a country one claims to be saving is brutal and cowardly. Everywhere we call in artillery and air rather than fight it out hand-to-hand with the guerrillas; this has been characteristic of our intervention from the beginning and this is the secret of why the rebellion grows ever stronger. It is we who rally the people to the other side.

The other incident took place at Khe San where we turned away not only civilian refugees but allied forces fleeing the fallen camp of Langvei. We not only refused them shelter but disarmed them before driving them away. The best account was a magnificent on-the-spot piece of journalism by Newbold Noyes in the *Washington Star*, 11 February. The decision was based it is clear on two motives. One was an unwillingness to share precious supplies, but had they been Americans our men would have shared their last crust to give them shelter. The other was the suspicion that there might be Vietcong among them. How can one fight a successful war when mistrust of one's own allies is so deep? Colonel Lownds, the commander at Khe San, acted only after consulting higher quarters and was in agony over the decision. 'This thing,' he told Noyes, 'can come back to haunt me – all of us. If these people say when the chips were down, after getting us to fight for you, you wouldn't protect us, then the whole civic action business here goes down the drain.' The truth is that when the chips are down we feel that the 'gooks' (or whatever the similar term of the moment) are expendable. To the darker peoples everywhere this incident will sound (fairly or unfairly) like 'whitey' all over again. Don't think it won't rankle.

The idea that we Americans are a superior race, and are justified in using any means of mass killing to save American lives will be the argument for using tactical nuclear weapons in defence of Khe San. It is this racial angle above all which would make it madness for us to add nuclear weapons to the suffering we have already imposed on the Vietnamese people. Let just one 'little' tactical nuclear weapon be used at Khe San and the moral devastation will be beyond calculation. It will stir race hate among the coloured peoples everywhere; they will feel that again they and not whites are the guinea pigs of these terrible weapons. The Chinese will bank this away as moral capital for the day when they can wage nuclear war on us. At home the awful split among our own people will be vastly deepened. The alienation among the youth and for every American of conscience will be beyond anything we have yet experienced. By far the strongest reason for getting out of this Vietnamese war as soon as possible is because sooner or later it will carry us to that fatal step, that crime against mankind.

It is time to stand back and look where we are going. And to take a good look at ourselves. A first observation is that we can easily over-estimate our national conscience; a major part of the protest against the war springs simply from the fact that we are losing it; if it were not for the heavy cost politicians like the Kennedys and organizations like the A.D.A. would still be as complacent about the war as they were a few years ago. A second observation is that for all the poppycock about the Vietnamese war clashing with our past traditions we have long been an imperialistic people. The Truman Doctrine and the Johnson Doctrine are only extensions of the Monroe Doctrine, new embodiments of that Manifest Destiny to which our expansionists appealed in a less cautious day. Bolivar once said that we plagued Latin America in the name of liberty; today we do it to a growing sector of the world. On other pages of this issue you may read the painful testimony of what Pax Americana means in practice in countries as distant as Guatemala and Greece. Everywhere we talk liberty and social reform but we end up by allying ourselves with native oligarchies and military cliques – just as we have done in Vietnam. In the showdown, we reach for the gun.

And this I fear is what we are going to do at home in dealing with the rising threat of a Negro revolt. We could be in the first stage of what Mao has envisaged – a world-wide colonial uprising against American power, accompanied by a complementary and similar rising of blacks in the racial colonies that our ghettoes have become. It is foolish to dismiss Mao's vision because the guerrilla movements in Latin America and Africa have so far proved unsuccessful and because most Negroes still want only to be accepted fully as fellow Americans. These facts give us time to save our country but only if that time is utilized wisely and quickly. So long as the war goes on it must deepen racial bitterness at home and abroad because coloured peoples are the victims and because coloured men make up so disproportionately large a share of our own combat troops while the cry rises to save the white boys from the draft for the graduate schools. And the longer the war goes on the less money we have for the giant tasks of social reconstruction at home. We put $2 billion into the French attempt to hold Indo-China. We have spent $65 billion since 1954 on our own. This year the war will easily cost $30 billion. The new 'defence' budget has already burst its seams with the Pueblo affair, and it was already $80 billion. These stupendous sums are the counterpart of the precious time and energy we waste.

Now Martin Luther King announces a new march on Washington for April. Negro moderates regard it as the last gasp of the non-violent movement. If it fails, they see race war in our cities. Dr King, as always, is playing it by ear. He is a mystic. He has no concrete programme. He has no clear aim except the full emancipation of his people. The nearest thing to a concrete objective is the Conyers bill which would spend $30 billion – the cost of one year in Vietnam – for the rehabilitation of our slums and the human beings twisted by life in urban jungles. That bill hasn't a chance in this atmosphere. The whole trend is to cut rather than to increase welfare expenditures. The emphasis is on repressing crime in the streets, which translates into repressing the Negro. Johnson gave in to that trend by calling in his crime message for enactment of a Federal inciting-to-riot bill which the Administration liberals have fought for two years. The Attorney General, like the new report on the Newark 'riots', has stressed that these racist convulsions are due to misery not conspiracy. But we are moving inexorably to the club, the gun and the jail, to a Vietnam at home.

Troops are being trained to fight urban guerrillas. G.I.s in Vietnam are being offered discharge ninety days early if they join an urban police force back home. Dr King promises nonviolence but he also projects a vast sit-down to bring Washington to a standstill unless it prepares to give the Negro what he wants. If he fails, more Negro youth will turn the revolutionary way. The chances of avoiding some outburst of violence during those April demonstrations will grow slimmer the longer they last. Some shooting, even accidental, may anger even Washington's apathetic Negro population and set off racial fighting here and by chain reaction in other cities. To move towards the end of the war, to show a readiness to spend for reconstruction at home instead of devastation abroad, would change the whole atmosphere. Must we wait until the fires that rage in Saigon set Washington ablaze too?

19 February 1968, vol. 16, no. 4

They Pleaded Guilty of Burning Paper instead of Children

In the days of the New Deal the W.P.A. had something called Living Theatre. Living theatre is what radicals have begun to produce. One example is the black comedy a wild horde of hippies and yippies wove around the House Un-American Activities Committee, driving it to suspend its hearings into the Chicago peace demonstrations. Those shopworn inquisitors did not know what to do with witnesses who acted out the procedure's essential irrationality.

Another example is the Morality Play the Catonsville Nine have been enacting. They staged their first act on 17 May when they entered a local draft board in Catonsville, Md, and burned up its files, with napalm they manufactured themselves from a recipe in the U.S. Special Forces Handbook. 'Our apologies, good friends,' said Father Daniel Berrigan, the poet-priest who was one of their leaders, 'for the fracture of good order, the burning of paper instead of children'.

The second act was in a Federal court in Baltimore last week before Chief Judge Roszel C. Thomsen. The Nine are all Catholic, clergy and lay. Their types are recognizable through history: the stuff of which saints are made, moved by a deeper sensitivity to human suffering. They joyfully admitted their guilt, like early brethren preparing for the lions. No legalisms spoiled the second act curtain.

The government in its own dramaturgy, picked a black man to prosecute them. First Assistant U.S. Attorney Arthur G. Murphy said the morality of the war was not at issue, though he admitted in passing that a reasonable man might think it illegal. The issue, he said, was simply destroying property and obstructing the law. The chief Defence Attorney, William Kunstler, insisted 'The trial is not as simple, any more than those of Jesus and Socrates were simple.'

Judge Thomsen, like a certain forerunner, kept washing his hands of the affair by allowing the defendants extraordinary latitude in explaining why they did it. The two most wondrous characters among the Nine, the ex-priest Thomas Melville and his wife, the ex-nun, were even allowed to touch on the sufferings they saw in Guatemala which ended by driving them into the arms of the guerrillas and out of the Church. Their quiet sobriety is in strange contrast to the traumas that so transformed their lives.

The trial drew some 2,000 zealots from all over the country. The deepest appeal of the spectacle for them was in Father Daniel Berrigan's testimony when he said, 'I was in danger of verbalizing my moral impulses out of existence. I sought a way to defy the state even if I was too old to defy the draft.' Of course they were found guilty. Not to acquiesce in murder, the chief and most ancient business of the state, is clearly subversive. On 8 November they will be sentenced. The third and longest act will be when they and their supporters use the appeals to put the show on the road. We cannot think if a finer way to stir the sluggish conscience of the nation.

21 October 1968, vol. 16, no. 21

The Con Game of 'Withdrawal' from Vietnam

On short range, as in the case of the thirty-six-hour cessation of B-52 bombings, the answer to the question puzzling the whole press corps – what is Nixon doing? – is (I suspect) quite simple. He doesn't know. He is thrashing about like a fish on a hook, trying desperately to find some way to get off. He is obviously hearing contradictory advice from civilian and military sources, and he vacillates, apparently depending on who talks to him last. If you look back, vacillation is the chief characteristic of this Administration, not only on Vietnam but on almost every question of policy, from tax reform through hunger to school desegregation. Nixon never changes his mind about appointments when they seem to have been firmly made, as in the Knowles case. The tiller of the ship of state has rarely had a more unsteady hand upon it.*

When looked at from a longer perspective, however, Nixon's course on Vietnam is not a thing of fits and starts. It was first projected by the Johnson Administration in 1968, and he is continuing it. A high Pentagon official phrased it very succinctly at the time to a friend of mine. 'We are going to reduce the fighting,' this military man said, 'to a level the American public

---

* To imagine that the B-52 'signal', if such it was, would get through one would have to believe (1) that Hanoi can read Nixon's mind better and faster than Washington can, and (2) that its communications with the guerrillas scattered around the South is far swifter than our super-duper electronic communications proved to be in the Pueblo affair.

will tolerate for a long pull.' The new course then charted was aimed not at negotiations with Hanoi or even at the 'Vietnamization' of the war but at mollifying, or conning, American public opinion. For the Pentagon the main enemy is American public opinion and its 'impatience' and even – for some silly generals – democracy itself, as the means by which that impatience expresses itself.* The course of events becomes clearer if one keeps in mind that the Vietnam strategy is primarily concerned neither with making war nor peace but with public relations – a 'snow job' to quiet unrest at home while pursuing the same objective in Vietnam. This is a Korean solution. The objective is a right-wing satellite regime, run by the native military with a constitutional façade but little or no civil liberty, in South Vietnam as in South Korea. To keep it in power we are prepared to maintain a reduced but considerable number of troops there indefinitely, as we do in Korea fifteen years after the war ended. The 55,000 U.S. troops still there cost us $600 million a year to maintain.

Though never publicly debated, the main lines of this programme have surfaced in the past year. Herman Kahn has had a secret withdrawal 'scenario' floating around town. Its content was indicated in his article 'If Negotiations Fail' in the July 1968 *Foreign Affairs* quarterly where he proposed that we appease opinion by Vietnamizing the war, reducing U.S. forces 'in the next two or three years to between two and three hundred thousand men' while keeping two or three combat divisions in South Vietnam for a considerable period in order to 'deter resumption of major hostilities'. The same idea reappeared in Secretary Laird's recent interview with *Time* magazine (29 August) when he suggested U.S. forces 'could be cut in half, to about 250,000 men, and kept in South Vietnam for an extended period'. Many columnists have picked up similar forecasts and *U.S. News & World Report* (September) said Nixon's hope last spring 'was to have almost all 250,000 combat troops out of Vietnam by the end of 1970. That would leave

* Two or three generals apparently have told dinner partners hereabouts that there would be no elections in 1972 because the military were going to end all this 'turmoil' by taking over!

slightly fewer than 300,000 support troops in the war zone.'

This was the plan Nixon was following in announcing a second reduction of 35,000 troops by 15 December. This would still leave 484,000 troops in Vietnam plus 28,000 naval personnel and about 45,000 air force men in Thailand. This adds up to 557,000 men tied down in the Vietnam war. Nixon's first two cuts total 60,000 men. The *Baltimore Sun* (16 September) quoted a 'high-ranking American official in Saigon whose views have been heard personally by Mr Nixon' as having estimated that 100,000 men could be pulled out without seriously reducing the fighting ability of the allied forces. One reason, he said, is that a number of soldiers sent to Vietnam to build airfields, logistical bases and outposts finished their tasks last year. We are still a long way from a real reduction in combat forces.

In a Senate speech, 9 September, on the eve of the latest Nixon announcement, Gore attacked the Administration line that a 'phased withdrawal, coupled with an unspoken but obvious pledge that we will keep enough troops there indefinitely to prevent collapse of the current Saigon regime, would convince North Vietnam that its cause is hopeless and therefore encourage Hanoi to negotiate.' To negotiate under such circumstances would be to accept the Thieu regime and a political defeat. 'In my view,' Gore went on, 'the history of the Vietnamese people does not support such a conclusion. They are accustomed to long struggles, spanning generations or even centuries.' The policy of phased withdrawal, he declared, 'holds no more promise of success than did the policy of bombing North Vietnam'. He said it might 'buy time for the Administration with the American people' but 'if it is used to tighten our embrace of the Saigon regime, the prospects for peace will be dim indeed.' Fulbright, supporting Gore, made the essential point when he told the Senate, 'It does not matter how much we talk about settlement, the war cannot be settled as long as we insist upon maintaining the puppet government in South Vietnam.' But that has always been the Johnson–Nixon strategy, and that is their common conception of an 'honourable peace'.

The peace movement is slowly waking up to this con game, but it's going to have to embark on a campaign of public education to thwart it. Even if this scenario worked, and we cut our troops – and the cost of the Vietnamese war – in half, we'd still be stuck for $12 to $15 billion a year indefinitely in Vietnam. Our military still have a low opinion of the South Vietnamese army; at the best, it will be years before it can do without U.S. air, artillery and logistics support. At the worst, what happens if U.S. bases are overrun, if the A.R.V.N. fails to protect them, if casualties rise among the U.S. troops left behind? What do we do, send more troops in and start this whole miserable process all over again?

We are being told that things are not going well in North Vietnam. That may be true, but they can hardly be going half as badly as here. North Vietnam has no stock and bond markets, to fall steadily even as inflation grows. As this is written the financial pages speculate that the U.S. may have to pay the highest interest rates since the war of 1812 – when the British burned Washington – to refinance debt coming due next week. It is the most dangerous nonsense to think that we can go on wasting 'even' $10 billion a year in Vietnam while inflation eats away savings and racial-urban problems eat away the very foundations of our society. The message we have to take to the country is that the war and the Pentagon have become the no. 1 threat to American security, and that we must get out of Vietnam and Asia before those quicksands are our ruination.

22 September 1969, vol. 17, no. 17

Strange Way to Cut Back

We can't read President Nixon's mind and we have long ago given up trying to understand Pentagon arithmetic. But when the October draft calls were announced we checked back and found that draft calls are up more than seventy per cent since Nixon at the beginning of June announced Vietnamese troop cutbacks were to begin. Here are the figures month by month:

	1968	1969
June	20,000	25,900
July	15,000	22,300
August	18,300	29,500
September	12,200	29,000
October	13,800	29,000
Total	79,000	135,700

22 September 1969, vol. 17, no. 17

The Atrocities Nixon Condones and Continues

The Pinkville massacre falls into perspective if we remember that from the first days of the struggle against the French, General Giap's strategy has been to fight a 'people's war'. Without our ever fully realizing it, ours has become an 'anti-people's war'. Some years ago an American colonel, who was never identified, put it very plainly. Mao Tse-tung, the foremost theoretician of the people's war, said that the guerrilla swims among the people as a fish does in the sea. The U.S. colonel said we would 'dry up the sea'. Our strategy has been to destroy the villages and the crops, to drive out or kill the people, wherever we suspect Vietcong. We set out to create a desert where no 'fish' could live. The soldiers at Pinkville may not have been ordered to kill women and children but they were certainly ordered to burn down the village and kill the livestock, to destroy their homes and their food supply. If the main target of a 'people's war' is to win the confidence and support of the peasantry, the main target of an anti-people's war is to uproot or destroy the peasantry the guerrillas may have won over. From such a strategy Pinkvilles come naturally.

In the rules of war, soldiers and civilians used to be separate categories. The strategy of the anti-people's war has given us that legal monstrosity we now read about – the 'innocent civilian'. This implies that some civilians are innocent and some are guilty. The latter are not only fair game but the safe rule when in doubt is to shoot first and investigate later, or just add them to the body-count. Horrible as this may sound, it has its logic and the logic grows stronger as the spiral of hate mounts on both sides. The guerrillas use civilians in their area – like the home population in any war – for many auxiliary tasks. The civilians – including women and children – take up those tasks ever more willingly as they see their homes and livestock, their menfolk and ancestral graves, destroyed by indiscriminate bombing and artillery fire and by 'search and destroy' missions like the one in Pinkville. Relations are not improved by calling them 'gooks' or – more politely, as in Lt Calley's indictment – 'Oriental human beings'. They retaliate with home-made mines and booby traps, including the 'ponji', the sharpened stick coated with excrement. The biggest and dirtiest booby trap of all is the filthy pit of this war itself, from which we emerge stinking in the nostrils of mankind.

There is a flurry of stories from Saigon about 're-indoctrinating' troops on the humane treatment of civilians. But we are dealing here not with an occasional atrocity but with a deliberate policy. What a fear-crazed and hate-filled G.I. may do in occupying a hostile village can be put down to the brutalization of war. The real crime is higher up. When the President announced that he was revising our chemical and bacteriological war programme and sending the Geneva protocol to the Senate for ratification, it looked like a gesture of contrition. It turned out to be the most hypocritical kind of public relations. For it excepted from these restrictions the two weapons of gas and chemical warfare from which the civilian population of Vietnam suffer most. These are the tear- and lung-gases which drive them out of their home-made bombing shelters into the open where our B-52s and fragmentation 'anti-personnel' bombs can destroy them, and the herbicides which kill their crops and threaten – like thalidomide – their unborn children.

How can we convince the world that we have not turned barbarian when a White House announcement, designed to take the curse off Pinkville and demonstrate our concern for international law, perpetuates a gross violation of it? We refer to the use of crop-killers. It is said that the Geneva protocol banning chemical warfare does not mention herbicides. True. But earlier treaties to which we are a party do. The Army Field Manual (F.M. 27–10) in paragraph 37 cites that provision of the Hague Convention of 1907 which says 'It is especially forbidden ... to employ poison or poison weapons.' The army interpretation which follows says this 'does not prohibit measures ... to destroy, through chemical or bacteriological agents, harmless to man, crops intended *solely* [our emphasis] for consumption by the armed forces (if that fact can be determined)'. But even this tortuous sophistry admits we may not destroy crops just because we believe *some* of the supplies may feed guerrillas, and that we may not employ chemical or bacteriological agents which *are* harmful to humans.

Two years ago the Japan Science Council* released a report on anti-crop warfare in Vietnam which said nearly 1,000 peasants and more than 130,000 livestock had been killed by it. Han Swyter, a former aide to Secretary McNamara, told the House Foreign Affairs Committee (2 December) that since 1962 we have sprayed about 100 million pounds of herbicides over four million acres, an area the size of Massachusetts. He said that since late 1967 there have been increasing reports and pictures in the Saigon press of a new kind of abnormality in newly-born children. These reports have found confirmation in a still secret report for the National Cancer Institute (see *Scientific Research* for 10 November) which found that one herbicide, 2,4,5–T was 'probably dangerous' and 2,4–D 'potentially dangerous' as teratogenic agents, i.e. capable, like thalidomide, of producing gross birth defects if ingested by pregnant women. As a result the Pentagon has 'restricted' the use of the first, but not the second substance to areas remote from human population. But how much reliance can be placed on this restriction remains to be seen and the crop-killing itself goes on.

So will the civilian killing via the tear-gas route. The government's position is that the Geneva protocol does not cover tear-gas. The protocol itself speaks of 'asphyxiating poisonous or *other* gases'. [Our emphasis.] The British government ever since 1930, like many other signatories of the protocol, has held that

* p. 153 of Seymour M. Hersh's indispensable recent book *Chemical and Bacteriological Warfare* (Bobbs Merrill).

tear-gases, too, are outlawed. Congressman McCarthy (D., N.Y.) told a Montreal audience (1 December) that when in London he heard the U.S. government was pressuring the British government to change its position on tear-gas. This is not academic in Britain. Imagine the massacre during the blitz if the Nazis had been able to flush people out of the subways and other shelters with tear-gases before the bombing, as we do in Vietnam.

The enormous quantities of tear- and lung-gas we use in Vietnam – almost fourteen million pounds since 1964, or more than half the total weight of the mustard-gas used by both sides in the First World War – testify how far we have gone from exceptional use in 'riot-like' circumstances to routine application before bombardment. These are the atrocities Nixon condones and continues.

15 December 1969, vol. 17, no. 23

Only the Bums Can Save the Country Now

The race is on between protest and disaster. Despite the first four martyr 'bums' of Nixon–Agnewism at Kent State, the college shutdown their deaths precipitated, the outpouring of student and other protesters here last weekend, the campus lobbyists beginning to flood the halls of Congress, the Senate resolutions to limit or end Indo-Chinese military operations, and the smouldering near revolt within the Nixon Administration itself, we are still on the brink. We are in the first stages of a new and wider war from which withdrawal will be difficult. The military hold the reins and can precipitate new provocations and stage new alarms. The only hope is that the students can create such a Plague for Peace, swarming like locusts into the halls of Congress, that they stop all other business and make an end to the war the no. 1 concern it ought to be. Washington must no longer be the privileged sanctuary of the warmakers. The slogan of the striking students ought to be: Suspend Classes and Educate the Country. I see no other visible and adequate means to stop the slide into a conflict that may sweep very suddenly beyond the confines of Indo-China if the man who gambled on Cambodia ends by gambling on the use of nuclear weapons.

In a dispatch from a landing zone in Cambodia, Jack Foisie of the *Washington Post* (8 May) described G.I.s jumping from helicopters under enemy fire with derisive denunciations of the war scrawled on their helmets. One of those he copied down sums up the situation of the whole country in this war. 'We are the unwilling,' it said, 'led by the unqualified, doing the unnecessary, for the ungrateful.' As usual the country is not being told the truth about why we went into Cambodia. In his war address of 30 April Nixon pictured the attack across the border as a pre-emptive exercise to hit an 'enemy building up to launch massive attacks on our forces and those of South Vietnam'. It was described as a swift preventive action from which we would soon withdraw and which was not part of any broader intervention in Cambodian affairs.

But thanks to the indiscretion of one Congressman, we now have the private – and more candid – version given members of Congress at special State Department briefings. This puts the origins and purpose of the Cambodian action in a very different light. The Congressman is Representative Hamilton Fish (R., N.Y.), a right-winger who has long questioned the logic of our heavy commitment in so peripheral an area as South-East Asia. In a letter to constituents released 13 May, Mr Fish summarizes a private briefing by Under-Secretary of State Richardson for selected members of Congress. Nixon said we moved across the border to nip enemy plans for an imminent attack. But from Richardson's briefing, Mr Fish reports, 'It was clear that the present military thrust into Cambodia hinged largely on the reportedly surprise overthrow of Prince Sihanouk.' Nixon said in his 30 April speech that for five years 'neither the U.S. nor South Vietnam moved against those enemy sanctuaries because we did not wish to violate the territory of a neutral nation.' But Richardson gave the Congressman a different story. He told them 'U.S. intelligence had known for years of those enclaves from which attacks on South Vietnam have been launched' but we had never attacked them before 'because it was feared that

Sihanouk would counter any invasion by allowing N.V.A. [North Vietnamese Army] forces to enlarge their occupied areas'.

Sihanouk was trying to maintain a precarious neutrality by playing one side against the other. Nixon was deceitful when he said in the 30 April speech that our policy since the Geneva Conference of 1954 'has been to scrupulously respect the neutrality of the Cambodian people' and adding – as proof of our virtue – that since last August we have had a diplomatic mission in Phnom Penh 'of fewer than fifteen' and that for the previous four years 'we did not have any diplomatic mission whatever'. The truth is that Sihanouk ousted our mission and broke relations in 1965 because he claimed the C.I.A. had been plotting against him for years and even tried to kill him. Sihanouk was especially resentful of the Khmer Serei (Free Khmer) mercenaries the C.I.A. and our Special Forces had enlisted from among Cambodians living in South Vietnam and Thailand to act as an anti-Sihanouk commando force. The C.I.A. gave it facilities to broadcast anti-Sihanouk propaganda from Saigon.

'For the past five years,' Nixon said with bland hypocrisy, 'we have provided no military assistance and no economic assistance whatever to Cambodia.' He did not explain that Sihanouk threw out our military mission because he said it had been trying to turn his armed forces against him and gave up economic aid, too, rather than have it used as a cover for U.S. agents trying to overthrow him. This was not a figment of Sihanouk's imagination. As far back as 1958, in a police raid on the villa of one of his generals, Sihanouk found a letter from President Eisenhower pledging full support to a projected coup and to a reversal of Cambodian neutrality. This was part of a 'Bangkok plan' worked out between the dictators of South Vietnam and Thailand (Diem and Marshal Sarit Thanarit) to dismember Cambodia and instigate civil war (see Wm Worthy's account in the York, Pa, *Gazette & Daily* of 30 April). When Sihanouk resumed relations last August, in his desperate see-saw between the two sides, his condition was that the U.S. mission be kept small. He didn't want too many C.I.A. agents roaming around.

That was poor Sihanouk's mistake. Cambodian neutrality was ended when the military we had long wooed finally overthrew Sihanouk on 18 March. The most complete account yet published of the events leading up to the coup is to be found in *Le Monde Diplomatique* for April. It is by Daniel Roy, a Frenchman with fifteen years' experience in Indo-China who was for a time press attaché to Prince Sihanouk. He claims that funds for the coup were provided by a Cambodian adventurer turned banker in Bangkok who was associated in the enterprise with the notorious Son Ngoc Thanh, puppet President of Cambodia under the Japanese occupation. The latter fled to Thailand after the war and according to M. Roy is 'today in the service of the C.I.A.' M. Roy also charges that the coup was prepared by Khmer Serei forces who went over the border with their arms and wives and pretended that they were defecting to Sihanouk. They infiltrated the army and the police as a Trojan Horse for the C.I.A.

Let us now return to Congressman Fish's account of the private State Department briefing. 'Following the fall of Sihanouk,' the Congressmen were told, 'the new anti-Communist government cut all supply lines [of the N.V.A. and Vietcong] except the Ho Chi Minh trail' which, of course, lies largely outside Cambodian territory. *'To re-secure their severed supply routes,'* the account in the private briefing continued, *'V.A. and N.V.A. began moving out of the enclaves, thereby threatening the overthrow of the Cambodian government.'* [Our italics.] It is 'against this background', Representative Fish's account of the briefing concludes, 'that the American–South Vienamese strikes into Cambodia were ordered'.

The sequence is quite different from that given publicly by Mr Nixon. Instead of preparing an attack on our forces in South Vietnam, the enemy was reacting to an attack on its supply lines. This upset the status quo, and risked a complete takeover of Cambodia by the other side. We intervened to save it from the consequences. Did our government give the new Lon Nol government of Cambodia assurances that we would defend it if its action in cutting all the supply routes precipitated an attack upon it?

It is true that at the State Department briefing 'it was stressed that the present attacks were not aimed at either the confrontation of the estimated 40 to 50,000 V.C. and N.V.A. believed operating in Cambodia or the defence of the present government of Cambodia. The raids were described as strictly "spoiling actions", aimed at supply, bunker and communication network destruction' and to give the South Vietnamese army additional time while the enemy rebuilds its supplies. But you have to be pretty feeble-minded to accept this at face value. What if Sihanouk, with N.V.A. and Peking support, is restored to power, this time not as a precarious neutral but as an ally of the other side? What if we are then faced with the prospect, not just of restoring the old supply lines and bases but of Cambodia turning into one big enemy base? Who can believe that the Nixon Administration will stand by and let this happen?

This is the wider war which lies ahead. The overthrow of Sihanouk was a grave political mistake. It gave the other side a new ally with legitimacy and mass support, basic necessities for the Indo-Chinese People's War which has already been proclaimed against us. The situation inside Cambodia was successfully summed up in an interview which the pro-Nixon and pro-war *U.S. News and World Report* for 18 May held by cable with its correspondent, James N. Wallace, in Phnom Penh:

Q. Have the allied attacks in Eastern Cambodia saved the rest of the country from a Communist takeover?

A. No. Unless the allied drive completely overwhelms the Communists, Cambodia's position remains the same ... the short-run result is even more chaos and confusion ...

Q. Did the Cambodians welcome the Allied move?

A. Again, No. Cambodians do not like ... the idea of South Vietnamese troops rolling across Cambodia ...

Q. What kind of reception would Sihanouk get?

A. Almost certainly he would receive more popular support than the Lon Nol government cares to admit. Sihanouk still is popular among a great many of Cambodia's 5.5 million peasants, who respected his traditional status as god-king and liked his earthy personal relations with villagers.

The French journalist, Max Clos, who has been covering Indo-

China for years during both the French and U.S. wars, foresees (in *Le Figaro*, 2–3 May) a Cambodian resistance based on peasant support, doing in their country what the Vietcong have done in Vietnam and creating a 'liberated zone' from which in time they will be able to take over Phnom Penh. 'Mr Nixon,' M. Clos wrote, 'hopes to withdraw his troops from Cambodia in a month and a half. Even if he succeeds, it is safe to predict he will have to send them back again.'

The political folly of our latest move is not limited to Cambodia. The newly enlarged war must add to the shaky character of the Thieu regime, which has had to close down all the South Vietnamese schools in a rising student revolt much like our own. The idea of South Vietnamese troops being used to bolster a government which has been massacring Cambodian citizens of Vietnamese origin must add to Thieu's unpopularity. The bitterness between the Viets and the Khmers of Cambodia is incomparably older and more bitter than the recent animosities of the Russo-American cold war. It is only two centuries since the Viets seized the Mekong delta from the Khmers. Sihanouk, unlike his successors, never stirred up the mob against the Vietnamese and the V.C. and N.V.A. intruders, unlike our forces, did not bomb and devastate Cambodian villages. This new shift strengthens the forces opposing our puppets on both sides.

This has been a political war from its very beginning against the French. We go on believing as they did that a political problem can be solved by military means. The annals of their war, like ours, are full of sensationally billed search-and-destroy operations which were finally going to cripple the rebels, like this latest 'Operation Total Victory' across the Cambodian border. The Communists under Ho Chi Minh seized national leadership in the war against the French, as the adroit Sihanouk did in Cambodia. Now they both are allied against us. Sihanouk will now make it possible for the other side to implement the basic strategy of a people's war on a wider scale. The strategy is to force maximum dispersion upon the hated foreign invader to make him widen the area of his activity and stretch his lines of communication so that the guerrillas can pick and choose the most advantageous weak points for their concentrated attacks. We have picked up their treacherous gambit by invading Cambodia and sooner or later, unless we get out of Indo-China altogether, we must send ground troops into Laos and Cambodia, perhaps even into North Vietnam where a fresh army of 250,000 or more awaits our landing. Nowhere has air power, however overwhelming and unchallenged, been able to win a war.

What will happen when the country wakes up to find that instead of withdrawing troops we are going to send in fresh divisions? What happens to inflation, the budget and the stock market? To student and racial unrest? Nixon, in a mood of self-pity, complained in his 30 April address that past war presidents did not have to face a nation 'assailed by counsels of doubt and defeat from some of the most widely known opinion leaders of the nation'. He seems to attribute this to some perversity. He takes it as personal. He does not stop to consider why this war has aroused so much more opposition than any past war, and done so in every class and every region and every age-group, from Wall Street financiers to campus radicals. Even National Guardsmen give the V-sign to students, and soldiers go into battle with peace amulets around their necks. He seems to think there is something wrong with the critics. He will not face up to the possibility that there is something wrong with the war. Certainly this generation of Americans would prove no less patriotic and brave than any other if our country were really in danger.

It is a measure of our stupid leadership that the Cambodian war was started on the phoney pretext that just across the border was a kind of enemy Pentagon and that we could cripple the enemy by smashing it. One measure of the mendacity may be found in an intelligence briefing the *New York Times* reported 4 April, two weeks after Sihanouk's overthrow. It said C.O.S.V.N., the enemy HQ., had been moved from Cambodian to South Vietnamese territory. The story even carried a map showing the old location at Mimot – which figures in recent accounts of the Cambodian operation – in the 'fish-hook' and the new location in a thick jungle area described as 'virtually inaccessible to ground troops' and 'probably not seriously vulnerable to air attacks'. It is difficult to believe that Nixon and his aides are such idiots as not to be aware of this intelligence information.

The Eichmann trial taught the world the banality of evil. Nixon is teaching the world the evil of banality. The man so foolish as to talk to protesting students about football and surfing is the same man who (like Johnson) sees war in the puerile terms of 'humiliation' and a challenge to his virility. He doesn't want us to be a 'helpless giant' (which we are in Indo-China) so he is plunging us into a wider quagmire where we will end up more helpless than ever.

The past week is the week in which the Nixon Administration began to come apart. Letters like Hickel's showed how isolated he is even from members of his own Cabinet where there seems to be a silent majority against him. The anti-war round robin signed by more than 200 employees of the State Department shows how deeply the Cambodian affair has stirred even the most timid, conformist and conventional section of the bureaucracy. Nothing Nixon says can be taken at face value. Even when he said on 20 April, in his troop withdrawal announcement, that a 'just peace' was at last in sight, he must have been planning this expansion of the war. Indeed, General Westmoreland as Army Chief of Staff had already begun to lobby for a Cambodian invasion in off-the-record briefings.

There were two remarks of the deepest significance in the Nixon press conference of 30 April. One was that if we withdraw from Vietnam 'America is finished in so far as a peace-keeper in the Asian world is concerned.' This revealed that he is still committed, despite that vague 'low posture' talk on Guam, to a Pax Americana in Asia. If we are to police Asia we are in for many years of war and internal disruption. The folly is as great as if China were to try and become the 'peace-keeper' of Latin America. The other remark was that unlike Johnson he would not escalate step by step but 'move decisively'. This is the Goldwater–LeMay thesis that we could have won the Vietnam war if we had smashed Hanoi and Haiphong in one great blow, perhaps with nuclear weapons. Hanoi, especially after the recent big bombing raids, expects something of the kind. Moscow and Peking are already trying to patch up their differences in expectation of it. If Nixon goes to nuclear weapons, the end result may well be the Third World War. Unless an army of students can fan out to the grass roots and make the country aware of these dangerous possibilities, terrible days may lie ahead.

18 May 1970, vol. 18, no. 10

Peace is Still a Long, Long March Away

After the Inquisition made Galileo recant the subversive notion that the earth revolves around the sun, he is said to have whispered, defiantly, 'Eppur si muove!' (but still it moves). In the euphoric wake of the huge anti-war gathering here on 24 April, one can only paraphrase Galileo and say of the government, 'But still it doesn't move!' There will be no peace in Vietnam until we get rid of Nixon as we got rid of Johnson. But the chances are slight that Nixon's successor will not be somebody like Muskie or Humphrey who will carry on the tactical retreat Johnson began. That retreat is designed to appease anti-war sentiment by withdrawing most, and if necessary all, of our troops from South Vietnam but to maintain a satellite regime in Saigon, supported by air power from the seventh fleet and Thailand. The aim is still the maintenance of U.S. power in East Asia as part of the Pax Americana. There can be no generation of peace until we somehow curb the militarism and imperialism which gave us Vietnam and will create new Vietnams. But the Pentagon is already utilizing the reduction in the cost of the Vietnam war to give it funds for a leaner but better equipped force with which to go on playing the world policeman role. Yet the dominant elements of both parties decry anti-imperialism as a return to isolationism.

From the top of Capitol Hill, the marchers looked like a mass of brightly coloured human confetti as far as the eye could see up Pennsylvania and Constitution Avenues. It took five hours for the last of the demonstrators to come within hearing range of

the speakers, and more bus and train loads were still pouring
into town when the demonstration was half over in mid-after-
noon. No one expected so huge a turnout, perhaps the biggest
since the Civil Rights March of 1963. The peace movement has
risen bigger than ever, from the ashes of Vietnamization and
withdrawal. But it still has a long, hard way to go. Though
sedately dressed older persons were visible amid the brightly
coloured rags that are chic with today's youth, the crowd was
still overwhelmingly the other side of thirty. There was a train-
load of 1,500 from District 65, many busloads from New York's
hospital workers (Local 1199), some U.A.W. and Teamsters, but
these were fringe elements long opposed to the war; clearly the
organized labour movement, rank and file as well as leadership,
is still wedded to the military–industrial complex by bread and
butter as well as ideology. The Third World contingent was far
less than one per cent of the 300,000 or more who turned out.
These, despite the favourite stereotypes of the Far Left, were
overwhelmingly white and middle-class. There is a lot of
missionary work to be done, in the ghettoes and out in the
country.

The stars of this year's demonstration were the Vietnam Veterans Against the War. The drama associated with their four-
day encampment on the Mall touched the heart of the country
and was mainly responsible in my opinion for the unexpected
size of the turnout. They stared down the Attorney General of
the United States in an episode without parallel in the history of
American constitutional law. He went to court to obtain an
injunction forbidding them to sleep on the Mall, and then after
winning a victory from Chief Justice Burger and later the entire
court, lost his nerve and went back to the District Judge who
issued the original order and asked him to reverse it!

The failure of nerve is understandable. I can remember as a
young newspaperman what happened after Herbert Hoover
called out the troops to drive the tattered Bonus Marchers, who
were also veterans, out of town in 1932; that was the biggest
mistake he made. If police or troops had driven the V.V.A.W.
out the night after the Supreme Court decision, it would have
been the biggest mistake Nixon ever made. Pictures of legless

veterans being carried out of the park could have precipitated riots in military encampments here and in Vietnam. Scores of men in the nearby 82nd Airborne Division, which would have been called up, sent word that they would join the vets rather than act against them. Contingents of active troops from Fort Bragg, Fort Meade, Fort Belvoir and Andrews Air Force Base turned up at the various affairs associated with the V.V.A.W. encampment: the candle-light procession around the White House, the parade of veterans throwing away their medals at the Capitol, the Memorial Service for the Dead at Washington Cathedral organized by the Concerned Officers movement and the march of the 24th itself.

Just as the relative handful of the Resistance saved the honour of France so these thousand or more veterans of Vietnam will some day be seen as men who saved the honour of America. Think of how differently Germany would have gone into the Nuremberg trials if it could have pointed to demonstrations in which German veterans had cared or dared to throw away their medals in shame and protest while the very horrors of the Second World War were still going on! I know of no war and no country in which there has ever been such a scene as that which took place on the west side of the Capitol that morning. It will be remembered with pride in our history books.

'We looked for leadership,' said the ex-officer who opened the medal ceremony, 'but found closed doors and closed minds.' The Armed Services Committees, always the faithful satellites of the high brass, refused to hear them. But Senator McGovern held an improvised session that afternoon to hear a succession of the veterans tell of the atrocities and the atrocious military tactics which had finally turned them off the war. And Senator Fulbright had the distinction of being the only committee chairman in Congress to hold an official session to hear a spokesman for the veterans, a twenty-seven-year-old Naval Lt, j.g., from Waltham, Mass., named John Forbes Kerry. His testimony was the most moving and eloquent we have heard in thirty years as a Washington correspondent. He spoke with a firmness, a tact and a grace that made the Senators seem elderly fumblers. The veterans have given the peace movement a fresh voice.

As this is written the second wave of protests has begun under the People's Coalition For Peace and Justice. The bold slogan is to shut down the government if it does not shut down the war. No one aware of the terrible immobility of the government can fail to have some sympathy with this effort. But it remains to be seen whether the People's Coalition has the troops. There were not more than 1,500 here at the start of what was billed as a major exercise in massive but peaceful civil disobedience in the Gandhi tradition. In all this anti-war theatre perhaps the pantomime which most undercuts the war is Nixon's sudden honeymoon with Chou En-lai. The containment of China is what it's been all about for two decades since we began to pour out first treasure and then blood in South-East Asia. Hanoi was Peking's tool, and we had to stop those hordes in Vietnam or fight them – remember? – on the beaches of California. What was billed as the Asiatic Armageddon now dissolves into a ping-pong tournament. So why go on with the killing? What's left of the war but inertia? Yet I have a terrible fear that if Nixon can pull off another rigged election in Saigon next October and keep Thieu in power with minimum cost the country may forget what we are doing in South-East Asia as easily as it forgets what we have done in Greece. There the controlled press and TV are playing up congratulatory messages from Nixon and Secretary of Commerce Stans on the fourth anniversary of the dictatorship we helped to impose on the very cradle of freedom. And who cares? As nobody would have cared about Vietnam either if it hadn't been made too painful and costly to bear.

3 May 1971, Vol. 19, no. 9

2: Cuba and Latin America

Botching the Cuban and Sugar Problems

Congress last weekend hurriedly passed a botched-up sugar quota bill few members understood, and set in motion a chain reaction that may end by ruining the last U.S. investments in Cuba. Under sudden pressure from a President who seems to have been spending most of his time playing golf since he reached Hawaii on his way home, Congress was forced into passing a piece of legislation involving complex questions of economics and foreign policy without committee hearings or adequate floor debate. Indeed, most of the work on the bill was done by a corps of lobbyists representing rival sugar interests while a sleepy House and Senate waited to ratify the results. The Sugar Act of 1937 was a successful experiment by the New Deal in stabilizing the sugar market and wiping out such social evils as child labour in the beet fields. Its latest embodiment, the four-year Sugar Act of 1948, expires at the end of this year but little had been done about its extension because of the unsettled Cuban situation.

Since a major aim of Castro's domestic policy is to end Cuba's dependence on a one-crop economy, it was clear that we would be getting less sugar from Cuba during the next four years even under the best of circumstances. The problem, sensibly considered, was to negotiate a revision downward of the Cuban quota, using the negotiations to save for American interests part of their sugar-mill investments, and to arrange a payment plan for expropriated U.S. properties. Only by such an orderly negotiation could we hope to keep the sugar market stable and to make new firm commitments to domestic and other foreign sugar-growers who can fill the gap of a declining Cuban output. Ellender of Louisiana pointed out that in any case forty-two per cent of the sugar now being produced in Cuba 'is owned and controlled by Americans' so that we would be in danger of cutting off our nose to spite our face.

Confronted by the first real social revolution Latin America has had since the Mexicans overthrew Diaz, not only conservative but liberal members of Congress so completely lost their balance that the more dangerous consequences of what they were doing went unmentioned. The Charter of the Organization of American States, for example, forbids (Article 16) the kind of economic warfare we are preparing to wage against Cuba. We have everything to lose by a conflict with the Castro regime. Mexico's seizure of our oil properties and Bolivia's of the tin mines, like Nasser's more recent expropriation of the Suez Canal, demonstrate that property rights can no longer be enforced by military means. We cannot march into Cuba as Russia marched into Hungary; the Russians had an army on the spot and a local and political apparatus to do their bidding; we would have to make landings on a hostile coast against a united people, for the Cuban revolution unlike the Hungarian one was not imposed from above by a minority with alien military backing. But to be 'soft on Castro' has become as dangerous a political sin as to be 'soft on Communism' – even Charlie Porter of Oregon now runs with the pack. Allott of Colorado called Castro's regime 'worse than Batista's' and Morse dismissed him as 'a Communist tyrant', leaving little discernible difference between them and such anti-Castro fanatics as Dodd and Keating.

Not a single vote was cast against the proposition of letting the President use sugar for economic war. Only Meyer of Vermont interjected the hope at the end that we were not going to see a new Hungary in Cuba, and the enlightened North Carolinian Cooley, chairman of House Agriculture, admitted the reluctance with which he was acquiescing in a plan to upset a twenty-four-year relationship with Cuba during which it loyally kept to its side of the bargain even during the war 'when', as he pointed out, 'world market prices were substantially above our own domestic prices'. A Congress blinded by anti-Communism seemed intent on pushing Castro farther into the arms of the Soviet bloc.

The simple-minded way that members of Congress indulged in rhetoric about Communist slavery in Cuba contrasts with what may be found in the independent left press here and abroad which agrees that the Cuban revolution is a peasant revolution of an indigenous type, maintaining many kinds of private property holdings. This is the view I understand that Paul Sweezy and Leo Huberman brought back and will expound in a forthcoming issue of their *Monthly Review*. It may also be found in the warmly appreciative portrait Simone de Beauvoir painted of Fidel in the 7 April issue of *France-Observateur*. Even in that pillar of anti-Communism, the *New Leader*, one finds a picture of Castro's Cuba quite different from the vapid nonsense in Congress.

I would call attention to three recent articles in the *New Leader* – by Harry Schwartz (14 March), by Robert J. Alexander (21 March) and by Theodore Draper (4–11 July). Mr Schwartz, the Soviet expert of the *New York Times*, pleaded for the U.S. to 'break out of its present bonds of resentments and legalistic fetishes and try to formulate an imaginative policy' which would include the fixing of sugar quotas by bilateral negotiation as the Cubans have long demanded. Professor Alexander, a leading anti-Communist expert on Latin America, also argued against a policy of economic reprisals, and defended the Cuban oil deal with Mikoyan. 'Newspapers which state that Cubans have fallen into a trap in this agreement,' Professor Alexander wrote, 'are mistaken.' He said that the U.S. has been buying 3 million tons of sugar a year from Cuba, leaving it with $2\frac{1}{2}$ million tons to be peddled elsewhere. The Russian agreement to take a million tons a year for the next five years will therefore, he wrote, give the Cubans, 'assured markets for almost 80 per cent of their output, instead of the previous 60 per cent'. Professor Alexander said 'Castro and his rebels have caught the imagination of the humble people who, in many countries, wish they could destroy their own military cliques as Castro destroyed Cuba's' and initiate 'similar land reforms'. Mr Draper, an authority on the history of the

Communist movement, reported that the Castro group and the Communists 'have fallen out in the past and it cannot be ruled out that they may fall out again in the future'. He said the revolution 'cannot be dismissed merely as a diabolical aberration because it does not live up to our expectations' and depicted it as 'a new type of system that is neither capitalist nor socialist, but contains elements of both, and emerges where capitalism has not succeeded and socialism cannot succeed'.

Congressional discussion took for granted that the event which precipitated its panicky action on sugar was justified. No one questioned the refusal of U.S. and British oil companies to refine Soviet crude oil which Cuba is getting at 80 cents a barrel cheaper than Venezuelan crude. The oil companies in Cuba are subject to its laws. It is hard to see any legal ground for this refusal. Cuba consumes about 3½ million tons of petroleum a year, and each of the three oil companies there has a capacity of about 4½ million tons annually. Each was asked to refine 300,000 tons of Russian oil a year, or about one-quarter of the island's requirements (London, *Economist*, 2 July). This would still leave the companies with the refining and distribution business, the major share of the crude, and good will for a future in which rising living standards will surely increase Cuban consumption of oil. In arrogantly preferring to provoke their own expropriation, they have created a situation for which the rest of us will pay.

11 July 1960, vol. 8, no. 27

What Do We Do in Cuba if We Win?

The German strategist, Clausewitz, in a famous chestnut, said war was the continuation of politics by other means. This implies that it has some rational purpose beyond vengeful or vindictive destruction. It is time we asked ourselves just what is the goal of our growing war on Cuba.

Let us suppose Fidel Castro were to surrender tomorrow and tell us, 'Do what you will with my country.' What would we do? If our aim is free elections, there is little doubt that these would be won by Castro. But few are naïve enough, after the long cosy years of our partnership with Batista, to believe that we are imposing economic sanctions on Cuba and encouraging counter-revolutionary preparations in order to force free elections. The sugar companies and the oil companies and the cattle companies want their property back.

And this is where we had better do a little thinking. It would not be difficult to restore certain kinds of U.S. property in Cuba. Indeed, much of it has been 'intervened' rather than 'expropriated' to facilitate return in future negotiations with the U.S. The restoration of Sears, Roebuck or the luxury hotels or even the oil refineries is a comparatively simple problem, whether by a military victory or by negotiation. But to take the land away from the peasantry and give it back to the sugar companies is another matter. Even if Castro surrendered tomorrow, the land would still be in the hands of the peasants, and once peasants get the land they till, it is an almost impossible task to take it away from them. The Bourbon restoration was never able to do it in France. Even Stalin, ruthless as he was, had to wage a long struggle of almost civil-war proportions to dispossess the peasants and collectivize the land in the Soviet Union. I cannot think of a single instance where land once distributed in an agrarian reform has been returned to its feudal or capitalist former owners.

Let us not confuse Cuba with Guatemala. In Guatemala, Arbenz was forced to resign by the army chiefs after we bought them over to our side. Land reform had hardly begun and the army was there to restore 'order'. But in Cuba Castro wisely liquidated both the Batista army and the Batista police. Since then he has given arms to the workers and the peasantry. What Castro has done for the Cuban peasants can never be undone, and we will incur the hatred of all Latin America and risk world war if we try it.

A new regime backed by the U.S. would have trouble enough undoing other Castro reforms, raising rents again, increasing electric rates, turning schools back into barracks, and beating the labour unions into submission. It would face an impossible task in the countryside. The mere effort would require measures

so repressive and brutal as to shame forever our pretensions to
being a champion of freedom. The best we can do is to obtain
compensation for the land and the restoration of those properties which can serve the Cuban people just as well under private ownership, particularly since the Cubans just don't have
the trained cadres to run a totally socialized economy. But these
sensible goals could best be reached by negotiation. To encourage counter-revolutionary forces to tear Cuba apart by
civil war first is to sow a harvest of bitterness which would
make any reasonable solution unlikely. We wish those two running for President would stop and think a moment about this.
One of them is going to have to deal with it. The problem is not
being made easier by the lynch-mob spirit both are whipping up
against Cuba in low and unscrupulous competition.

31 October 1960, vol. 8, no. 39

The Deed was Done Quickly, But It's Macbeth Who's Dead

Here in Washington and earlier at the U.N. in New York, it was
being whispered that if the Cuban deed were to be done, it
would be best if it were done quickly. And so, it seems, these
Shakespearean prayers have been granted, except that it is Mac-
beth and not the king who lies slain. The rebel invasion of
Cuba, as this is being written, seems to have been crushed.
There is an atmosphere of deep gloom at the State Department.
The President, due to 'the press of business', has just announced
that he will be unable to witness that weekend naval training
exercise off the Florida coast, and the Navy followed this a few
minutes later by cancelling the exercise altogether, though it
was supposed to have been routine. Several hours before the
news came over the U.P.I. ticker that rebel headquarters had
lost all contact with the troops on the beachhead in Las Villas
('Do you want me to evacuate you?' seems to have been the
last words transmitted to them by the commander of an
offshore supply vessel), the A.P.'s State Department correspondent John M. Hightower had already filed a dispatch saying

that the rebel invasion 'was reported on excellent authority today' to have failed to set off 'the political defections and up-risings' on which the expedition had counted. The failure was a failure of intelligence, and it is being said jokingly in the State Department press room that after the U-2 incident and the débâcle in Laos, the Cuban defeat is the third strike against the C.I.A., and on three strikes it should be out. Fidel Castro will have done us a favour if his clean-up of the invasion also leads to a clean-up of Allen Dulles and the C.I.A. They have again demonstrated their incompetence.

The shattering of the invasion hopes may also shatter the Kennedy honeymoon. The post-mortems had begun before the defeat was confirmed. On the hill, a Senate Internal Security subcommittee under Dodd of Connecticut has been holding executive sessions today to hear complaints from the wilder right wing of the Cuba emigration against the Miro Cardona coalition. A preview was provided in last night's *Washington Star* where its right-wing columnist Constantine Brown attacked the Miro Cardona coalition as too far left, and predicted on the basis of earlier hearings by Internal Security 'should the present counter-revolution succeed, there will not be much change in the totalitarian policies of Castro'. On the other hand, the left wing of the emigration had already begun to grumble bitterly about Kennedy. Those who had hoped for a new Fidelism with-out Fidel were disappointed on two scores. The first is that they had been forced to accept an economic and social programme tailored to the moderate right and inconsistent, in their view, with the hopes aroused by the *alianza para progreso*. The second is with the invasion itself, in which they had had little hope from the beginning.

One of the key points to watch, I had been told earlier, was the choice of military leader for the invasion forces. There were two candidates. The candidate of the anti-Castro left led by Manolo Ray was Colonel Ramon Barquin, the most respected military figure in the emigration, an army officer who had been imprisoned by Batista for revolting against him. Colonel Bar-quin was named military commander of Havana by Fidel and defected last summer. Colonel Barquin was against any large-scale invasion, predicting that it would be disastrous if attempted because the time for it was not ripe; he is reported to have said that it would be militarily difficult and psychologically bad, uniting the Cuban people behind Castro against what would inevitably appear to be a foreign-inspired invasion. He was in favour of infiltrating small groups and working from within. The candidate of the right-wingers was Captain Manuel Artime, a young man in his late twenties, a member of the Agrupcion Catolica, who had served for a month or two with Castro in the Sierra Maestra. He was described to me as 'the pin-up boy of the C.I.A.' and the darling of the right-wing Diario de la Marina, which only last Saturday appealed for a new government which would exclude all who had ever served with Castro. Captain Artime was, however, to be forgiven his short stay under Fidel's banner and it was Captain Artime who was chosen to command the invasion. The right wanted a man of its own in charge of the troops, and a man who shared its objective. This was not a new popular uprising but a beachhead on which a provisional government could quickly be established and then appeal for American arms and American military support. The paymasters of the counter-revolution, the big sugar and oil and other companies which helped finance the invasion, didn't invest their money to buy themselves a new revolution.

No doubt the defeat will be disguised as lack of matériel. I have never seen a military force equipped so quickly with tanks and jets, at least in the headlines. A few days ago it was being leaked by the C.I.A. that we had to mount an invasion quickly before Soviet M.I.G.s arrived. They seem to have been supplied more quickly than anyone expected by the Lem Jones firm which was hired to polish up public relations for the rebel forces. On Tuesday afternoon, Lem Jones put out a bulletin (see the account in the *Wall Street Journal*, 19 April), saying that Soviet tanks and M.I.G.s had destroyed 'sizeable amounts of medical supplies and equipment' on the Mantanzas beachhead 'humanitarian supplies . . . destined for the Cuban freedom fighters who are shedding their blood to overthrow the shackles of Communism'. Thanks to this communiqué, the headlines in this morning's papers were full of Soviet tanks and jets, although smaller, more sober stories buried inside the *New York Times*, the *Herald-Tribune* and the *Washington Star* explained that heavy tanks would be useless on that swampy terrain, questioned whether Fidel had M.I.G.s and pointed out that these planes would be of dubious value against small bodies of troops with mountain forest cover. These side stories, which seemed to originate from responsible sources in the Pentagon, said the fighting was essentially a small-arms operation but the Soviet tanks and M.I.G.s fought on undeterred in the headlines.

On the stock market Monday, the stocks of American firms which lost property in Cuba rose hopefully (see the survey on the *New York Herald-Tribune* financial page, 18 April), but wiser estimates were already available. Albert M. Colegrove in the Scripps-Howard papers (see *New York World-Telegram*, 18 April) said most businessmen operating in Latin America disagreed with the rosy hopes of the rebels and quoted one U.S. businessman from Panama as saying, 'Why don't you folks up there in Florida stop kidding yourselves? Sure Castro has lost some support among the middle-class people who still remain in Cuba, but most of the peasants, who comprise the great bulk of the Cuban population, still think he's great.' These businessmen seemed to have a more realistic view than such liberals as the editors of the *Washington Post*, the *New Republican* and Max Lerner who lined up so quickly – and as it turns out so prematurely – with the war crowd. Now it is difficult to see what the anti-Castro forces can do. With no bridgehead, there can be no provisional government and it is too late for direct action by the Marines. This is not 1917.

At the United Nations earlier this week, one felt that the Cuban invasion was destroying Adlai Stevenson and the U.S. morally. How defend the indefensible and deny the undeniable? But the defeat of the rebel forces has suddenly turned high tragedy into low comedy. The Latins who spoke so bitterly in private and were so conspicuously silent in public will now laugh at the U.S.A. It is better that the defeat came now and quickly before the flames could spread. I hope we are not going to try and retrieve our prestige by jumping into a jungle war in Laos, and that the bigger Latin countries will rescue us by firmly pressing for negotiations between Washington and Havana. We're lucky if we can liquidate this David and Goliath affair with no more than this minor bloody nose. It is too bad that our own folly gave Khrushchev a cheap and easy chance to win a victory of prestige, but that is an irretrievable error. Let's not compound it with greater folly by continuing our vendetta against Castro.

24 April 1961, vol. 9, no. 15

U.S. Public Not Informed of Guevara's Olive Branch at Punta del Este

Writing on the eve of the new Punta del Este conference, we want to call attention to a significant omission in the new State Department White Paper on Cuba. The White Paper quotes Che Guevara as saying to the Punta del Este conference last August that the Cuban revolution had set an example for the rest of Latin America. This was used to paint a picture in the White Paper of a Cuba intent on exporting its revolution by military means to other countries of the hemisphere. What the White Paper omits is that Major Guevara went on to say that while Cuba could not give up the moral effect of its example, it was prepared to guarantee that it would not give military aid to revolutionary movements elsewhere in the hemisphere. This olive branch was not reported in any American newspaper we have seen. Indeed, we did not become aware of it until we saw it quoted some weeks ago in *Le Monde* of Paris.

In effect Guevara was offering Cuban non-intervention in Latin America in return for U.S. non-intervention in Cuba. This is relevant to the new Brazilian proposal for 'creating the conditions of live and let live between a socialist Cuba and other members of the O.A.S.' (*Washington Star*, 14 January). The Brazilian Foreign Minister, Dantas, in proposing it at Rio (12 January) expressed the belief, according to the *New York Times* (13 January) that in return Castro 'would accept the idea of a limitation on Cuba's attempts to interfere with other American states'.

Brazil's proposal for a hemisphere code of peaceful co-existence is resented at the State Department which issued a special statement against it, calling for 'continued and positive resistance to totalitarian ideology'. We wonder how this will be equated with Secretary Rusk's recent visit to Franco, when he invited the Fascist dictator to join Washington in a 'triangular' relationship with Latin America. Franco, overtly as an Axis ally before the war and covertly as an American client since, has tried to spread anti-democratic and anti-Yankee conceptions of 'Hispanidad' in this hemisphere, ideas as alien as those of Marxism-Leninism and the lineal descendant of the Holy Alliance clerical-authoritarianism which the Monroe Doctrine was designed to keep out of the New World.

The Kennedy Administration to its credit searches for compromise over Berlin, and over Laos. It urged India to negotiate over Goa and it urges Indonesia to negotiate over West Irian. It not only coexists with, but gives aid to other regimes which are at least as 'Marxist-Leninist' as Castro's. We help Tito and Gomulka. We give aid to Guinea and Ghana. Why is Cuba alone the object of economic blockade, hostile diplomatic action and secret cloak-and-dagger activities which support in Cuba exactly the kind of bombings and assassinations we condemn when committed by the other side in South Vietnam? In any adequate answer two names would figure: United Fruit and Standard Oil.

22 January 1962, vol. 10, no. 3

The Reprieve and What Needs to be Done with It

Last week was the world's first thermonuclear crisis. It will not be the last. This issue of the *Weekly* might never have been written. You who read it might have been one of the lucky few, huddled half-mad with anxiety about missing loved ones, in the ruins of New York or Washington. Mr Kennedy's gamble paid off. But what if it had failed? Unless we can achieve a fundamental change of behaviour among nations, the Cuban confrontation is only a preview. Is the fate of the world again to be decided in a test of will and nerve between two men? Or among three? As the news slowly begins to trickle out from behind the secrecy imposed, we get a glimpse of close contact between Russian submarines and U.S. warships hunting them. A U-2 was shot down. Other U.S. planes were fired upon. Incident and accident thrive on such tension. What if one of them had led to an outbreak of fighting? What if on some lonely aerial or naval patrol next time, someone's nerve or judgement fails?

In an article written before the Cuban crisis but published just after it in the London *New Statesman* (26 October), under the title 'Can Nuclear War Be Prevented?', Bertrand Russell wrote it was essential 'to prevent the spread of nuclear weapons to powers which do not at present possess them' because 'increase in the number of nuclear powers augments the danger of nuclear war at a rate greater than the increase in the number of nuclear weapons'. Cuba demonstrated this vividly. In this, the first thermonuclear crisis, we saw the debut of the first Nth power. Though Khrushchev assured us, as we have so often assured him, that the ballistic missiles passed out to an ally were kept in close control of officers from Big Brother, what if Castro refuses to give them up? We are reminded by an Assistant Secretary of State (Martin, in a *Voice of America* broadcast) that Castro still has preponderant power in the island itself. He could seize the missiles and the Russians in charge of them. He could, with fewer than the thirty nuclear missiles he is supposed to have, blackmail the U.S. and the world. This is what Khrushchev risked. I would feel more grateful for his backdown if he hadn't made this terrible gamble to start with.

What happens when a bigger Nth power than Cuba is in a position to threaten the world's end to get its way? *Time* (2 November) reported Bonn's Defence Minister Franz Josef Strauss 'worriedly saw a cynical deal trading off bases between the U.S. and Russia, *which would weaken his own long-range goal to obtain nuclear missiles for West Germany*' (our italics.) What happens when last year's models of atomic weapons are available on the world's armaments market? What if Israel and Egypt had atomic weapons in the Suez crisis? If

India and China had them now? If Chiang could lob one at Peking? This is what the reprieve gives us time, precious time, to prevent.

National sovereignty has now become the right of any nation to decree everybody else's extermination. Either we end it or it will end us. Major Raul Castro, Fidel's brother, said in a speech at Santiago (Reuter in the *New York Times*, 30 October) that 'a world-wide holocaust was risked because President Kennedy has "set himself up as supreme judge of the planet" '. There was justice in the gibe. He had arrogated to himself the right to decide when to press the button. The Pope appealed for negotiation. U Thant asked for a stand-still. Lord Russell appealed to both sides. Mr Kennedy insisted on a backdown by Khrushchev first. Fortunately, he got his way. But the happy relief should not blind us to the monstrous situation in which all humanity found itself. Any ruler, with nuclear weapons, as the head and symbol of a sovereign state, now had a Divine Right beyond that any king ever dreamed of, to condemn mankind to hell. Before the backdowns began, Kennedy, Castro and Khrushchev were all making like Joves, with their thunderbolts. As for the rest of us, ours was but to do and die, like the Light Brigade but not so glamorously, huddled in the cellar with canned goods and candles. The nation-state system that enables one or two men to decide life or death for the planet is the common enemy, not Russians or Americans, Communists or capitalists. The rest is delusion. 'It is in the nature of political bodies,' Jung wrote in *The Undiscovered Self*, 'always to see the evil in the opposite group.' Only this bigger and truly human perspective can light the way to peace.

We Americans emerge from the crisis the strongest power on earth. Man's fate depends on whether our collective intelligence can be made to match our strength. Mr Kennedy, vastly strengthened politically by his victory, stands at a fork in the road. One way, the easy way, the line of least resistance, leads in the direction of a bigger arms and civil defence build-up so that next time we can be in an even stronger position to dictate terms. The military bureaucracy is already demanding heavier arms appropriations; the scare will lead to a strong demand for more and better stocked cellars in which to huddle. The President, however, according to a remarkable interview with James Reston (*New York Times*, 29 October), 'is rejecting the conclusion of the traditional "hard-liners" that the way to deal with Moscow everywhere in the world is to be "tough" as in Cuba'. It is good to know that the President sees that the world cannot be governed by crisis and ultimatum.

Will Mr Kennedy, then, take the other fork in the road? This requires courage and leadership of a far more difficult kind. The crisis showed the curious limitations of presidential leadership in our society. The President can easily take the nation into war. He can only with difficulty lead it towards peace. When he seems ready to push the button, albeit for universal destruction, few voices are raised against him. But let him decide for peace and negotiation – the bipartisanship ends. The Republicans and the right-wing Democrats and a sizeable section of the bureaucracy are already complaining that we tied our hands on Castro. Their motto is Better the whole world dead than Cuba Red. The President is going to need the support of the peace forces, and he is going to have to help create a stronger peace movement, if we are honourably to live up to our assurances on Cuba in return for the removal of missile bases in the trying days ahead. A way out of the crisis can only be found if Mr Kennedy now sets out to do what he has never done before – actively to educate and to lead the American people to a saner view of the world, to a more sophisticated view, to a less self-righteous view. This may be his and our last chance.

All this would require taking the really hard line – the line which runs athwart unthinking prejudice and hateful preconception. What are the lessons which need to be drawn from the crisis and driven home? One is the indispensability of the United Nations – it offered a face-saving way for Khrushchev and Kennedy to back off from a direct blockade confrontation, a way to deal with Castro without offending his dignity and Cuba's. U Thant's efforts would have been impossible unless the United Nations had preserved sufficient universality and independence to remain a moral force. To maintain this universality and independence should be the aim of a wise American foreign policy; this dictates the admission of China and an end of the attitude which has treated the U.N. as if it were a U.S. errand boy. A second lesson of the crisis is that it followed inexorably from our unwillingness to coexist with Cuba in the hemisphere. The stationing of Russian nuclear missiles in the island, the crisis which brought all of us so close to destruction, was the climax of the hateful attitudes and policies with which we have long sought to dominate, to destroy and to starve out an island neighbour in violation of the U.N. Charter and the Inter-American treaties. Until we face up to the truth about our own guilt towards Cuba, we cannot find our way safely and finally back from the brink.

The third and main lesson is that human beings everywhere must band together to get rid of this monster, the bomb. We need to act now to prevent its spread; a denuclearized Latin America, Africa and Middle East is still easy to achieve; a denuclearized Pacific has been asked by Communist China on several occasions. A disengaged and denuclearized Europe between the U.S. and U.S.S.R. is the one way to prevent future crises that would dwarf Cuba and from which extrication would be much more difficult. A noteworthy survey by Jonathan Spivak in the *Wall Street Journal* (29 October) revealed the dwindling importance of our nuclear bases abroad not only in places like Turkey but even in England. 'Indeed, U.S. military strategists,' he reported, 'would not [by a curious misprint we verified, the "not" had disappeared in the edition we saw] be seriously perturbed if no new nuclear striking force were stationed on the British Isles. The independent British deterrent is considered far more important as a morale booster for Britain than as strategic protection for the U.S.' Such facts need to be brought home to the widest possible audience if we are to find the road to peace. Both Khrushchev and Kennedy in their final exchanges showed themselves sobered by their look into the abyss, ready for a fresh start. The urgent place for them to begin is with this wholly irrational war between India and China. If it is allowed to continue, the two big nuclear powers may slowly find themselves drawn in. A senseless quarrel which

began over a few square miles of desolate Himalayan wasteland
could end by engulfing the planet.

5 November 1962, vol. 10, no. 40

Why Peron Happened and Can Happen Again

In the editorials celebrating the fall of Peron, two major items
in his rise to power are passed over in a discreet silence. One is
how much he owed to the Cold War. The other is how much he
owed to the Catholic Church. Indeed the Cold War may be said
to have begun with the Argentine question. The first of Yalta's
broken promises was not Stalin's promise of free elections in
Eastern Europe, but our promise that Argentina, the Axis base
in the Western hemisphere in the Second World War, would not
be admitted to the United Nations.

Peron as vice-president and minister of war and labour was
already the real power in Argentina when, in the interest of
welding the Western hemisphere into a solid anti-Soviet block,
we broke that promise and sponsored Argentina for membership. Molotov finally gave in, but at a price: 'You can have
Argentina if we get Poland.' The unity of the victors was
breached, and power politics took over. The Lublin regime was
thereby established in Poland and a regime Cordell Hull had
stigmatized as Fascist was admitted to respectability in the Americas. When Peron ran for President the year after and con-
solidated his power (with the help of some $13,000,000
contributed by Nazis), Acheson and Spruille Braden tried to
defeat him with a 'Blue Book' exposing his pro-Axis record and
backing, but it was then too late.

We didn't try again. The mythological rhetoric of the Cold
War propagated the view that Peron's Argentina was part of the
'free world'. We hope Mr Truman in his memoirs will find
space to recall that two months after Peron suppressed *La
Prensa* he hailed a Latin American Foreign Ministers Conference (with the Argentine present) as 'proof of the vitality of
free men and their institutions'. A Brazilian newspaper, *Correio
a da Manhã* of Rio de Janeiro, noted sadly that there wasn't

enough vitality present to discuss the suppression of Argentina's leading newspaper. 'Freedom was sacrificed,' it wrote, 'to the diplomatic convenience of having General Peron's representative sign the conference declarations ... Unanimity ... was not really achieved. *La Prensa* is a reality. Peron's solidarity is at best an equivocation.'

Another incident is worth recalling, lest it be imagined from the events of the last few months that Peron and the Catholic Church were always at loggerheads. In Argentina, as in Germany and Italy, the Church was ready to sacrifice liberty and Catholic anti-Fascists to its own purposes. In Peron's 1945–6 campaign for the presidency, thoughtful Argentines realized this might be their last chance for a long time. An extraordinary event occurred. The Radical, Socialist and Communist parties joined forces, with the unofficial support of the Conservative Party, in a Democratic Union which put an opposition ticket into the field. Peron was supported by all the rightist, pro-Axis, nationalist and anti-Semitic hate groups, by a captive labour movement and a renegade split-off from the anti-clerical Radical Party. It was with this motley collection that the Church took its stand for Peron. On the eve of the election a pastoral letter was issued urging Catholics to vote against candidates who advocated separation of Church and state, secular education or legal divorce. This meant vote for Peron.

In Argentina, as in Italy, there were brave churchmen who fought Fascism. But the majority of the hierarchy, led by the Primate, supported 'the revolution of 1943' in which Peron played a leading role. Argentina's 'Father Coughlin', Padre Filippo, told his people during the 1945–6 election campaign, 'you must shut your mouths because Jesus Christ himself was a great dictator.' The Church's reward was the re-introduction of compulsory religious instruction in the schools, where secular education had been the rule since 1884. The new press law forbade, among other things, publication of matter which might undermine Christian morals. 'We are pleased,' Pius XII said in a message to Peron, 'by this recognition of the rights of the Church in the field of Christian education.' We may be sure that clerical influence played its part in the behind scenes

manoeuvres which had made a place for this 'new' Argentina in
the United Nations.

This is not ancient history. The same forces which helped
Peron into power are still at work, and are an obstacle to the
creation of a free Argentina. The Church fell out with Peron
only because in the end he turned anti-clerical; the logic of
totalitarianism pushed Peron as it once pushed Mussolini into
conflict with the Church. We may be sure that the Argentine
hierarchy is shopping around for a safe general who will carry
on in the spirit of 1943. We may be sure that the State Department is also looking for a cooperative military man. U.S. firms
have some $400,000,000 invested in Argentina; Standard Oil of
California has an exploitation contract with Peron, as yet
unratified, which was so juicy that we were willing even to
overlook church burnings for the sake of it.

In the context of Argentina these forces may fashion a new
'strong' regime. The context is one in which free traditions
never took deep and wide root. The democracy overthrown by
successive generals from 1930 on was in too many respects an
oligarchy to win mass support. The underprivileged working
classes were too easily open to the bribery of compulsory wage
increases and a dictator's social-welfare benefits. To overlook
these fundamental factors in the Argentine picture is to fail to
see why Peron lasted as long as he did, and why a new Per-
onismo could so easily be established.

26 September 1955, vol. 3, no. 35

The Bitter Harvest in Central America

A revolutionary wave is sweeping over Central America, but
the State Department's reactions show that it has learned
nothing useful from the Cuban experience. On 26 October the
Lemus regime, which had grown increasingly harsh and author-
itarian, was overthrown in El Salvador. On 11 November an
uprising began in Nicaragua and two days later in Guatemala.
It would not be at all surprising if trouble were to erupt next in
Honduras. These four tiny republics – lands which live on

coffee and bananas – are alike in being sinks of human misery in which the old Latin American triumvirate of landowner, general and priest has long held back basic reform. In two of them, Guatemala and Honduras, they have had the aid of two big American fruit companies, United Fruit and Standard Fruit. These revolts are their bitter harvest.

So long as the army was strong enough in these countries to hold down discontent, the State Department paid little attention to them. No reporters were called in for private briefings to spread alarm about the violation of basic human rights. It is only when popular revolt breaks out that the U.S. takes a hand, and then only to spread alarm about the danger of Communism and now of that new bugaboo Castroism. Of the four, the most miserable is El Salvador. Nowhere in Latin America is the gulf deeper between the few rich at the top and the many poor at the bottom. Our government viewed the situation with a self-deceiving equanimity. But now that the Lemus regime has been overthrown, the prisons opened and reform promised, the U.S. has decided not to recognize the new regime 'until', as the *New York Times* reported, 5 November, 'it is satisfied with the political coloration of the civilian members of the Junta' which took over 'and of their independence from leftist groups'. The government fears that it will fall unless recognized and its members are reported (*New York Times*, 11 November) as 'particularly resentful that their political leanings are being questioned while they have not had a chance to expound their views'. They deny that they are either Communists or Castro followers but the denial will do them little good with diplomats determined to see Red.

Instead of scare headlines about Castro's hand in Central America, the Department and the press ought to be educating the American people on the facts of life in Central America. Only Costa Rica with a relatively wider distribution of land and a high level of literacy has had stable democratic government. The other four have economies in which the bulk of the land is in the hands of a few great landowning families or U.S. corporations, dependent on a pool of uneducated, landless rural proletarians for their harvest help. The average annual income per capita is about $200 a year, a very deceptive figure since it includes many big incomes at the top; in El Salvador a third of the people have an annual income of less than $200 *per family*.

None of us North Americans have any conception of the hateful memories these revolts awaken among our Latin neighbours. The Somoza dictatorship in Nicaragua, one of the oldest in the hemisphere, was established in the thirties by Anastasio Somoza, one of the leading figures in the National Guard our U.S. Marines organized in their long fight to put down the national hero, Sandino, who rebelled against U.S. control of Nicaragua. The Somozas thus began as U.S. stooges against their own people, and have ruled over them since with our support. The Guatemala memories are more recent. We helped overthrow the Arbenz government in 1954 and then looked on complacently as its successors undid the Arbenz reforms, reforms we claim to favour. Arbenz enacted a moderate income tax in 1954, it was soon afterwards abolished by Castillo Armas; 'the Agrarian reform was halted and most of the land expropriated under the Arbenz regime was returned to the landowners' (Robert J. Alexander, *Communism in Latin America*). Is it any wonder that Castro is a hero in Latin America, and that we appear to be the main obstacle to aspirations for a more decent life below the border? Yankee imperialism, to our shame, is not just a propaganda slogan in Central America. It is a reality. To recognize this, and to stop blinding ourselves with nonsense about Cuban plots, is the first essential to wiser policies and better relations.

21 November 1960, vol. 8, no. 42

Speaking Loudly, But Carrying a Twig

Like Mr Kennedy's other economic messages, his long awaited Latin American programme turned out, when unwrapped from its tinsel, to be warmed-over Eisenhower. The strategy of keeping his actual legislative demands to a bare minimum is understandable in view of the Congress with which the new President has to deal. But the disparity between the rhetoric and programme is beginning to give these performances a distinct flavour of the mock heroic. Mr Kennedy strides out on the field of battle declaiming in high and urgent tones, but brandishing no more than a twig. Since he dare not wound and must instead cajole the Congressional dragon, it would be better if our St George began to adapt his prose style to his humble necessities. At home these realities are so well understood that the wide gap between advance announcement and product is taken for granted as it is in any form of advertising copy. But in Latin America, which expected a new era with the new President, this programme will be dangerously disillusioning, and there Mr Kennedy has competition. He has to produce a product to compete with the hopes aroused by Castroism. And though few Americans will be aware of it – for Latin America is still the stepchild of our concerns – our neighbours will recognize at once that this *alianza para progreso* boils down to the same meagre fare cooked up hastily by Mr Eisenhower's banker advisers at the Bogotá conference.

To see this programme as our neighbours will see it, one must take a good look at the agency which will administer the bulk of the new programme. This is the Inter-American Development Bank. In 1959, after Castro had launched the most complete agrarian reform the land-hungry masses of Latin America have ever known, we finally rushed steps to match him with a revolutionary step of our own – a bank. Ever since 1889, Latin America has been trying to sell us the idea of establishing an Inter-American Development Bank. It took the threat of Castroism to give this project the necessary push. In June 1959 hearings were finally held and it went through Congress with the support of such radical organizations as the American Bankers Association and the U.S. Council of the International Chamber of Commerce. As a concession to our hungry friends to the south, a 'Special Operations' till of $150,000,000 in soft currency loans was provided but the rest of the $1 billion in capital was to be loaned out on a sound banking basis for social purposes not attractive to private business investment and for technical assistance in planning other projects in which private investors *would* be interested. The underlying purpose was to create a better climate for private investment in Latin America.

Only $400,000,000 was actually to be paid in capital; the rest was to be raised on the private money market with $450,000,000 in callable capital providing the investor with a guarantee. By tying the bank's operations so closely to the money market, Latin America was to be taught a lesson. As Dean Acheson told the House Banking and Currency Committee, in the tone of a schoolmarm discussing a recalcitrant pupil, 'The foreign investor is not encouraged by the knout in the hand of the nationalist demagogue. Since the bank's success in expanding the resources available for development loans will depend on its ability to sell its own securities to the investing public, Latin Americans – through the bank – will have the clearest possible demonstration of the effect of their conduct upon their credit.' By this ingenious device, the landless peon was to be taught to think like a National City Bank vice-president.

The purpose of the bank, as the Hon. T. Graydon Upton, then Assistant Secretary of the Treasury, told the Senate Foreign Relations Committee, was to assist Latin American countries 'in mobilizing their own resources and in encouraging domestic and foreign private capital to undertake desirable investments'. To make sure that this institution did not somehow turn *sans culotte*, Eisenhower's friend, Robert Cutler, the Boston banker, out of Old Colony Trust, was made president. Mr Upton, who had been vice-president of the foreign department of the Philadelphia National Bank before going to the Treasury, was made vice-president. Under such circumspect direction, the bank's first five months of operations have been marked by an exemplary freedom from hasty action. It has made only two loans – one hard-money loan of $3,900,000 at $5\frac{3}{4}$ per cent to Arequipa, Peru, for a water system, and a $10,000,000 loan at $4\frac{1}{2}$ per cent out of its 'Special Operations' till to hard-pressed Bolivia. These driblets and their interest rates will be compared elsewhere in the hemisphere with the $100,000,000 ten-year credit for petroleum-development machinery which the Russians gave Argentina at $2\frac{1}{2}$ per cent.

It is to this sedate institution that Mr Eisenhower at Bogotá last year proposed to assign the task of administering his new Latin American aid programme, and thus to fight the inroads of Castroism in the hemisphere. And it is this unimaginative policy which Mr Kennedy's message for all its drama is implementing. Of the $500,000,000 programme, $394,000,000 will be assigned to the Inter-American Development Bank 'under a special trust agreement' to apply 'on a loan basis with flexible terms, in-including low interest rates *or* repayment in local currency' (our italics) for a carefully specified list of activities, none competitive with private investment. In this list agrarian reform re-emerges sanitized as 'land settlement and improved land use' – far from anything as crass as the expropriation of semi-feudal estates. The other purposes specified in the message to Congress are 'housing, water supply and sanitation, and technical assistance related to the mobilizing of domestic financial resources'. Mr Kennedy said apologetically at one point in his message that of course 'social progress is not a substitute for economic development'. But this, he indicated in the message, is to be left to private enterprise. The idea of loans to enable these countries to develop their own resources is as conspicuous by its absence from the message as it is evident in the thinking of almost every Latin American regime. 'U.S. business concerns,' Mr Kennedy said pointedly, 'have also played a significant part in Latin American economic development. They can play an even greater role in the future.' If the Latin American masses will only wait.

This programme is triply inadequate – in financial size, in the character of the administering agency, and in the thinking which underlies it. 'Our approach,' Mr Kennedy told his White House reception for Latin American diplomats the night before he sent his message to Congress, 'must itself be bold . . . a vast effort, unparalleled in magnitude and nobility of purpose.' A rhetoric so far out of proportion to the realities is the very kind we like to think of as typically Latin. Why talk as Mr Kennedy did of 'the endless exploration of new frontiers' when he holds back so plainly from the new frontiers of fresh social thinking and looks to a banking institution and a banker mentality to give Latin America a peaceful but revolutionary substitute for

Castroism? I want to deal next week with the magnitude of the Castroite challenge and with the dimensions on which any programme must be built which hopes to compete with it. Mr Kennedy is a long way off from effective answer.

20 March 1961, vol. 9, no. 10

Debasement of the Coinage and Corruption of the Word

Let's take it slow and easy, like a first-grade class. We live in the free world. In fact we are the leader of the free world. The other world is a world of one-party dictatorships. There people are denied the right to vote. If they try to demonstrate the police rush them off to jail. Or set the dogs upon them. That's bad. To combat such wickedness, we spend $50 billion a year on arms. We spare no expense anywhere to combat the forces of evil. Our armies, our secret agents, are on all the continents, alert. But somehow all these big words and high purposes seem to evaporate when things happen in Le Flore County, Mississippi, or Birmingham, Alabama, or Albany, Georgia. It's as if the free world were a myth, a fairytale, a bit of advertising copy not intended to be taken seriously. Men trying to exercise the right to vote are shot at. Men and women kneel to demonstrate in prayer and dogs are set upon them. Men are beaten, and then jailed for resisting arrest. They've even begun to arrest them for resisting the dogs. The machinery of the state governments, their courts, their law-enforcement officers, are mobilized to maintain rule by one party and one race. But Congress and the press, the lawmakers and the opinion-makers, the White House and the Church, don't really get excited about this the way they do about events, let us say, in Berlin.

We have grown accustomed as a nation to living in a fine haze of big words nobody really takes seriously. This debasement of our ideological currency, this corruption of the word, confronts us on every hand. It's not the Negro alone to whom the free world appears as a fraud. President Kennedy at Costa Rica had hardly finished calling for 'an unyielding defence against all who seek to impose new tyrannies on the Americas' when a new military tyranny was established in Guatemala, the third in a year: first Argentina, then Peru, now Guatemala. In each case the military took over in fear of free elections. Though free elections bulk large in our official rhetoric, there is some evidence that we shared that fear. C.B.S. (4 April) and Bert Quint from Guatemala City in the *New York Herald-Tribune* (7 April) both reported that the Guatemalan army chief, Peralta, made discreet soundings as to what the U.S. reaction would be before venturing to take power. Quint wrote that, like the Guatemalan army, the U.S. believed free elections would bring Juan José Arevalo to power again and 'Washington felt he could not be trusted'. Dictatorships are allowed to stage fake elections in Paraguay, Nicaragua and Haiti without U.S. interference or loss of Alliance for Progress aid. But free elections are stopped without protest from us, if not with our connivance, where we fear the results. The test is not whether Guatemalans trust Arevalo but whether we do. This is what people below the border call Yankee Imperialism.

The Alliance for Progress bathes Latin America in speeches calling for agrarian and social reform. Arevalo gave Guatemala some measure of both while he was President between 1945 and 1951. After the long night of the Ubico dictatorship (a very pleasant period for United Fruit Company), Arevalo gave Guatemalans a taste of civil liberties. Apparently this was not to our liking. Though the Communist Party was never able to achieve legal status until after he left office and he even upheld the closing down of its paper, *Octubre*; though United Fruit lost none of its lands to agrarian reform while Arevalo was President and though it took four years for him just to legalize agricultural trade unions, Arevalo figures in our newspapers as 'an extreme leftist'. If Arevalo was an 'extreme leftist', Franklin D. Roosevelt was an anarcho-syndicalist.

At Costa Rica, Mr Kennedy said we and the six Central American governments would 'build a wall around Cuba . . . a wall of dedicated men determined to protect their own freedom and sovereignty'. Of the six countries, two are now plain military dictatorships; two, Panama and El Salvador, are ruled by hated oligarchies; only two, Costa Rica and Honduras, have freely elected popular governments. Their secret-services chiefs met together in Nicaragua to erect an Iron Curtain around Cuba, to apply stricter police-state methods to their own people. This was a wall not of dedicated men but of little Metternichs. In one sphere at least these backward countries have now come fully abreast of us. 'Representatives of the Central American and U.S. governments,' the A.P. reported from Managua, 5 April, 'recommended last night that their citizens be kept out of Cuba by stamping their passports, "Not Valid for Travel to Cuba". The U.S. uses the same system to bar Americans from Red China.' Thus technology marches on. But how keep Latin American youth from asking, 'If conditions in Cuba are as bad as the U.S. says, why is it so anxious to keep us from seeing for ourselves?'

We Americans used to pride ourselves on being a plain-spoken people. But the windy euphemism affects our relations with all the world. An example, around which the annual legislative battle has begun, is the case of foreign aid. Most of this is really an annex to our military budget. The Clay Committee reported that seventy-two per cent of this year's foreign aid went in direct military or related economic assistance to maintain 2,000,000 men under arms along the Sino-Soviet border. The committee calls this 'frontier of freedom'. It is in fact almost entirely a chain of military dictatorships. The otherwise chilly Clay Committee gives this part of the programme warm support, though it recommends some cuts, particularly where 'sophisticated weapons' are going to armies 'of value largely for internal security purposes'. Ordinary guns and tanks are good enough to hold people down. The humane aspects of foreign aid are only a thin sugar coating on a Pentagon pill. Since the Marshall Plan ended, we have spent $50 billion on foreign aid. Of this, $30 billion were for armament, another $15 billion to bolster the economies of those same dictatorships so they could support such large armies. Of the remaining $5 billion, $3.5 went for development, $1.5 for technical assistance. Thus of every dollar of foreign aid, only 10 cents went for constructive purposes, 90 cents for military. No wonder we can no longer afford to speak plainly. Unfortunately the validity of free speech, free elections and free institutions suffers in the minds of a whole new generation from our abuse of fine words for shabby purposes.

15 April 1963, vol. 11, no. 9

What Chile Needs Is an Opening to the Left

While the centre of gravity in U.S. politics is moving towards the right, the centre of gravity elsewhere in the hemisphere is moving left. Here a broad national front has been formed behind a Texas conservative to defeat the danger of Fascistic influence in the White House. In Chile a broad national front was formed behind a Catholic leftist to defeat a Popular Front candidate with Communist Party support. This divergence in development forecasts trouble unless the time the U.S. gained by the Chilean victory is put to good use. The first essential is to understand better what happened in Chile and what might have happened in the U.S. The election of a Communist-supported Socialist in Chile, pledged to nationalize U.S. copper and nitrate properties, would have pushed U.S. politics farther rightwards. The prospect of another Castro in the hemisphere, this time in one of South America's Big Three, would have let loose a burst of hysteria worse than that we have seen over Cuba. It would have given the Goldwaterites a boost in this election, impelled Johnson to new demonstrations of toughness this time in Latin America, set back the fragile beginnings of peaceful understanding with Moscow and the hope after the election of negotiating an end to the Indo-Chinese war with Peking. When a power as big as the U.S. has fits, the whole world shakes, and fits we would have had if the left had won in Chile.

If we are to use the reprieve wisely, it is important to realize that Frei Montalva's victory in Chile was not a victory for democracy or free enterprise as they are defined in the simpleminded U.S. lexicon. Chile is barely beginning to be a democracy in our sense of the word; it is a nation in which a landed aristocracy has played the game of parliamentary musical chairs much as it was played in England before the nineteenth-century Reform Bills gave lower-class Englishmen the right to vote. It is only in recent decades that pressure from below has forced Chile's oligarchy to utilize one makeshift after another to protect its privileges. The latest was to support a Catholic leftist as a lesser evil. This oligarchy is anti-democratic and anti-capitalistic. The paradox in Chile, as elsewhere in Latin America, is that U.S. capitalist interests allied themselves with the big landowners in policies designed to *prevent* industrial and capitalist development. U.S. copper and nitrate companies have been interested in getting raw materials out of Chile as cheaply as possible, not in developing native industry. For landowners and copper magnates alike this would mean higher labour costs. The biggest push towards industrialism and capitalism in Chile came from its first Popular Front government, which was elected in 1938 and launched the Chilean Development Corporation, the first of its kind in Latin America. It initiated a wide variety of public, semi-public and private enterprises, giving Chile its first steel plant, its first oil industry and its first public power company. The most important measure required for peaceful relations with Latin America and peaceful reform there is to educate the U.S. to the need for such governmental planning and direction if development is to get off the ground in time to match the population explosion and popular aspiration.

U.S public opinion will also have to accept the fact that this new regime will not 'stand firmly with the West' if that means isolating Cuba and embargoing trade with the Communist countries. Even Frei's conservative predecessor had begun making copper deals with Moscow, Prague and Peking. Frei deplored the break with Cuba and in a press conference after his election expressed the hope that Cuba could be brought back within the hemispheric fold on the basis of the principles of self-determination after the U.S. elections. U.S. public opinion must also be prepared for domestic measures in Chile more drastic than those proposed by Bosch in the Dominican Republic, Villeda Morales in Honduras and Goulart in Brazil before U.S. interests encouraged their overthrow by the military.

The first necessity of the new Chilean regime is to stop Latin

America's second-worst inflation (after Bolivia), a bonanza for landowners and primary producers but a savage capital levy on its working class. This means effective taxes on large incomes and properties. The second necessity is swift land reform. Only about one-fourth of its best arable land is under cultivation, forcing Chile to import food. With 600,000 landless peasants and most of the land in the hands of a few great families indifferent to its wise use, the big estates must be broken up. On top of this, Frei Montalva's Christian Democrats, while on record for the ultimate nationalization of the big copper mines, want immediate control of the industry to expand refining at home and marketing abroad. Here there will be a frontal conflict with U.S. interests.

The inner weakness of the Christian Democratic majority will make itself felt as soon as these conflicts begin. For in Chile, as in Western Europe after the war, all kinds of re-actionary interests jumped on the Christian Democratic bandwagon because they had nowhere else to go. Only anti-Communism put together the big majority in Chile. As soon as Frei moves to implement his programme in the Chilean Congress, to which elections are scheduled in March, his coalition will begin to fall apart. He will be reduced to a minority regime unless he can, like the Christian Democrats in Italy, achieve an 'opening to the left' and form an alliance with those elements of the Popular Front which favour peaceful reform rather than revolution. Here Frei's friendship with Allende and the latter's own Socialist background should prove fruitful. It should also be facilitated by the shift in the position of the Chilean Catholic hierarchy in recent years from support of feudalism to support of social reform. Only a new alliance of this kind can give Chile the social reform it needs if major convulsion and perhaps war are to be avoided. But can U.S. public opinion be educated to understand this? Or will we back a military coup if the Chilean oligarchy and the U.S. copper companies cannot corrupt a Frei regime? Last January the *Engineering and Mining Journal*, wel-coming the appointment of Thomas Mann as Johnson's policy 'tsar' for Latin America, expressed satisfaction with his 'tough, no nonsense approach' and said Chile would be his first test. In

Chile the U.S. can easily destroy the last bulwark to what it fears.

Brazil Provides an Ironic Footnote on Wars of National Liberation

Joint U.S.–Latin American war games were held last month in Peru. The Chilean government declined to let its army participate. Chile, with one eye on Brazil, fears a fresh rise of militarism in the hemisphere. The purpose of the manoeuvres was to teach Latin regimes how to deal with 'wars of national liberation'. Unfortuntely such wars are rarely suppressed by military means. A wiser policy is not to provoke them.

Brazil threatens to become a pilot model in how to brew a future uprising. There the military dictatorship has just given the Hanna Mining Company and Bethlehem Steel concessions they had sought in vain from the predecessor democratic regimes. For five years both the moderate left and the nationalist right (including Lacerda, the favourite Brazilian of *Reader's Digest*) opposed the efforts of the Hanna Company's George H. Humphrey to obtain control of rich iron-ore deposits.

A week before Castelo Branco, the new Brazilian military dictator, signed the decree Humphrey wanted, the Alliance for Progress announced it would make available $450 million to Brazil in 1965. Humphrey was Ike's Secretary of the Treasury and Goldwater's most influential supporter. Yet he seems to do better under the Democrats. The 'give-away' policies his candidate deplored have bought Humphrey concessions in Brazil its own Congress had refused to grant. Such are the wonders which foreign aid, in its mysterious ways, can perform.

In April we will hold the second Special Inter-American Conference in Brazil. It is to deal with 'human rights and measures to strengthen democracy in the hemisphere'. The site would seem to be well chosen, since many of Brazil's leading statesmen and intellectuals have been proscribed, jailed or exiled by its military, were it not that the purpose is to deal with Cuba not

Brazil. Its Foreign Minister (Reuter in the *Washington Post*, 29 December) looks favourably on allowing a Cuban government in exile to establish itself on Brazilian soil. The military who destroyed democracy in Brazil would then, by an exquisite turn of fate, provide the base for restoring democracy in Cuba, or if not democracy at least United Fruit.

11 January 1965, vol. 13, no. 1

Will Brazil Some Day Be Our Algeria?

The *Washington Post* is more and more losing its editorial independence under pressure from the White House and the State Department. A scandalous example of what this can do to a liberal newspaper was its editorial (29 October) on the military take-over in Brazil. The less liberal but more independent *Baltimore Sun* (31 October) commented with acidity on Castelo Branco's claim that he was suspending the Constitution and dissolving Brazil's political parties in order to achieve 'tranquillity for the nation's economic development'. The *Sun* responded with a defence of democracy. 'Repression,' it said, 'can tranquillize but hardly energize an economy.' The *Washington Post*, on the other hand, published a long and fatuous defence of the Brazilian military. This faithfully reflects the line which is being handed out by the State Department and by Lincoln Gordon, who in his passionate advocacy acts like Brazil's Ambassador to Washington instead of our Ambassador to Rio.

'Doctrinaire reactions against the role of the military are unrealistic,' said the *Washington Post*. Brazil's workers had too much 'coddling' under the Goulart regime. 'Brazil,' it said, 'was an example of a situation in which a militarily-based regime has proceeded with dedication in areas where politicians had failed.' This recalls the language in which Mussolini's seizure of power in Italy was once welcomed.

'With the mammoth economic problems in Brazil and the razor balance between reform and revolution,' said the *Post*, 'it is especially important for Americans to have a sympathetic insight into what President Castelo Branco and his colleagues have been trying to do.' A better insight into what the military have been trying to do was afforded by the stock market in Rio. The day after the decrees wiping out free government in Brazil, the market had the biggest and most bullish day in its history. Bull markets are not precipitated by agrarian reform and higher minimum wages. Democracy had to be suspended because the Castelo Branco regime is putting the burden of deflation on the backs of Brazil's poor. They not only have to bear it. Their spokesmen are even forbidden to complain. The very day the *Washington Post* wrote that editorial explaining that Castelo Branco had not 'interfered so far with freedom of the press', severe restrictions were being announced in Rio. Newspapers were forbidden to publish news 'likely to stir the people against the government' (*Baltimore Sun* from Rio, 29 October). Presumably this would apply to such items as the forty-per-cent rise in the cost of living during the first nine months of this year, despite the sacrifices imposed on wage-earners in the name of stopping inflation. Newspapers were also forbidden to publish statements by persons who have had their political rights taken away from them by the military, persons like former President Kubitschek. To focus on Kubitschek is to light up what is happening in Brazil. The Alliance for Progress really originated in Kubitschek's proposal two years earlier for an Operation Pan America. Under his presidency, 1956–60, Brazil had one of the greatest periods of development in its history. Its growth rate was about double its rate of population increase. Though this was accompanied by the galloping inflation endemic in Latin America, the benefits of prosperity were widely shared. It is revealing that today Kubitschek is the no. 1 target of the Brazilian military. He has been deprived of political rights and subjected to constant interrogation at the expense of his health. It was the victory of his party in five of the recent gubernatorial elections which led the military to suspend the Constitution, and to forbid the press to publish anything he might say. The man who comes closest to being Brazil's hope for leadership in the direction of democratic and peaceful reform is regarded as no. 1 enemy by the military we support. Our primary concern under Johnson and Mann is not social change for the benefit of the masses as envisaged by Kennedy but the maintenance, by force if necessary, of what is called a favourable climate for U.S. investment in Brazil. Such climates, though made favourable today, risk being paid for by an explosive popular resentment tomorrow.

Another primary concern of the Johnson–Mann era is to maintain in power in Brazil the one major military force in the hemisphere on which we can count for such joint operations as our recent intervention in the Dominican Republic. There is something risible about a crusade to make the Western hemisphere safe for democracy when its chief supporters with our approval set up a military dictatorship in their own country.

All this merits more than a casual glance as if at a distant error of policy. What if the military in Brazil were to be confronted by a mass uprising for the restoration of democratic liberties? What if the military were to split, as they did in the Dominican Republic and one faction to fight for restoration of the Constitution? What if Castelo Branco and his hard-line Army Chief of Staff, Costa e Silva, were in danger of being overthrown? Would we be asked to intervene in their defence? Would another Communist menace be conjured up, with the names and addresses of fifty-seven agitators? Would we be told that American lives and property were in danger? Whether in Brazil or elsewhere in Latin America, future crises of this sort can easily be envisaged. The time to think about them is now before they happen. 'After Indo-China,' a U.S. Special Forces lieutenant in Vietnam told the French novelist Jean Larteguy (*Paris-Match*, 16 October), 'we will have our Algeria. It will be South America.' It could some day cost a lot of American lives to try and undo what our military protégés are now doing in Brazil.

8 November 1965, vol. 13, no. 37

Why Washington Would Be Wise to Be Patient with Chile's Allende

It is fortunate for us and for Chile that the Republicans are in power here. If the Democrats were in the White House, the

Republicans would be attacking them for standing idly by while 'a new Castro' takes over in the hemisphere. Humphrey would never have dared the low-key, low-posture stance Nixon has so far been following, as he did over Peru. The Chilean election marks another step in the liquidation of U.S. investments in Latin America, but it will be cheaper to let U.S. copper and steel companies in Chile take their nationalization as a tax loss than to set out on the path of an intervention which could convert South America into a giant Vietnam.

Chile has been moving left for a long time. For 101 turbulent days during the depth of the world depression in 1932 Chile was declared a Socialist Republic. In 1938, after native Nazis attempted to seize power, Chile elected the first Popular Front regime in the hemisphere, an anti-Fascist coalition of the Radical, Democratic, Socialist and Communist parties. A new Popular Front in 1958 came within 35,000 votes of electing Dr Allende President in a three-way race. In 1964 the right and the U.S. supported Frei and gave Chile its first Christian Democratic regime in fear of a Popular Front victory. But while the oligarchy gave Frei the votes for a majority, it blocked the 'revolution in liberty' he had promised. The result was to push the Christian Democratic movement left. A split-off joined the Popular Front.

The traditional order in Chile, as in most of Latin America, rested on the trinity of the priest, the army officer and the landowner. This has broken down. While the armed forces have become socially adventurous, the Church has moved left. The Christian Democratic candidate, Tomic, ran on a platform almost as radical as Allende's; both called for complete nationalization of the U.S.-owned copper companies. Allende promises recognition of Cuba, and an end of the economic blockade, but Frei had already been doing a sizeable business with Cuba in foodstuffs.

This convergence of the two movements makes any deal to deny Allende the presidency unlikely. Normally it would seem hazardous to launch so fundamental a change as Allende promises on a mandate which represents thirty-six per cent plurality, only fractionally larger than the thirty-four per cent given the conservative candidate. But a sizeable portion of the 'other third', the Christian Democrats, is as radical as the Popular Front. It needs only twenty-one of the seventy-five Christian Democratic votes in Congress for Allende's election. *The* (London) *Times* reports from Santiago (11 September) that there are about twenty Christian Democrats 'who would support Dr Allende under any circumstances'. Since the election Dr Allende has repeated his assurances of freedom of expression, multi-party politics, and adherence to the constitution. Dr Allende, an aristocrat and a Socialist, is temperamentally and philosophically neither a Castro nor a Lenin.

Chile is already highly socialized. Its main exports, copper and iron, are in too short supply to be boycotted as we boycott Cuban sugar. In charting a take-over of the big landed estates, the monopolies and the banks, while leaving middle and small business in private hands, Dr Allende seeks agrarian reform and social planning for full employment. His most dangerous enemies may be on the left. He must hold down wages to curb galloping inflation and curb the violence of Chile's own 'instant revolutionaries'. He must achieve results fast enough to win mass support for austerity. If he fails, the result may be a collapse into civil disorder which could easily spread elsewhere in South America and make it more difficult for the U.S. to keep hands off. That's why Nixon would be wise to be patient with Allende.

21 September 1970, vol. 18, no. 17

3: Israel
and the
Middle East

What Should Not Be Forgotten in Israel's Crisis

As many readers know, I saw a good deal of the birth of Israel. I visited Palestine every year for six years from 1945 to 1950 inclusive. In 1946 I travelled as an illegal immigrant from the Polish–Czech frontier through the British blockade to Palestine. In 1947 I was on one of the prison ships which took illegals to Cyprus, and I celebrated Passover in one of the British detention camps on that lovely Greek island. I got to Palestine again in 1948 just before statehood was declared and stayed on until after the first truce, covering the Arab-Jewish war for *PM*. I remember cowering in an open ditch in the border settlement of Negba when it was bombed by the Egyptians and I remember stumbling along by starlight with the human pack train that volunteered to carry supplies at night past the Arab fortress at Latrun and over rocky Bab-el-Wad to besieged Jerusalem.

Though it was only as a newspaperman, I had the privilege of seeing my people in some of the greatest moments of their long history – as they emerged from the hells of Auschwitz and Buchenwald, packed into the old freighters which served as their Mayflowers on the Mediterranean, fighting against odds which seemed overwhelming to establish a Jewish nation. I cannot write of those years or of Israel with objectivity. But as a new crisis looms up in its existence, I would like to recall some aspects of those all too recent events which Jews dare not forget, and which I would ask non-Jews in all kindness to remember.

It is much too early to forget what happened with the rise of

Hitler, the indifference of the State Department towards the pre-war refugees, the shiploads the British Foreign Office turned away from Palestine in 1939–41, the hopeless who blew themselves up in mass suicide on the *Patria* and the *Struma*, the cruel farce of the Bermuda Conference at that very moment in 1943 when the remnants of the Warsaw Ghetto were staging their uprising. Had there been the tiniest semblance of a Jewish state in Palestine, it could have saved many of those who later went to the crematoriums. If nothing else it could have supplied those precious *papers* without which a man was no longer a man in pre-war Europe but stateless, with no right to remain where he was yet no right to go elsewhere. There have been too many Hitlers too often to be sure that new persecutions may not occur, in which the existence of a Jewish state would offer a haven. A bitter history warns us that this might make a difference to our children or our children's children.

In this crisis it is also much too soon to forget exactly why and how war broke out in Palestine between the Jews and the Arabs. Sixteen days before the United Nations General Assembly voted by more than the required two thirds for the partition of Palestine between them, Britain's delegate, Sir Hartley Shawcross, said 'If states are to permit themselves – and to be permitted – to cooperate with the [United Nations] Organization when it suits them and to stand aside, or to attempt to sabotage it, when it does not, this Organization would be rendered wholly abortive ...' The occasion was a debate over the Soviet veto but the words applied as neatly to Britain's attitude towards that partition decision. Bevin had asked the U.N. to act on Palestine. Every other member of the British Commonwealth had voted for partition. The U.N. resolution called for a Jewish and an Arab state to be linked economically. It sought to provide for a peaceful transition by directing the British, as the mandatory power, progressively to hand over the functions of government to two provisional state councils, Arab and Jewish. Bevin declined to cooperate with the U.N. and encouraged the Arabs to defy the U.N. decision. So did the State Department by reversing the American position and on 19

March 1948 asking the Security Council 'to suspend ... the proposed partition plan'.

Then as now, behind the moralizing, was a concern only for oil and bases. The Arab states were confident, and looked forward to easy pogroms. 'This war,' boasted Azzam Pasha, the Secretary General of the Arab League, 'will be a war of extermination and a momentous massacre which will be spoken of like the Mongol massacres and the Crusades.' Yet the State Department six days after partition was voted imposed a unilateral arms embargo on the Middle East which had the effect of shutting off arms to Israel while leaving the Arabs free to obtain arms from the British. When Bevin was asked in the Commons on 28 April 1948 whether Britain would go on supplying the Arab states with arms though their armies were massing on the Palestine borders, his cynical answer was 'we must honour our contracts'. Thus Anglo-American influence, which might have brought about a peaceful transition, was utilized to encourage war against the U.N. decision. The Jews had no recourse but to fight for their lives, and the war was stopped only when the Foreign Office and the State Department suddenly realized that the Arabs were losing.

The Arab refugees weigh upon my conscience, and I believe it the moral duty of Jews everywhere to contribute when peace is made towards their resettlement. They are the tragic victims of a tragic war, in which both sides felt that they were fighting a war of national survival. But as another crucial moment arrives, when the great powers must again decide whether to bring about peace or foment renewed war, it is important to remember that the earlier war might possibly have been avoided if the Foreign Office and the State Department had honoured their obligations to the United Nations.

And qualitatively the situation is made no different because this time the Soviet Union has embarked with zest on the same game, competing with the West to furnish with expensive arms poverty stricken feudal principalities whose people need bread and peace, even as do those of Israel.

6 February 1956, vol. 4, no. 5

An Affluent Society But Living Beyond Its Means

To see Israel again after eight years is to be struck at every turn by the triumphant evidence of progress. The flood of new immigrants, which has more than tripled its population since the achievement of independence eighteen years ago, is reflected in a continuous building boom. The dismal acres of shanty towns (*ma'abaroth*) hastily erected for new immigrants were still distressingly visible in 1956. Today they have given way (except for a hard-core of 3,000 which still clings to the old hovels) before whole new neighbourhoods – and cities – of towering apartment houses. The roads have widened, the traffic jams grown worse. The country throbs with expansive vitality. Israel has become an affluent society. Even in the once Spartan kibbutzim, the outhouse and the cold outside shower have been replaced by private lavatories and running hot water, provided by individual solar heaters. Everywhere there are flowers. Even in Tel Aviv the whole new northern extension of that rather grubby city has become downright pretty with tree-lined boulevards and flower gardens. Not all the changes are to the taste of those who loved the old Palestine. The Dan Hotel in Tel Aviv has become as over-sumptuous as its counterpart in Miami. The Desert Inn outside Beer Sheva, no longer a sleepy Bedouin town, might be in luxurious Palm Springs, except for the *mezuzoth* beside every door and the Arab-with-camel on duty at the entrance. The dolce vita has arrived, as the old-timers complain, complete with juvenile delinquents and call girls.

The other big change since the spring of 1956 is in the sense of security. Then infiltrating fedayeen from Egyptian training centres in the Gaza Strip and Sinai were shooting up settlements at night and making travel after dark hazardous. The Sinai campaign later that year may have been a humiliating setback for England and France, but for Israel it put a stop to these terrorist raids, smashed Czech and Soviet arms dumps across the Egyptian border and established a U.N. force at the narrow straits where Eilat's access to the Red Sea had been shut off by Nasser. This much was accomplished, whatever the wisdom of the retaliatory spiral which led up to the Sinai campaign, and its cost in the alienation of Afro-Asian sympathy from Israel.* Today one can travel everywhere with assurance. Unusually heavy rains had turned the country greener and lovelier than we had ever seen it in seven previous trips. Our visit was a succession of unforgettable scenes: Haifa's gleaming harbour from the top of Mt Carmel, the wide lawns of Mishmar Ha-Emek, the rich green vistas of the once malarial Valley of Israel, the holy places of Nazareth, Tiberius and Safad, lunch on the eastern shores of Lake Galilee at Ein Gev within the shadow of the Syrian border, the mauve hills at twilight which look down on the fertile collectives in that narrow 'finger' of Israel which stretches northwards between Lebanon and Syria. Later we saw Ashdod, Israel's biggest seaport, rising on the dunes where the Philistines once dwelt, and Kiryat Dan, a new complex of factories and farms to the north of Beer Sheva. We saw old friends in kibbutzim like Shoval and Hatzor nearby which were once lonely military outposts and are now thriving centres of rural industry as well as agriculture, for since 1959 the industrial by-products of the collective settlements equal or surpass their agricultural output. The climax was our climb up those venerable hills to Jerusalem. There one can still step backwards in time, and savour ways of life centuries apart. A fashionable crowd takes tea on the verandah of the King David overlooking the walls of the Old City, and a few blocks away little boys in ear curls and suspenders rock back and forth over their pious schoolbooks in the back-alley *yeshivahs* of Mea Shearim, keeping alive a medieval universe of orthodox Jewry.

Beneath the prosperous and picturesque surface there are problems grave enough to threaten Israel's future. But for those who have seen the crisis of its earlier years it is impossible not to be optimistic. I first saw Palestine on 2 November 1945, the day the Haganah began the war against the British by blowing up the watchtowers from which they laid in wait for illegal immigrant ships; it seemed hopeless for so small a force to challenge

---

* See Michael Bar-Zohar's, *Suez: Ultra Secret*, newly published in Paris, and Simha Flapan's critical article on it in the May issue of the *New Outlook*, a Middle East monthly devoted to Arab–Jewish reconciliation.

so great an empire. In the spring of 1946 I travelled with the illegals on one of those Jewish Mayflowers. In 1947 I saw the British impose martial law on Tel Aviv in an effort to wipe out the terrorist campaign against them. In 1948 I was a witness to the joint attack of the Arab states on what was then an ill-prepared tiny community of 650,000 Jews.* In 1949 and 1950 I saw the lack of food and the letdown in morale which followed the war and the onset of the Arab blockade. To have seen such odds overcome makes it hard to take too tragically the problems of the dynamic, confident and expanding Israel of today.

They are nonetheless serious. The first is fiscal: Israel is living beyond its means. Its rate of economic growth is topped only by Japan's and few countries can match its steep rate of increase in exports. But in 1963 its adverse surplus of imports over exports was still $420 million and in the first quarter of 1964 its trade deficit rose to three times that in the first quarter of 1963. Capital imports have been running ahead of the trade deficit so that the government's cash reserves have been growing. But of total capital imports in 1963 of $500 million, $162 million was in German reparations and restitution payments which will now decline sharply. Israel will soon have to meet the challenge of austerity and better distribution of income. Its affluent society, like America's, has little-seen but wide fringes of poverty. An ostentatious luxury by the rich does not make this more bearable. And there, as in America, the problem of poverty is intensified by colour and 'race'. Israel has a double 'Negro' problem. The darker Jews from the Orient and North Africa, as well as the Arab minority, suffer from prejudice.

The usual Jewish attitude towards the Arabs is one of contemptuous superiority. Our driver northwards was a Jew who had fled from the Nazi advance into Hungary but that did not save him from racist habits. When I suggested that we give a boy a lift, he refused, saying the boy was an Arab. When I asked what was the difference, he said Arabs smelled bad. I said that is what anti-Semites said of us Jews in the outside world but this

* In *Underground to Palestine* (1946) I told the story of the illegal trip and in *This is Israel* (1948) the story of how Israel won its war of independence.

made no impression. His attitude, it is painful to report, is typical. Israel is a country not only of full employment but of
labour shortages. Thousands of Arabs do the menial tasks of
Tel Aviv. They find it as hard to obtain decent lodgings as
Negroes do in America and for the same reasons; many 'pass' as
Jews to circumvent prejudice. In Haifa I visited the only secondary school attended by both Jews and Arabs but even there
the classes turned out to be separate. The State of Israel has
done much in a material way for the Arabs but the sense of
humiliation outweighs any improvement. The spectacle fills one
with despair. For if Jews, after all their experience of suffering,
prove no better than the rest of mankind once in the majority,
what hope for a world as torn apart as ours is by tribalism and
hate?

More progress is being made in dealing with Israel's other
integration problem – that of the Jews from the Orient and
Africa. For these – unlike the Arabs – are people Israel wants.
That does not save them from being looked down upon. Half
the people of Israel are now from countries where Yiddish is
unknown. But in Israel, for the first time, the tender language of
East European ghettoes has become an upper-class tongue. The
Ashkenazi, the Yiddish-speaking Jews, hold the commanding
positions in the community. The Sephardi, or Oriental Jews,
speaking Arabic, French or the Old Castilian of the Spain from
which they were driven five centuries ago, are the hewers of
wood and drawers of water. They make up half the population
but their children are only fifteen per cent of those in secondary
schools and only five per cent of those in the university. Their
cultural level is lower. They cannot afford to send their children
to the higher schools. Discrimination has given them solidarity
and 'communal' tickets have begun to appear in local elections,
pitting Sephardi against Ashkenazi. The right-wing parties are
making demagogic appeals to the Oriental Jews. On the other
side one Yiddish-speaking *meshuganah* has just published a
book to prove that the Yiddish-speaking from the West are the
only true Jews! The government is trying its best to give prefer-
ences to the Orientals where equally qualified. It fears lest Israel
run into a situation like that of Belgium where after 150 years

the conflict between Walloon and Fleming divides the nation. Fortunately the common language of Hebrew, and the melting pot of school and army, are available to ease Israel's divisions. Education is seen as the key to amalgamation but education costs money and here we come to Israel's other big headache, that of defence.

The amount spent on defence is a secret but some notion of its magnitude may be gathered from a veiled figure in the budget. This shows that about a third goes for an item called 'security, special budget and reserve'. This has been rising. It was less than $300 million or 28.3 per cent of the 1963/4 budget and close to $400 million or 30.9 per cent of the 1964/5 budget. The next largest item was education, but this is less than 8 per cent of the budget. Were the arms race in the Middle East to end, Israel could afford to make secondary education free, too, as elementary education is now. Nothing could do more to develop her human resources and end the rankling inferiority of Oriental Jew and Arab. Another way to measure the impact of the arms race is to notice that 'security, special budget and reserve' amounts to more than German reparations, U.J.A., private gifts and donations of food surpluses put together. If Israel enjoyed real peace, she would no longer be dependent on the bread of charity. However one looks at it, peace is Israel's overriding problem. It's hard for a poor country to keep up with the Joneses in armament. 'In the war for independence,' said one of those tireless old-timers who make Israel the dynamic community that it is, 'a Spitfire was hot stuff. We could buy one second-hand for £2,000. Now the Mystere costs us $750,000; the Mirage, $1,000,000; the Super-Mirage, $1,250,000. But planes and tanks are given to Egypt by the Russians for very little. They gave Nasser fifteen submarines and a flotilla of Komars, swift mosquito boats armed with missiles which can shoot from thirty kilometres offshore. Now we're afraid Egypt may get enriched uranium from Moscow, too.' Between Russian aid and German scientists there is a real fear that Egypt may some day be the instrument for a second go at Hitler's 'final solution'. Khrushchev's visit stirred deep anxiety. 'The Government of Israel regrets,' Prime Minister Eshkol told the Knesset pointedly, 20 May, 'that in spite of the Egyptian ruler's aggressive declarations against Israel he receives political support and supplies of arms from sources that generally advocate peace and coexistence.' It is tragic that Israel could not have joined its neighbour in rejoicing over so fruitful and historic an achievement as the Aswan Dam. And it was mischiefmaking demagogy for Khrushchev to join the Arab states in stigmatizing as an imperialist plot the beginnings of the Jordan water scheme which could benefit the whole area and does no more than put to use millions of precious gallons otherwise wasted in the Dead Sea.

To inflame the Arab–Israeli quarrel is to risk no small conflagration. Eshkol's statement on the eve of his visit to the United States reiterated previous denials that atomic development in Israel was designed for other than peaceful purposes. But doubts persist. There are circles in Israel which see nuclear arms as a necessity for survival. They fear that neo-Nazi German scientists are using Egypt as a proving ground for 'unconventional' weapons. The arms race between Egypt and Israel can become the next hot spot in the proliferation of nuclear arms. A committee of distinguished scholars and scientists in Israel have begun to agitate for a denuclearized Arab–Israeli area but there is no echo from Egypt, where a police state represses free opinion. Behind the quarrel which is dividing Israel's ruling party, the Mapai, the quarrel between Ben Gurion and Eshkol over the irrepressible Lavon affair, is a struggle between younger military men who put their faith in force and an Old Guard which wishes to steer a course of moderation away from the apocalyptic adventurism of Ben Gurion. The Suez affair showed that B.G. and the military were able to carry on secretly behind the back of civilian government. They might do so again. If the conversations with President Johnson strengthen Eshkol, they will make a contribution to peace. Now is the time to prevent Egypt and Israel from wasting their substance and endangering the world in the blind alley of a nuclear arms race. I hope to report further on this in a later issue.

The Harder Battle and the Nobler Victory

Israel's swift and brilliant military victory only makes its reconciliation with the Arabs more urgent. Its future and world peace call for a general and final settlement now of the Palestine problem. The cornerstone of that settlement must be to find new homes for the Arab refugees, some within Israel, some outside it, all with compensation for their lost lands and properties. The world Jewish community, already girding itself for a huge financial effort to aid Israel, should be thankful that its victory has come with so little loss of life or damage to either side. The same funds may now be diverted to a constructive and human cause. It was a moral tragedy – to which no Jew worthy of our best prophetic tradition could be insensitive – that a kindred people was made homeless in the task of finding new homes for the remnants of the Hitler holocaust. Now is the time to right that wrong, to show magnanimity in victory, and to lay the foundations of a new order in the Middle East in which Israeli and Arab can live in peace.

This alone can make Israel secure. This is the third Israeli–Arab war in twenty years. In the absence of a general settlement, war will recur at regular intervals. The Arabs will thirst for revenge. The Israeli will be tempted again to wage preventive war, as in 1956 and now again. The Israeli borders are so precarious, the communications between Jerusalem and the coast, on the coast between Tel Aviv and Haifa, and up the finger of eastern Galilee, are so narrow, so easily cut, as to be untenable in static defensive warfare. A surprise attack would cut Israel into half a dozen parts. A long war would be suicidal for a community of not much more than 2,000,000 Jews in a sea of 50,000,000 Arabs. Only total mobilization can defend it, and total mobilization is impossible for any extended term in Israel since it brings the wheels of the economy to a crawl. The strategic and demographic circumstances dictate, and blitzkrieg is a dangerous gamble. To be forced to keep that weapon in reserve is ruinous. It is ruinous financially and it is ruinous morally. It imposes a huge armament burden. It feeds an ever more intense and costly arms race, as each side seeks frantically for ever newer and more complex weapons. It brings with it a spiral of fear and hate. It creates within Israel the atmosphere of a besieged community, ringed by hostile neighbours, its back to the sea, sceptical with good reason of the world community, relying only on its own military strength, turning every man and woman into a soldier, regarding every Arab within it distrustfully as a potential Fifth Columnist, and glorying in its military strength. Chauvinism and militarism are the inescapable fruits. They can turn Israel into Ishmael. They can create a miniscule Prussia, not the beneficient Zion for which the prophets hoped and of which the Zionists once dreamed. The East will not be redeemed by turning it into a new Wild West, where Israel can rely only on a quick draw with a six-shooter.

In justice to Israel no one can forget the terrible history that has turned the Jewish state into a fighting community. Events still fresh in living memory illustrate how little reliance may be placed on the conscience of mankind. Long before the crematoria were built, in the six years of Nazi rule before the Second World War, refugees met a cold shoulder. Our State Department like the British Foreign Office distinguished itself in those years by its anaemic indifference to the oppressed and its covert undertone of admiration for the Axis; our few anti-Fascist ambassadors, like Dodd in Berlin and Bowers in Madrid, were treated miserably by the Department. The welcome signs in the civilized world were few, and even now if events were reversed and Israel were overrun it could expect little more than a few hand-wringing resolutions. Both sides would play up to the Arabs for their oil and their numbers. If the upshot of this new struggle is the expropriation of Western Europe's oil sources in the Middle East, it will only seem to history a giant retribution for the moral failure that forced the survivors of Hitlerism to seek a refuge in the inhospitable deserts, drawn by a pitiful mirage that pictured them as an ancestral home.

The precedent of the cease-fire resolution at the U.N. *is* a most disturbing one. It accepts preventive war and allows the one which launched it to keep the fruits of aggression as a bargaining card. But Israel has a right to ask what the U.N. was prepared to do if Nasser had been able to carry out his threats of total war and the complete destruction of Israel. Who would have intervened in time? Who would take the survivors? These are the bitter thoughts which explain Israel's belief that it can rely on itself alone. But to understand this is not to accept it. The challenge to Israel is to conquer something more bleak and forbidding even than the Negev or Sinai, and that is the hearts of its Arab neighbours. This would be greater and more permanent than any military victory. Abba Eban exultantly called the sweep of Israel's armies 'the finest day in Israel's modern history'. The finest day will be the day it achieves reconciliation with the Arabs.

To achieve it will require an act of sympathy worthy of the best in Jewry's biblical heritage. It is to understand and forgive an enemy, and thus convert him into a friend. A certain obtuseness was unfortunately evident in Abba Eban's brilliant presentation of Israel's cause to the Security Council. To rest a case on Jewish homelessness and refuse at the same time to see the Arabs who have been made homeless is only another illustration of that tribal blindness which plagues the human race and plunges it constantly into bloodshed. The first step towards reconciliation is to recognize that Arab bitterness has real and deep roots. The refugees lost their farms, their villages, their offices, their cities and their country. It is human to prefer not to look at the truth, but only in facing the problem in all its three-dimensional frightful reality is there any hope of solving it without new tragedy.

Just as Jews everywhere sympathize with their people, so Arabs everywhere sympathize and identify with theirs. They feel that anti-Semitic Europe solved its Jewish problem at Arab expense. To a rankling sense of injustice is now added a third episode in military humiliation. Zionist propaganda always spoke of the role that the Jews could play in helping to modernize the Arab world. Unless firm steps are taken now to a general and generous settlement, this will become true in a sense never intended. The repercussions of this new defeat will lead a new generation of Arabs to modernize and mobilize for revenge inspired (as are the Jews) by memories of past glory.

Considering their numbers and resources and the general rise of all the colonial people in this period, the Arabs must eventually prevail. Those who shudder to think that Israel, with all it cost in devotion and all it won honourably in marsh and desert, might be destroyed after a short life as were the Maccabean and Crusader kingdoms before it, all who want it to live and grow in peace, must seek to avoid such a solution. Israel cannot live very long in a hostile Arab sea. It cannot set its face against that renaissance of Arabic unity and civilization which began to stir a generation ago. It cannot remain a Western outpost in an Afro-Asian world casting off Western domination. It cannot repeat on a bigger scale the mistakes it made in Algeria, where Israel and Zionism were allies of Soustelle and Massu and the French rightists. It must join them. The Jews played a great role in Arabic civilization in the Middle Ages. A Jewish state can play a similar role in a new Semitic renaissance. This is the perspective of safety, of honour, and of fraternity.

One crucial step in this direction is, in the very hour of victory, to heal wounded Arab pride as much as possible, and in particular to reach a new understanding with Nasser. Both American policy and Israeli policy have sacrificed long-range wisdom to short-sighted advantage in dealing with the Egyptian leader. He is a military dictator, he wages his own Vietnam in Yemen, he uses poison-gas there against his own people, he runs a police state. But he is also the first Egyptian ruler to give Egypt's downtrodden fellahin a break. It is fascinating to recall that Egypt has been ruled by foreigners almost since the days when David and Solomon ruled in Israel. Not until Nasser's time and the eviction of the British and French at Suez have the Egyptians at long last become the master in their own ancient house. Nasser's programme has given Egypt its first taste of reform, on the land, in the factory, in health and education services. His accomplishments certainly surpassed those of a comparable military figure, Ayub in Pakistan. The U.S. oil interests, Johnson's animosity and Israel's ill-will have been united in recent years in efforts to get rid of him. They have all favoured feudal monarchs like Saudi Arabia's whose day is done. It is Nasser who represents the future and who can create the internal stability so necessary to peace. The alternative if he is overthrown will ultimately be some far more fanatical and less constructive force like the Moslem Brotherhood. If war makes sense only as an extension of politics by other means then Israel's victory will make political sense only if it leads to a new era of friendly relations with Nasser. This is the biggest challenge of all to objectivity and insight in both Washington and Jerusalem.

The bigger picture as we write is ominous. The price of bogging down American military power in a peripheral and irrelevant theatre like Vietnam is a huge shift in the balance of power in Europe and the Middle East. If the Arabs go through with nationalization of oil resources the effect on the pound sterling will be catastrophic. This will be another giant step in the disintegration of West European empire. Western Europe in a sense has already lost the Third World War. To avert its outbreak steps are needed as quickly as possible to reduce world tension. The U.S. could contribute mightily by calling off our barbarous and futile bombing of North Vietnam and making peace in South Vietnam. One crisis at a time is enough, indeed too much. The super powers have taken a first step in the U.N. cease-fire resolution to damp down the dangers of a wider war in the Middle East, at least temporarily. Can't the same initiative be widened to the Far East?

12 June 1967, vol. 15, no. 21

Golda Meir and God's Cruel Prank

This year, happily, the guns of August were stilled. It would be a crime against humanity if they were allowed to blaze up again this fall. It would also be a disaster for both branches of the Semitic people. The extremists on either side are mad if they think they can attain their aims by war. Al Fatah's dream of destroying the Jewish state cannot be accomplished. It would end only in a new holocaust, this time for Jew and Arab alike, and it would be a miracle if the flames did not engulf the world.

Equally foolish are those Israelis who think they can go on for another generation besieged and dependent on an ever more frantic and costly effort to maintain air superiority. A fourth of Israel's gross national product and 85 per cent of her taxes are already going to defence. In the tense and clamorous weeks ahead the one essential point should not be lost to sight. The international climate, and particularly the relations between the two super powers, have unexpectedly provided a precious opportunity in which it may be possible at last to guarantee the existence of Israel and to construct a Palestinian State in which Arab refugees may be helped to build a new life. That opportunity must not be lost.

Two steps are urgent. One is to set up some joint system of inspection which will deal quickly with the charges of cease-fire violation. The other is to speed up the Jarring mission by making the Arabs spell out just how they are prepared to recognize Israel and its rights in a settlement and at the same time making the Israelis spell out just how and where they are prepared to withdraw. When parallel discussions have forced both sides to begin putting their cards on the table, it will then be the task of the U.N. and the superpowers to pare down the positions of both sides so they will fit into the framework of the 1967 Security Council resolution. The faster this is done the better. Contending peoples who haven't agreed in 3,000 years are not going to come to terms in thirty days. Basically the agreement will have to be imposed, as the cease-fire itself was imposed.

In a real sense the coerced agreement to begin talks may be seen not so much as an imposition by the big powers as a liberation of Israeli and Arab politics from sacrosanct but stale rigidities. What had long been deemed politically impossible turned out to be politically popular. The war-weary people on both sides greeted news of the cease-fire with relief. The big powers have not only isolated the extremists but unleashed hopes for peace which make it more difficult for the leadership to turn back from negotiations.

For many years here and in Israel I have heard it said that Nasser alone among the Arab rulers was strong enough some day to make peace with Israel. Now that this day seems precariously to be dawning, Israeli leaders are unwilling to acknowledge what is happening. It took courage for Nasser to accept the U.S. proposal, and Israel has already reaped political dividends from this action. Arab unity has been shattered. The ranks of the fedayeen are split. Nasser shut down the radio facilities of the guerrillas in Cairo and they may lose their subsidies from Saudi Arabia, Libya and Kuwait, all of which have accepted the cease-fire. *Al Fatah* has termed the talks a crime. What better earnest could Nasser and Hussein give of their sincerity? Would Israel prefer Arab unity and continuation of the war?

In a period of World-wide *detente,* the Israeli leadership is in danger of becoming the last stronghold of the cold war. The joint moves towards a Middle Eastern settlement are part of a larger trend. When West Germany and Moscow make peace, when Moscow embraces the hated Social Democrats and *revanchards* of yesterday, when Bonn accepts the Oder-Neisse line, and Washington acquiesces, we are in a new period of history. If Germans and Russians can agree, why not Arab and Israeli? The Israeli leadership finds it hard to adjust to this. As recently as 20 July Mrs Meir in an interview with the German weekly *Der Spiegel* suggested that N.A.T.O. and the U.S. should force the Russians out of the Middle East in a confrontation like that of the Cuban missile crisis!

The basic trouble between the Israeli government and the Nixon Administration is that Nixon is becoming too much of a dove to suit Jerusalem's taste. The Israeli government hoped for confrontation, and Nixon seems set on negotiation. The divergence extends beyond the question of Soviet relations. The Israeli government for some time has sought to polarize the situation, to push the Arab states so completely into the arms of Moscow that Israel would become the one firm friend of the U.S. in the Middle East. This would assure U.S. support in a continuous arms race. 'Do you think President Nixon's era of negotiation with the Soviet Union,' Mrs Meir was asked on C.B.S. *Face the Nation* 30 August, 'is reacting to Israel's disadvantage?' Mrs Meir dodged the question with a lengthy answer to a previous inquiry. The recent suggestion from San Clemente of joint Soviet-American teams to safeguard the new borders must have alarmed the Israel government because it fears great power collaboration. But what kind of security would Israel have if the Cold War intensified and grew hot in the Middle East?

U.S. policy is to save U.S. interests in Egypt and the Middle East by bringing about a settlement. The oil companies which draw $2 billion a year for the U.S. balance of payments from the Middle East and have a growing investment in Egypt want peace. If the price of that settlement, realistically, is a kind of super-power partnership in enforcing the peace, the oil companies are prepared to pay it. So is Nixon. I myself believe this is to Israel's interest, and that it is far better for Israel if the Arab states are not completely dependent on Moscow and if the U.S. maintains sufficient leverage on both sides for peace.

Fulbright sees the conjuncture of forces as providing an ideal opportunity not only for peace in the Middle East but to revive the United Nations. His speech of last week on the Middle East, from which we present excerpts in these pages, gives Nixon and Rogers valuable help. From all indications the Nixon Administration has been giving Israel assurance of new safeguards if it goes along with a settlement within the framework of the 1967 U.N. resolution. Nixon's hand is strengthened when Fulbright, the leading foe of America's effort to be a world policeman, declares his readiness in this case to support a U.S. treaty underwriting a U.N. settlement and guaranteeing Israel's security. Three fourths of the Senate in two open letters to Nixon in the past two months have put their names to hawkish declarations of support for confrontation in the Middle East and new arms shipments to Israel. Fulbright's speech on the other hand provides support for negotiation rather than confrontation. This accounts for the sour response it received in hawkish and Israeli quarters.

The Fulbright speech, in its humanity, its idealism and its concern for both Arab and Jewish rights and susceptibilities, is one of the greatest he ever delivered. But we must confess considerable misgiving about a security treaty between the U.S.

and Israel. History too often has seen such relationships begin in benevolence and end in imperialism. It would create serious risks for both America and Israel, and the Israeli reactions indicate that they also are doubtful. Israel's security would be better served by strengthening the United Nations and solidifying the world *detente*. Her long-range future depends on her becoming an accepted part of a Semitic Middle East, not an outpost of any super-power. But Fulbright's suggestion, even if it never materializes in a treaty, must give added assurance to Israel that the U.S. will not let her down in a peace settlement. A consensus which extends from Nixon to Fulbright is more assurance than any treaty.

The peace talks flow from the carefully drawn 22 November 1967 resolution of the Security Council. Its cornerstone is 'the inadmissibility of the acquisition of territory by war'. The principle is important from the standpoint of world law and its reconciliation with Israeli security needs is not as difficult as may appear at first glance. The problem is eased first of all because the bulk of the inhabited areas taken over by the Israelis in the 1967 war are occupied territories in a double sense. They are occupied by Israeli forces but they are also occupied by Arabs. That occupation is an obstacle to Israeli annexation. The Gaza Strip is jammed with refugees from the 1948 and 1956 wars. On the West Bank this time the Arabs did not flee or let themselves be frightened into flight. Gaza and the West Bank together have so many Arabs that their annexation would at once threaten soon to create what *Al Fatah* seeks: a Palestine with an Arab majority. The only way to preserve a Jewish state is to relinquish those territories.

This leaves three genuine security problems: the Golan Heights, from which Jewish settlements in the Jordan valley were so long shelled by Arab guerrillas; Sharm El Sheikh, which guards the Tiran straits and Israel's access to the Red Sea; and Latrun, which protects the vital road from Tel Aviv to Jerusalem. Some form of demilitarization and international force should be a feasible compromise at the first two points. According to the able Israeli journalist, Victor Cygielman, in *Le Nouvel Observateur* (24 August), the U.S. would not be op-

posed to rectification of the old Israel-Jordan frontier at Latrun
(and the retention by Israel of Kfar Etzion in the hills to the
North) if Israel is ready to cede a territory of the same extent to
Jordan in a peace settlement. Cygielman reported that Israel
was disposed to cede the region of Oum-el-Fakham which is
inhabited by Israeli Arabs.

This leaves the problem of Jerusalem. Cygielman says the
Rogers proposals would demilitarize Jerusalem, leave the city
united but with Israeli police and municipal authorities in the
Jewish section and Arab authorities in the Arab. There would
be a common council for Greater Jerusalem representing both
sides with free access to the Holy Places guaranteed for all.
There is no reason why Jerusalem under some such ingenious
scheme should not become an open city for Jew and Arab,
perhaps some day the joint capital of a Palestinian confederation. The Holy City deserves a solution of imagination
and magnanimity. Its present Mayor, Teddy Kolleck, has paved
the way by his own liberal and large-minded policies for an
evolution of this kind.

The crux of the problem, the key to future peace, lies with
the Palestinian Arabs, whether in the occupied territories or in
the refugee camps. Unfortunately the Rogers plan does not provide for their representation. Nathan Yalin-Mor, head of the
so-called Stern Gang in the Jewish terror against the British in
the 1940s, and now one of the leading spokesmen in Israel for
Arab-Jewish reconciliation, spoke of this on Radio Stockholm,
20 August. 'Without the Palestinians being part of, and partner
in, any political settlement, as an autonomous body,' Mr Yalin-
Mor said, 'no solution will be of lasting value. A new selling out
of the Palestinian people would amount to planting a time
bomb bound to explode after a few years.' Unfortunately, he
added, the Arabs in the occupied territories, though they favour
Nasser's decision for peace talks, have no representative body.
On the other hand those in the refugee camps are under guerrilla leadership which opposed the ceasefire and any kind of
compromise. This is the same intransigent and frantic line
which has led Arab resistance into one debacle after another.
'The result,' Mr Yalin-Mor said, 'may be the same as for the

last fifty years: disaster for the Palestinian people and the missing of a promising historical opportunity for national self-determination.'

Friends of peace must deeply regret the way in which Mrs Meir handled questions about the Palestinian Arabs in her appearance on *Face the Nation*. She rejected any idea of talks with them and any responsibility whatsoever for the Arab refugees. She implied that they had only themselves to blame because they had not accepted the 1947 U.N. partition plan. But how can Mrs Meir invoke the 1947 partition resolution, the legal basis of Israel's existence, and then ignore the 1948 U.N. refugee resolution, which is the legal basis of Arab rights to repatriation or compensation?

We know the situation is a complex one for Israel but we wish Mrs Meir had voiced some sympathy for their plight, some readiness to help, some hope for reconciliation. Her coldness was unworthy of a Jewish leader. It is said that Moses kept the Jews forty years in the desert to purge them of the habits acquired in slavery. Leadership, like hers, in forty years of siege and war, will purge the Jews of the compassion acquired in Exile. While the Palestinian Arabs are beginning in their homelessness to talk like Jews in a new Diaspora, the Israeli leadership is beginning to sound more and more like unfeeling *goyim*. This reversal of roles is the cruellest prank God ever played on His Chosen People.

7 September 1970, vol. 18, no. 16

Part Five:
Three Themes
and an
Epilogue

Note to the Rest of the Universe

Within two years you may see a flaming ball rocket up from the earth's surface and swing into position in an orbit around it. Do not regard the spectacle with complacency. These satellites will grow larger and more numerous; men will go up with them. Voyages to the moon will follow. After that the distant realm of planet and star will lie open to Man. Beware in time. This is a breed which has changed little in thousands of years. The cave-dweller who wielded a stone club and the man who will soon wield an interstellar missile are terribly alike. Earth's creatures feed upon each other, but this is the only one which kills on a large scale, for pleasure, adventure and even – so perverse is the species – for supposed reasons of morality.

Should you drop a secret mission of inquiry in alarm, you will find that the sacred books on which the young of the various tribes have been brought up for thousands of years glorify bloodshed. Whether one looks in Homer, or the Sagas, or the Bible, or the Koran, the hero is a warrior. Someone is always killing someone else for what is called the greater glory of God.

This is not a creature to be trusted with the free run of the universe. At the moment the human race seems to be temporarily sobered by the possession of weapons which could destroy all life on earth except perhaps the mosses and the fungi. But the planetary rocket may revive recrimination. The currently rival tribes, the Russians and the Americans, fear the other may use the new device against it. They may soon be transferring to outer space the hates that in every generation have brought suffering to the earth. It might be wise to stop them now, on the very threshold of the open and as yet unpolluted skies.

The Pax Americana Brings Fascism to Our 'First Frontier of Freedom'

In modern as in ancient times, the Greeks have shown a genius for civil war. Fraternal feuds have made them the prey and the protectorate (it is hard in practice to tell the two apart) of foreign powers from the days of the ancient Persian, to those of the modern American, Empire. The liberation of Greece from the Nazis, like its struggle for independence from the Turks a century earlier, broke down at the moment of success into civil war. The British reimposed the monarchy in 1945 and backed the right (including those who had collaborated with the Nazis) against the Resistance movement and the Communists as part of a strategy designed for more than a hundred years to keeping the Russians from access to the Mediterranean. The U.S. took over in 1947 from the exhausted British with the Truman Doctrine, carrying on the classic British policy under the new name of 'containment'. This is when and where the Pax Americana began. Greece was our first Vietnam.

Now twenty years and $2 billion later the façade of success has crumbled and Greek politics face polarization again between a monarcho-Fascist military dictatorship and the threat of a new Communist-led Resistance. Not all of this is America's fault. You have to go to Latin America to find parallels for the Greek oligarchy, with its propensity for making money on America's obsession with anti-Communism and salting the proceeds away in foreign countries. And you have to go to the John Birch Society to understand the political mentality behind the coup. Only the kind of paranoid who suspects Eisenhower of being a Communist tool could see a Red menace in Papandreou and his Centre Union party. *Papandreou was Churchill's tool and Prime Minister in the restoration of the monarchy and in launching the civil war to crush the Communists.*

To a majority of the Greek people he now seems an elderly Franklin D. Roosevelt, though Papandreou* is really about as

* His son, Andreas, whom Cyrus Sulzberger in the *New York Times* has smeared so shamelessly as a Red, is about as far left as our A.D.A.

liberal as Herbert Hoover. The clocks of conventional Greek politics still run on nineteenth-century time.

Until 1964, rigged elections, fear of a new civil war and a conservative peasantry kept the oligarchy in power. In 1964 a revived and growing middle class made it possible for Papandreou to obtain an absolute majority and give Greece its first taste since the last war of genuinely free institutions. These threatened control of the army by the King and the right. For months Greek political life has been thrown into convulsions as the crown sought by bribery and U.S. pressure to destroy Papandreou's majority in Parliament and now to establish a dictatorship rather than risk the 28 May elections he might have won. Apparently the quick take-over plan used by the military was drawn up months ago (the best account is in the reports Bernard Nossiter filed to the *Washington Post*, 30 April, on his return from Athens) by the King and the army for the eventuality of a Papandreou victory or a Communist coup. They equated the two, and so – there is every reason to believe – did the U.S. military mission, the C.I.A. and the American Embassy which have treated Greece as a protected province since 1947. We have neither broken relations with, nor ended military aid to, the military dictatorship. For this the thousands they have imprisoned and the press they have gagged can justifiably blame the United States.

The result, by forcing opposition into illegal channels and giving the leadership to those skilled in illegal ways, may ultimately benefit the Communists. Thomas T. Fenton, in a dispatch from Athens to the *Baltimore Sun* (30 April) reports a conversation with a Western diplomat who was there during the civil war and estimates that in those days the insurgents had the support of only thirty per cent of the Greek people. 'He now estimates,' Mr Fenton cabled, 'that if a counter-revolution de-

---

We note (in *Le Monde*, 28 April) that the new head of the A.D.A., John Kenneth Galbraith, and his colleague, Carl Kaysen, another New Frontiersman (both men knew Andreas as an economics professor in this country) have cabled his American-born wife that they asked the White House to intervene for her husband. He faces death on trumped-up charges of treason in a military court-martial.

velops against the military regime, it might enjoy the support of sixty per cent of the population.' So after twenty years and $2 billion in aid, a new rebellion would have twice as much support as before.

In Defence of the Campus Rebels

I hate to write on subjects about which I know no more than the conventional wisdom of the moment. One of these subjects is the campus revolt. My credentials as an expert are slim. I always loved learning and hated school. I wanted to go to Harvard, but I couldn't get in because I had graduated forty-ninth in a class of fifty-two from a small-town high school. I went to college at the University of Pennsylvania which was obligated – this sounds like an echo of a familiar black demand today – to take graduates of high schools in neighbouring communities no matter how ill-fitted. My boyhood idol was the saintly anarchist Kropotkin. I looked down on college degrees and felt that a man should do only what was sincere and true and without thought of mundane advancement. This provided lofty reasons for not doing homework. I majored in philosophy with the vague thought of teaching it but though I revered two of my professors I disliked the smell of a college faculty. I dropped out in my third year to go back to newspaper work. Those were the twenties and I was a pre-Depression radical. So I might be described I suppose as a premature New Leftist, though I never had the urge to burn anything down.

In microcosm, the *Weekly* and I have become typical of our society. The war and the military have taken up so much of our energies that we have neglected the blacks, the poor and students. Seen from afar, the turmoil, and the deepening division appear to be a familiar tragedy, like watching a friend drink himself to death. Everybody knows what needs to be done, but the will is lacking. We have to break the habit. There is no excuse for poverty in a society which can spend $80 billion a year on its war machine. If national security comes first, as the spokesmen for the Pentagon tell us, then we can only reply that the clearest danger to the national security lies in the rising revolt of our black population. Our own country is becoming a Vietnam. As if in retribution for the suffering we have imposed, we are confronted by the same choices: either to satisfy the aspirations of the oppressed or to try and crush them by force. The former would be costly, but the latter will be disastrous.

This is what the campus rebels are trying to tell us, in the only way which seems to get attention. I do not like much of what they are saying and doing. I do not like to hear opponents shouted down, much less beaten up. I do not like to hear any one group or class, including policemen, called pigs. I do not think four-letter words are arguments. I hate, *hate*, intolerance and violence. I see them as man's most ancient and enduring enemies and I hate to see them welling up on my side. But I feel about the rebels as Erasmus did about Luther. Erasmus helped inspire the Reformation but was repelled by the man who brought it to fruition. He saw that Luther was as intolerant and as dogmatic as the Church. 'From argument,' as Erasmus saw it, 'there would be a quick resort to the sword, and the whole world would be full of fury and madness.' Two centuries of religious wars without parallel for blood-lust were soon to prove how right were his misgivings. But while Erasmus 'could not join Luther, he dared not oppose him, lest haply, as he confessed "he might be fighting against the spirit of God".'* I feel that the New Left and the black revolutionists, like Luther, are doing God's work, too, in refusing any longer to submit to evil, and challenging society to reform or crush them.

Lifelong dissent has more than acclimatized me cheerfully to defeat. It has made me suspicious of victory. I feel uneasy at the very idea of a Movement. I see every insight degenerating into a dogma, and fresh thoughts freezing into lifeless party line. Those who set out nobly to be their brother's keeper sometimes end up by becoming his jailer. Every emancipation has in it the seeds of a new slavery, and every truth easily becomes a lie. But these perspectives, which seem so irrefutably clear from a pillar in the desert, are worthless to those enmeshed in the crowded

* Froude's *Life and Letters of Erasmus*.

struggle. They are no better than mystical nonsense to the humane student who has to face his draft board, the dissident soldier who is determined not to fight, the black who sees his people doomed by shackles stronger than slavery to racial humiliation and decay. The business of the moment is to end the war, to break the growing dominance of the military in our society, to liberate the blacks, the Mexican-American, the Puerto Rican and the Indian from injustice. This is the business of our best youth. However confused and chaotic, their unwillingness to submit any longer is our one hope.

There is a wonderful story of a delegation which came here to see Franklin D. Roosevelt on some reform or other. When they were finished the President said, 'Okay, you've convinced me. Now go on out and bring pressure on me.' Every thoughtful official knows how hard it is to get anything done if someone isn't making it uncomfortable *not to*. Just imagine how helpless the better people in government would be if the rebels, black and white, suddenly fell silent. The war might smoulder on forever, the ghettoes attract as little attention as a refuse dump. It is a painful business extricating ourselves from the stupidity of the Vietnamese war; we will do so only if it becomes more painful *not to*. It will be costly rebuilding the ghettoes, but if the black revolt goes on, it will be costlier *not to*. In the workings of a free society, the revolutionist provides the moderate with the clinching argument. And a little *un*-reason does wonders, like a condiment, in re-invigorating a discussion which has grown pointless and flat.

We ought to welcome the revolt as the one way to prod us into a better America. To meet it with cries of 'law and order' and 'conspiracy' would be to relapse into the sterile monologue which precedes all revolutions. Rather than change old habits, those in power always prefer to fall back on the theory that all would be well but for a few malevolent conspirators. It is painful to see academia disrupted, but under the surface were shams and horrors that needed cleansing. The disruption is worth the price of awakening us. The student rebels are proving right in the daring idea that they could revolutionize American society by attacking the universities as its soft underbelly. But I would also remind the students that the three evils they fight – war, racism and bureaucracy – are universal. The Marxism-Leninism some of the rebels cling to has brought into power a bureaucracy more suffocating than any under capitalism; the students demonstrate everywhere on our side but are stifled on the other. War and imperialism have not been eliminated in the relations between Communist states. Black Africa, at least half-freed from the white man, is hardly a model of fraternity or freedom. Man's one real enemy is within himself. Burning America down is no way to Utopia. If battle is joined and our country polarized, as both the revolutionists and the re-pressionists wish, it is the better and not the worse side of America which will be destroyed. Someone said a man's character was his fate, and tragedy may be implicit in the character of our society *and* of its rebels. How make a whisper for patience heard amid the rising fury?

19 May 1969, vol. 17, no. 10

Notes on Closing, But Not in Farewell

Last September I had been a Washington correspondent for thirty-one years. Next February I will have been a news-paperman for fifty. This month represents a double milestone. In December 1933, I made my debut in the Big City, as an editorial writer on the *New York Post* for J. David Stern who had just purchased it. This month also marks the completion of nineteen years for the *Weekly*, now *Bi-Weekly*. Regretfully, this is the last issue. I will be sixty-four this month and I have de-cided to heed the familiar warning signals and shift to a less exacting pace. On 1 January I move to the *New York Review of Books* as a contributing editor. I have written for it off and on with pleasure since 1964 and look forward to a new challenge. I also have in mind a major work on the problem of freedom.

In this final issue it seemed appropriate to talk a little about myself. Almost as far back as I can remember I wanted to be a newspaperman. At fourteen, while in my sophomore year at high school in Haddonfield, N.J., the small town in which I grew up, I began to publish a monthly called *The Progress*. The very first issue struck that note of impractical idealism which was, I suppose, to become characteristic. I attacked Hearst for his Yellow Peril campaign and called for the cancellation of the First World War debts on condition that the debtor nations agreed to a twenty-five-year holiday from the arms race. The paper was printed in the job shop of a local weekly, and the linotypist, after setting some of these early radical effusions, opined between meditative squirts of tobacco juice, that I would come to a bad end.

The paper was a commercial success. It carried advertising I obtained after school on my bicycle from merchants in the area. But my father, returning from a convalescence to find me a publisher, wisely made me stop publication after three issues when it became clear that I was falling behind in my school work. This draconian measure was too late. Within a few months I was working for a local weekly paper, and in my junior year I became a full-fledged reporter. J. David Stern, who owned the Camden, N.J., *Evening Courier*, stopped by my father's store one Saturday night, said he had heard of me and asked whether I would like to cover Haddonfield for his paper. That at fifteen was the real beginning of my career. I was a natural at the business from the start. But one result of working as a reporter after school is that I graduated from high school forty-ninth in a class of fifty-two, was turned down by Harvard (which I still long to attend) and made it – thanks to open enrolment for high schools in the Philadelphia area – to the University of Pennsylvania.

I loved learning and hated school. I devoured books from the moment I first learned to read but resisted every effort to make me study whatever I saw no sense in learning. A few teachers I loved, the rest I despised. At college I was a philosophy major, and Penn had two philosophy teachers of stature, Newbold and Singer, whom I revered. I thought I might teach philosophy but the atmosphere of a college faculty repelled me; the few islands of greatness seemed to be washed by seas of pettiness and mediocrity. The smell of a newsroom was more attractive. I was full of romantic nonsense and looked down on college degrees as artificial. I quit college in my junior year, when I was working ten hours afternoon and night after school on the Philadelphia *Inquirer*. In the mornings, feeling like Jude the Obscure (how I loved Hardy's dark vision in those days!), I would go to the library and read. The high points of my self-education in that period were two books of the *De Rerum Natura* of Lucretius in Latin and one poem of Sappho's in Greek. The other books I gobbled are too numerous to mention, but I still feel like a drop-out whose education was cut short.

I became a radical early. The first book I remember which began (about twelve) to open my eyes to the modern world was Jack London's *Martin Eden*. By the time I was *bar mitzvah* I had read Herbert Spencer's *First Principles* and become an atheist. My idol a few years later was Kropotkin. Engels's *Socialism Scientific and Utopian* was enthralling and I joined the Socialist Party, becoming a member of the New Jersey State Executive Committee before I was old enough to vote. But Kropotkin's communist anarchism, his vision of a voluntary society without police or oppression of any kind, seemed to me then and still seems now the noblest human ideal.

My basic attraction to anarchism did not keep me from more normal politics. In 1924 I was for La Follette, the Progressive candidate for President. In 1928, though I had considerable respect for Al Smith, I worked as a volunteer for Norman Thomas. I immensely admired his capacity to deal with American problems in Socialist terms but in language and specifics that made sense to ordinary Americans. I was a passionate anti-Fascist and got into trouble with the business manager of the Camden, N.J., *Courier* after I was sent to cover a Rotary Club meeting on Italy. The speaker was a pro-Fascist propagandist. I denounced him from the press table when he was through. Fortunately for me the *Courier*'s editorial policy was anti-Fascist, despite the presence of a large Italian minority in Camden which was for the most part unthinkingly pro-Fascist. Though nominally Republican in what was then a G.O.P. stronghold, the *Courier* fought the local Republican machine, praised La Follette and was the only paper in the Camden-Philadelphia area which was pro-Sacco and Vanzetti. I quit the paper because the city editor wouldn't let me cover their execution, and walked out of the city room with a $5 bill and an extra pair of socks to hitch-hike my way to it – but that is another story.

It sounds strange coming from a loner like myself but I liked just about every boss I ever worked for. The first, a boyhood hero who recently died, was Stern. I worked for him on the Philadelphia *Record* after several stints on the *Courier*. When he bought the *New York Post* in December 1933 I went to New York with him as editorial writer. Among the others were Freda Kirchwey of the *Nation*, a sympathetic and courageous liberal editor, then Ralph Ingersoll who founded *P.M.* and John P. Lewis his managing editor. Ingersoll had genius, and taught us all new ways of writing; Lewis was a small town newspaperman who ran a team of temperamental big-city intellectuals and won their respect and affection. Then there was the late Joseph Barnes who edited the *New York Star*. The last was Ted O. Thackrey who fought so hard against such heavy odds to keep the New York *Daily Compass* afloat, and had finally to give it up the day before election day in November 1952. Every one of them gave me freedom. They also set an example. In its small way, my newsletter has carried on where they left off.

My first move, when the *Compass* closed, was to ask for my old job back as Washington Editor of the *Nation*, which I held from 1940 to 1946. But the *Nation* was, as usual, in financial difficulties, and I waited several weeks without being able to get either a yes or no answer. There would have been no *Weekly* if the *Nation* had taken me back. I only started the newsletter as a last resort. In the 1948 Arab-Jewish war in Palestine, the Israelis said their secret weapon was *ain breira*, which is Hebrew for 'no alternative'. That was my situation. I had been thinking of a newsletter for several years. Georges Seldes had shown the way with his 4-page newsletter *In Fact* a decade earlier. I had seen one experiment after another in liberal-radical journalism go down to defeat. I thought the time had come to cut the cloth to the dwindling market, and try a paper so small and inexpensive it could pay for itself even in bad times. With the help of my energetic and resourceful younger brother, Marc, I set about preparing to launch a newsletter.

Since others may try the same course in the future, the financial details may be interesting. The *Weekly* was made possible first of all because it had a kind of piggy-back launching. The shock of the closing of the *Compass* provided a receptive audience; the existence of mailing lists of *Compass* and *P.M.* subscribers provided an easy way to reach them. The second factor which made it possible was that I had $3,500 severance pay in escrow when the *Compass* closed; and we owned our little home in Washington so our expenses were low, even with three children. Then there was an unexpected angel. A fan, the late Arthur Wiener, took me to lunch in New York and lent a sympathetic ear. I walked down the street with him after lunch at the Museum of Modern Art. 'I'm going to keep on fighting,' I told him, 'if I have to crank out a paper on a mimeograph machine in the cellar.' He loaned me $3,000 without interest (which I am happy to say I repaid in full before he died). There were a few others who helped, but none on that scale. With less than $10,000 in two mailings my brother and I managed to get 5,300 subscribers with which to start, and the *Weekly* made its debut on 17 January 1953.

Its survival and growth were made possible by several factors. One was the relatively low level of costs at that time. The second-class mail rate made it possible to mail the *Weekly* in those days at only one-eighth of a cent per copy, the minimum piece rate then; it is 1.5 cents now. I shall always be grateful that the Post Office not only granted second class quickly but gave me a refund for the first few issues mailed at a higher rate. Second class made my survival possible. Though I was regarded in the paranoid atmosphere of those McCarthy years simply and plainly as a Red, I had no trouble whatsoever with the Post Office. No political questions were asked me. I was treated with the utmost courtesy by the postal authorities then and since. It is no small testimonial to the strength of the First Amendment that a new publication could be launched in those years with what amounts to a postal subsidy to a left-wing journalist.

I had two basic decisions to make when I started, one

business, the other editorial. The first was whether to go out and raise money for promotion and try to grow fast, or concentrate my energies on doing as good a job as possible and hope that the quality would sooner or later attract a larger audience. I felt that no matter how much money I could raise, a radical publication in the atmosphere of 1953 could only grow slowly anyway; that money-raising was too exhausting and humiliating, and would leave me too little time and strength for reporting and writing. I have never regretted that decision, though the *Weekly* at first grew very slowly.*

The other, the editorial, decision was the character of the new paper. I decided to do a radical paper in conservative format, with lovely typography (Garamond, an old French face, was the basic type I chose), to eschew sensational headlines, to document what I had to say from governmental and standard sources. I wanted a paper which would be sober in statement and as accurate as I could make it. I wanted a paper which a campus reader, in the hostile atmosphere of that time, could pass on to a conservative colleague without having it dismissed as just another hysterical rag. People on the other side might not agree but, if they read me at all, would have to take my findings and analysis seriously. I decided to make no claim to 'inside stuff' or private sources in the government since I had none and was unlikely to get any in the McCarthy era, when public officials were too intimidated to leak material to a left-wing newspaperman, or even be seen talking to one. Finally I wanted the paper to have readability, humour and grace. I dreamed of taking the flotsam of the week's news and making it sing. I had a vision of a paper which would be urbane, erudite and witty; with substance, but as light as a soufflé. Needless to say I rarely felt that I had succeeded but that was my idealized image of what I wanted the *Weekly* to be.

The early years were lonely. I am naturally gregarious but

* Here are some basic figures on average circulation as reported every September to the Post Office under second-class mail regulations. I hit 10,000 in 1955 but it took eight years more until I reached 20,000 in 1963. In 1968, the first year of publication as a bi-weekly, I reached 40,000. It was 50,000 in 1969, 60,000 in 1970 and 70,000 this year.

found myself ostracized. I was sustained by my readers. No one ever had a more loving audience, and the letters (few of which – please forgive me – I was ever able to answer) made up for the coldness of Washington. No one could have been happier than I have been with the *Weekly*. To give a little comfort to the oppressed, to write the truth exactly as I saw it, to make no compromises other than those of quality imposed by my own inadequacies, to be free to follow no master other than my own compulsions, to live up to my idealized image of what a true newspaperman should be, and still be able to make a living for my family – what more could a man ask?

I have been able to live in accordance with my beliefs. Politically I believe there cannot be a good society without freedom of criticism; the greatest task of our time is to find a synthesis of socialism and freedom. Philosophically I believe that a man's life reduces itself ultimately to a faith – the fundamental is beyond proof – and that faith is a matter of aesthetics, a sense of beauty and harmony. I think every man is his own Pygmalion, and spends his life fashioning himself. And in fashioning himself, for good or ill, he fashions the human race and its future.

14 December 1971, vol. 19, nos. 21 and 22

Index

Index

Penguinews *and*
Penguins in Print

Every month we issue an illustrated magazine, *Penguinews*.
It's a lively guide to all the latest Penguins, Pelicans and
Puffins, and always contains an article on a major Penguin
author, plus other features of contemporary interest.

Penguinews is supplemented by *Penguins in Print*, a
complete list of all the available Penguin titles – there are
now over four thousand!

The cost is no more than the postage; so why not
write for a free copy of this month's *Penguinews*? And if
you'd like both publications sent for a year, just send us a
cheque or postal order for 30p (if you live in the
United Kingdom) or 60p (if you live elsewhere), and we'll
put you on our mailing list.

Dept EP, Penguin Books Ltd, Harmondsworth,
Middlesex

Note: *Penguinews* and *Penguins in Print* are not
available in the U.S.A. or Canada.

The Greening of America

Charles A. Reich

'There is a revolution under way. It is not like the revolutions of the past. It has originated with the individual and with culture, and if it succeeds, it will change the political structure only as its final act. It will not require violence to succeed, and it cannot be successfully resisted by violence . . .'

Thus Charles Reich in this extraordinary book which raced to the top of the American non-fiction best-seller lists and which (according to the *Sunday Times*) 'has unleashed a debate that reminds some in its impetuosity and effervescence of the one that followed Rachel Carson's *Silent Spring*, and others of the *Kinsey Report*.'

Optimistic, lucid and wide-ranging (across economics, history, law, sociology, psychology and philosophy), *The Greening of America* shows not only how the corporate state has usurped all values but how the young generation – in their creativity, their rediscovery of community and freedom – has set in train a movement that may transform America . . . and even the world.

'Enormously interesting . . . It will affect political thinking and behaviour . . . I am greatly impressed with his central idea . . .' J. K. Galbraith.

Not for sale in the U.S.A. or Canada

A Penguin Book

Soledad Brother

The Prison Letters of George Jackson

When he was eighteen, George Jackson was sentenced from one year to life for stealing $70 from a gas station. In all he spent ten years in prison, seven and a half of them in solitary confinement. In 1970 when he was twenty-eight he was charged with the murder of a prison guard in Soledad Prison and would have faced a mandatory death sentence if he was convicted.

On 7 August 1970, just a few days after George was transferred to San Quentin and seven months after he was accused of the murder of the guard, his brother Jonathan, who had just turned seventeen, invaded the San Rafael courthouse single-handed, with a satchel full of handguns, an assault rifle and a shotgun hidden under his raincoat. As he left the courtroom with the three black convicts he had armed and the five hostages they had taken Jonathan shouted 'FREE THE SOLEDAD BROTHERS BY 12.30.' Within minutes Jonathan was dead.

Finally in the course of a prison riot in August 1971 George Jackson himself, the author of these moving letters, was killed, and a martyr born.

Not for sale in the U.S.A. or Canada

A Penguin Book

American Power and the New Mandarins

Noam Chomsky

This is, quite simply, the most profound study yet written of what makes America's continuing behaviour in Vietnam possible. With its publication the anti-war movement comes of age. Not in any sense of achieving 'respectability' (although Noam Chomsky is one of the world's greatest linguistic scholars) but because its morally impassioned scholarship digs deep beneath the external events to their cultural and ideological bedrock within America itself.

American power is wielded not by napalm-crazy reactionaries who wish to bomb Vietnam back to the Stone Age, but by the New Mandarins. This élite of liberal experts professes to analyse problems in a scientific, value-free language. Any human reaction to the war it condemns as 'sentimental'; or, more accurately, the categories in which protests are formulated (honesty, indignation) simply do not exist for the tough-minded social scientist. They cannot be programmed on the RAND Corporation computers.

But are the new pragmatists as objective as they claim? Chomsky proves that unconscious bias systematically distorts their view of the world, from Vietnam today to historical events such as the Spanish Civil War. The New Mandarins have rejected the traditional role of the intellectual as conscience of the community. Their sophisticated techniques rest on dogmas about America's rectitude which are naïve, crude – and frightening.

Not for sale in the U.S.A. or Canada

America's Receding Future

Ronald Segal

An analysis of the American way of life that
could be called an indictment of the whole nation.

'Undoubtedly, Mr Segal's book is significant. It deserves
careful attention. For it voices all the grievances about
democratic institutions and the market economy that are
shaking the United States and causing tremors in Britain
as well' – Charles Curran in the *Sunday Telegraph*

'His invective is brilliant, his research meticulous . . .' –
Karl Meyer in the *Sunday Times*

'His examples of the horrors and sadness of places like
Dallas and Los Angeles are well chosen. He is shrewd
on American presidential failings . . . he offers a perceptive
account of American radicalism past and present' –
Marcus Cunliffe in the *New Statesman*

'. . . meant to make liberals seethe. They ought to read it' –
Jonathan Steele in the *Guardian*

Also available
The Race War